GETTING TOUGH CUSTOMERS TO YES!

BY WILLIAM R. HUGGINS

DARTNELL is a publisher serving the world of business with book manuals, newsletters and bulletins, and training materials for executives, managers, supervisors, salespeople, financial officials, personnel executives, and office employees. Dartnell also produces management and sales training videos and audiocassettes, publishes many useful business forms, and many of its materials and films are available in languages other than English. Dartnell, established in 1917, serves the world's business community. For details, catalogs, and product information, write:

THE DARTNELL CORPORATION
4660 N. Ravenswood Ave.
Chicago, IL 60640-4595, U.S.A.
or phone (800) 621-5463 in U.S. and Canada

Except where noted, this book may not be reproduced, stored in a retrieval system, or transmitted in whole or in part in any form or by any means (electronic, mechanical, photocopying, recording, or otherwise) without prior written permission of The Dartnell Corporation, 4660 N. Ravenswood Ave., Chicago, IL 60640-4595.

This publication is designed to provide accurate and authoritative information in regard to the subject matter covered. It is sold with the understanding that the publisher is not engaged in rendering legal, accounting, or other professional service. If legal advice or other expert assistance is required, the services of a competent professional person should be sought.

From a Declaration of Principles jointly adopted by a Committee of the American Bar Association and a Committee of Publishers.

Copyright 1996 in the United States, Canada, and Britain by
THE DARTNELL CORPORATION
Library of Congress Catalog Card Number: 96-083846
ISBN 0-85013-250-9

Printed in the United States of America by
The Dartnell Press, Chicago, IL 60640-4595

CONTENTS

CHAPTER 1: Who Are These Guys? 1

CHAPTER 2: The Changing Buyer 21

CHAPTER 3: The Sales Profession—
How Important Can It Be? 35

CHAPTER 4: Getting Started 41

CHAPTER 5: The Perfect Presentation 55

CHAPTER 6: Who Needs It? 67

CHAPTER 7: The Mechanics of Selling 75

CHAPTER 8: What It Takes To Sell 95

CHAPTER 9: Magic Words and the Magic
in Words 107

CHAPTER 10: Promoting Sales 117

CHAPTER 11: The Business Letter 133

CHAPTER 12: Asking Questions, Being Quiet,
and Getting Answers 155

CHAPTER 13: The Battle of the Buddy System 167

CHAPTER 14: Finding the Market 175

CHAPTER 15: Creating Markets, Creating Needs 189

CHAPTER 16: The Cold Call 199

CHAPTER 17: Selling Sense, Common Sense 213

CHAPTER 18: Staying Motivated and
Saving the Sales 231

CHAPTER 19: Direct Sales 247

CHAPTER 20: Tips for Success in Direct Sales 265

INDEX 277

ABOUT THE AUTHOR

Bill Huggins has more than three decades of practical and marketing experience. An outstanding sales producer and international sales award winner, Huggins has crafted sales training programs for companies both large and small. Currently, he acts as a sales and marketing consultant to an ever-changing variety of companies. In addition, he holds sale seminars both here and abroad, lectures, and writes about his favorite subject: selling.

Huggins believes that two challenges face the salesperson of today: A declining demand for salespeople in the traditional marketing structure, and the almost total lack of sales training available through company channels. His book addresses both these challenges and provides answers available nowhere else.

Huggins has a Bachelor of Science degree from the University of Missouri and a Master's degree in Business from Southern Illinois University. He lives with his wife and two daughters in Southern California.

1

Who Are These Guys?

A career in sales can be the best-paying or the poorest-paying job you can find. Sales can be a complex, demanding business or a simple, elementary business. It can be difficult, easy, frustrating, exhilarating, rewarding, punishing, depressing, uplifting, dull, exciting, active, and passive — all at the same time and in the same day. In sales, every day is different. Every customer, new or old, is a fresh canvas — challenging, demanding, waiting for the artistry of the professional salesperson. It is that difference which makes sales so exciting and so much fun.

Is it any wonder that salespeople are the objects of envy in so many businesses? Chained to their desks, screened from the world outside their immediate areas of interest are the bookkeepers, personnel managers, and purchasing department buyers. They look at the salesperson as a free spirit — overpaid, undisciplined, and incredibly lucky. Buyers, I suspect, are particularly conscious of this notion, and that is why they are sometimes so tough on us.

Buyers can make our day either wonderful and fulfilling or miserable and empty. They are the motivation we need to plan carefully and think and improve. They force us to push our companies for better prices, improved products, and innovative promotions.

Buyers are vital to their companies. Indeed, they are vital to business in general, and they are a dying breed. They come in all shapes and sizes, all genders, colors, and levels of competence. Some are very good; some, just fair; and others, downright bad. Quite often a good buyer is also a tough buyer. At the same time, I have never found a bad buyer to be a tough buyer. If that sounds like a conflict of terms or logic, let me explain.

BUYERS

Not many people understand what buyers do or (more important) how vital their job is in the operation of any business. A buying job is very special, and some buyers are very special. Whereas salespeople run a gauntlet of emotions during a day, buyers also deal with similar emotions and pressures that few others ever know or appreciate.

A buyer's job is demanding, stressful, and filled with pressure. Just think about it for a moment: When a person is given the authority and responsibility to buy the goods that a company will sell for profit, he or she is making decisions that will affect everyone in the company, from the CEO to the merchandise manager, from the store clerk to the entry-level employee. The buyer's decisions are constantly questioned, analyzed, second-guessed, and criticized. If the decisions are mostly right, his or her company will prosper and grow. Generally, a buyer receives no special recognition or rewards for those decisions — after all, "That's why we pay you the big bucks!" If the buyer's decisions are mostly wrong, however, the company will suffer losses, lose market position and consumer favor, and may even collapse. (In another chapter, I will present examples of companies that have faded or failed, thanks in large measure to poor buying practices.)

Of course, not all buyers buy products for resale. Some buy items that every office, factory, store, and shop must have to operate internally. These buyers are invisible to most of us, yet their function is no less important. Office workers expect adequate supplies of paper, pencils, pens, clips, staples, and other supplies when they come to work. The assembly-line employees expect to have a full stock of the oils, greases, tools, nuts, and bolts they will need each day. The cooks and serving staff expect all the foods, napkins, dishes, glasses, pots, pans, and kitchen implements to be on hand. Everyone expects towels, tissue, soap, and other restroom products, along with coffee, tea, soft drinks, bottled water, and snacks to be available. No one gives a second thought to how those products are always there and in adequate supply. Those things and thousands of other goods and services have been provided by a buyer, and all have been sold to the buyer by a salesperson.

Buyers spend thousands, hundreds of thousands, and even millions of dollars of their employers' money every year. This can and does have an intoxicating effect on some buyers and can change them from pleasant, honest, and sincere people into swelled-headed, arrogant egomaniacs who become almost impossible to see and who, when seen, don't listen. They suddenly know it all and can't be bothered with new ideas and innovative thoughts. This condition, regrettably, is becoming more common, as consolidations, mergers, and acquisitions increase and as accounting and legal department executives begin to fill the top jobs which, heretofore, were filled from the sales and marketing ranks.

As with any other group, it is dangerous to generalize and paint all with a broad brush. Some buyers, important and powerful, retain the characteristics that propelled them to the top of their profession. These people insist on continuing an open-door policy to the salespeople who call on them. They recognize that salespeople are messengers who educate, inform, and enlighten. Without that flow of information, buyers can, and usually will, quickly become out of touch with their own industry.

As a group, buyers are too cumbersome to handle. They are too diverse in the products they buy and the industries they serve. A buyer of steel, for example, cannot be compared with a buyer of ladies' wear, except in the most general terms. A buyer for a small card shop cannot be compared to a buyer for a major retail chain. They all buy, but the similarities stop there. So, for our purposes, we will consider only the buyers who purchase products for resale in medium to large retail operations. Even if you don't sell or plan to sell to that category of buyer, you will find common characteristics, regardless of your industry or marketing level.

In large retail chains, the buying responsibility is divided among many people, usually by category. Obviously, no single person could handle all the buying necessary to stock a Sears, Wal-Mart, or Montgomery Ward chain. Obtaining the mountains of goods (just physically placing the orders) that these companies and others like them buy and sell each week would overwhelm any one person. Even buying for one department can't be handled by a single individual. Take the sporting goods department, for instance. Skiing equipment, ice skates, cold weather wear, tents, camping equipment, baseballs, gloves, bats, bases, uniforms, masks, guards, footballs, pads, shoes, uniforms, soccer balls, nets, lures, tackle boxes, bait buckets, gaffs, knives, hunting equipment, rifles, shotguns ... Well, you get the point.

To make certain that each department has the latest full range of goods in terms of quality and price, some merchandise managers feel it is necessary to closely supervise and even eliminate the buying decision of the buyers that they monitor. If no one person should be vested with the power to supply a department, they reason, then each "team member" should share in the decisions of every other team member. This is called "buying by committee." Many buyers will try to cover up or hide behind this emasculation, since it is an embarrassment and a reflection on their abilities. Nevertheless, word soon gets out that the company buys by committee, which makes the salesperson's job very difficult. It robs him or her of the opportunity to present the product or service to the decision maker. It dampens the verve, passion, and excitement of a strong presentation. In short, it removes emotion from the sales process.

Of course, the whole idea behind buying by committee is to take emotion out of buying decisions, and I suppose it does that effectively. However, it denies that spark, that special quality found in topnotch buyers — namely, the gambling, innovative instinct that makes the product mix special to the consumer, builds a cultlike following, and causes profits to soar. I fear that that kind of buyer, that kind of talent, that kind of opportunity is being squashed by today's robotlike, "we-all-look-alike," "me-too" retailers — the bottom-line mavens of mediocrity.

With their power diluted, the buyers' worth is also weakened. They can be easily replaced — and frequently are — by almost anyone of average intelligence, regardless of experience or education. After all, the team makes the final decisions; therefore, the credit and fault are spread over many, with the all-knowing merchandise manager actually making the final decisions.

All these buyers do is decide if it is worth their time and trouble to bring the product to the attention of the committee. Unfortunately, without experience, few can detect the sales potential of new products from smaller, less well-known vendors. Hence, they often discount an unknown vendor out of hand, passing over products that could be sales sensations if only given the opportunity. This is the safe road to travel. They take no risks and make no decisions. These buyers supposedly save the company money, since their salary is considerably lower than the professional buyers they replaced. But, in my opinion, and from the vantage point of experience, these buyers eventually cost much more than any savings they represent.

The quality of buyers — in fact, the whole buying process — has lost the luster, intelligence, and piquancy that it had less than a decade ago. The fun has gone out of the buyers' job. They used to be risk takers. They took pride in their ability to sniff out a product line that was a "comer." Today, in many companies, buyers are little more than computer programmers, puppets that dance to the corporate tune as played by the merchandise manager.

Not all companies buy by committee. Some still recognize the importance of individual decision making and individual initiative. Their buyers work hard to understand the markets, anticipate the competition, and seek out products that will give their stores something a little different, which is not easy in today's world. These buyers must know how and when to close out a model or an entire line of goods. They must decide on which models, colors, or styles to stock and promote, and they will fight for ad dollars, extended terms, guaranteed sales, or other concessions to make their departments more competitive. They must guess what is hot and what is not, and their ever-vigilant eyes search out trends among the trendsetters — the young and the admired.

In recent years, buyers have also been forced to be alert to ecological concerns and a whole range of government regulations. Their duties extend beyond simply buying, often reaching into merchandising, retail sales training, promotion, and even store management. Their purview stretches worldwide, and they may have life or death power over many suppliers.

WHAT BUYERS DO

The preceding account makes buyers who are not shackled to committees sound rather grand, and their duties seem staggering. All that is true, but simply put, a buyer's job is to buy. Many buyers forget that. It is understandable, but not forgivable. Buyers must try to interview every sales person who takes the time to call on them. They must learn from salespeople about new products and systems, about the competition, and about what is selling across the street and across the country. Buyers learn about upcoming advertising campaigns, promotions, and ideas, and their knowledge helps them buy wisely.

In our litigious society, buyers protect their companies from consumer lawsuits and government penalties. They are sensitive to the needs of various age, gender, ethnic, and religious groups. They must beware of buying from a supplier whose advertising or association with some political cause can be damaging to sales. Likewise, not buying from that same source may be equally damaging. Buyers must know which way to jump and exactly when.

I hope you now have a better understanding of what the job of buying entails. It's a tough job and if buyers are really buyers and not just a front for a committee, we must respect them and their time (of which they always have far too little). As I stated earlier, there are good buyers, fair buyers, and bad buyers. We can define buyers by their traits. I've given them names, or labels. Maybe you'll recognize some of your customers among them.

INTROVERTS AND EXTROVERTS

My definition of introverts and extroverts differs from Webster's. In the language of sales, introverts are people who always want to be right. They are studious individuals. Introverts test the salesperson's product knowledge and honesty, no matter how long they have known him or how much they trust him. By traditional terms, these buyers may be difficult to identify as introverts. They may be breezy, flippant, and outgoing. They may be the life of the party, full of witty remarks and hilarious jokes; nonetheless, at some point, they will reveal deep-seated stubbornness and an unwillingness to give in to the most trivial point. At lunch, an introvert may quarrel with the waiter about how a wine should be served or what kind of fish a "baby salmon" really is. This person will express strong views about current affairs, sports teams, or the condition of the stock market, and will furiously argue this point of view. Always, the introvert will end a contact with a smile, a warm handshake, and the impression that the "little tirade" is over and forgotten. It isn't.

I urge you to study your target buyer and try to immediately identify him or her as either introverted or extroverted. This is not easy to do. Contrary to popular belief, the extrovert does not always smile, crack a joke, wear loud sports jackets, smoke cigars, or pat you on the back. In fact, extroverts may not necessarily be outgoing at all, in the common understanding of the word, and their interests may not be external.

The extrovert could be the person who does kind and thoughtful things for others as the Community Chest organizer or member of the church choir. He or she may head up a fund-raising drive for the homeless, participate actively in church, volunteer to lead a youth group at a local school, and may well belong to a host of charity groups. Almost certainly, he or she will be heavily involved in community welfare projects.

Extroverts are known by friend and foe alike as nice people. You may hear them referred to as "real gentlemen" or "sweet gals," and they probably are. They usually are self-deprecating, modest people. Inwardly, they want and appreciate praise and recognition. They truly enjoy helping others, even to the point where their families may suffer. Their involvement may affect their job as well.

Selling to extroverts is sometimes difficult. First, they are likable people, pillars of the community, almost saints. When they say, "Gee, Alice, I wish I could buy your line, but I just don't have an open-to-buy right now," you will find it hard not to believe them. But don't. Extroverts will use that nice-guy façade to turn you away. But this nice-guy image and affable personality also works against them. If you persist, if you close hard and don't take no for an answer, they will have a very difficult time saying no — just as they have a hard time saying no to any request or favor asked of them. If you have diagnosed your target correctly, you will know how to direct your presentation to a successful conclusion. Selling to an introvert or an extrovert will require a somewhat different set of approaches, but the most important thing is knowing where your buyer fits. It's easy to misdiagnose, but it's fun to try guessing correctly. Watch television, listen to radio commercials, and read newspaper and magazine ads to see if you can tell to whom the ads are directed. Sellers of household products, soaps, cleaners, breakfast foods, vacuums, and even waxes and deodorants, seem to have determined that most homemakers are extroverts. "Your family will love you for (buying some product)," is a common refrain. In other words, the family will love the extrovert for buying the product, but it will withdraw that love if the product is denied them. Let's take a few other examples.

A breakfast cereal that is growing in popularity aims its ads at the introvert. "It's the right thing to do," these ads proclaim. "The wise investor ... " is the lead-in for a mutual fund aimed at the introvert. Beer ads always suggest that drinking this or that particular brand of beer includes consumers in a fraternity of happy, attractive young people who spend their days on a sunny beach. There are no homely women or ugly men in these ads — their world is perfect. These ads are aimed at the extrovert who wants to be liked. "My husband raves about the feel of my skin since I started using XYZ soap," is still another zinger aimed at the extrovert.

Automobile ads are excellent examples of advertising messages sent to introverted and extroverted personalities. Sporty models are generally aimed at the extrovert. Beautiful girls seated alongside the driver or tossing admiring glances from the sidewalk clearly send the male extrovert a message. Stately sedans and sturdy four-wheel-drive vehicles are aimed at introverts. Volvo, for example, stresses safety and durability. Can you guess whom they have targeted?

This is not to say that some part of virtually every ad isn't pointed toward both sides of the introvert/extrovert fence, but a specific, target consumer is always there. It's fun to search for the target, and you'll discover how useful this skill can be in your career.

THE STRONG, SILENT TYPES

Many buyers are the strong, silent type. These characters are egocentric and confident (the two traits go hand-in-hand). They are noncommittal about almost everything. They will ignore you or rush you through your warm-up and will refuse to become involved in small talk. In effect, they stand above the fray, forcing salespeople to struggle and sweat through their presentation with no feedback whatsoever. They almost never ask questions. If they do, rejoice, because a question indicates that they are listening and have a mild interest at least.

It doesn't take a genius to recognize these strong, silent buyers. Their body language gives them away: arms folded across the chest, head tilted back and cocked to one side. These nonverbal clues tell the salesperson that he or she is not important, and the buyer has bigger fish to fry. These stalwart buyers wear a bored or tired expression, the mouth turned down at the corners, with a "how long is this going to take?" look. They will be brusque, preoccupied with seemingly more important things to do and with little time to do them.

Strong, silent buyers are usually introverts. Strike that, they are *always* introverts. Recall that an introvert is someone who wants to be right. An extrovert is someone who wants to be liked. Think about these definitions and what they really mean. If you can determine if your buyer is introverted or extroverted, you will be operating from a distinct advantage. Of course, most people have elements of both, but one characteristic will usually dominate. When dealing with the strong, silent type, play to reason more than emotion. Be armed with backup materials, reports, charts, and outside endorsements.

Strong, silent buyers have few friends, but they admire certain competitors. If you can determine who those might be and produce evidence that they sell your products or services successfully, you will be close to a sale. Be careful how you introduce that evidence, because these buyers will not be seen as followers and will take umbrage at the hint that they are. "I don't give a damn what Wilson's selling," he might say and, at that moment, he means it.

The strong, silent types are loyal to their vendors. That often means they will be very difficult to sell, because buying from a new vendor usually means replacing an old vendor. On the other hand, they are confident and sure of themselves and their position. They don't worry about their managers' opinions of the decisions they make. They are informed about their market and know the customers. Always be honest with these buyers. If they catch you in a fib or discover that you're trying to slip something over the outside corner, you will be finished forever.

Usually strong, silent buyers will refuse your luncheon invitations, but if you do get them to lunch, it will be sincerely appreciated. They will be tough to entertain because you will be the only one dancing. Don't try to be the life of the party. Be content to pry and probe, until you discover something about which they are interested. Their opinions are firm and strongly held, but don't concern yourself if yours are different. They often admire someone who has differing opinions, if those opinions are logical and presented with little passion and strong reasoning.

Be prepared to be investigated if they are considering you as a potential vendor. These buyers are cautious and slow to act. They will want to know all about your company and will conduct an investigation without your help. They will examine your samples carefully, shop your products in other stores, ask the retail clerks about consumer response, and research the product line's track record over a period of time.

Once they are satisfied that you meet their standards, they may continue to be cautious and place a "test order." Don't be impatient, but be persistent without being pushy. Strong, silent buyers don't respond to pressure in a positive way; you could blow the opportunity. However, once they are in the fold, you will find the strong, silent types to be the best customers. They will work to make your products successful in their stores and cooperate with you on promotions and advertising campaigns.

They expect honesty and fair treatment and will never ask for unreasonable discounts or price concessions, but, like any good buyer, they will push for the best deal they can get. If you do a favor, get a special deal, or perhaps offer first refusal on close-out merchandise, make sure they know it is a favor. Do it subtly and without too much fanfare.

The strong, silent buyers may envy the flamboyant salesperson, because they are so far removed from flamboyancy. They may envy the freedom that a sales job provides and will have a distorted view of what a salesperson really does. Since they usually lack social graces and are a disaster at small talk, they may have a deep-seated, poor self-image and a lack of confidence in their interpersonal skills.

Although most strong, silent types I have known are good buyers (but annoyingly slow to act), there are some who are bad buyers — very bad. These bad strong, silent types harbor a powerful dislike for people with social skills (namely, salespeople) and are frequently rude and nasty. They lack self-confidence, which accounts for their silence. They simply don't know what to say! These buyers are *extreme* introverts. Like the good strong, silent types, they will watch the salesperson twist in the wind and enjoy the discomfort they've created. The bad types are more likely to enter into a dialogue, not because they are truly interested, but because they like to set traps. They'll discover a tiny, insignificant flaw in your product, or an error in your presentation and base refusal to buy on that. You'll be infuriated, of course, but don't let them know it. Stay cool, smile, and be courteous. You may not get the sale, but it is never a good idea to burn bridges, no matter what.

One of the favorite tricks of the bad strong, silent types is to ask for concessions they know you cannot give. They might quote competitive prices that are impossible to meet (and are fabricated anyway), just to see your reaction.

If you really know your product, the market, and your competition's product, together with prices, ad allowances, promotions, and other terms of sale, you will be operating from strength. The bad strong, silent types will not be able to play their games. They will be quick to know that you are on top of your game and that their silly ploys are transparent.

General rules apply to all types of buyers with some variations. For the strong, silent types (good and bad) you must follow these rules:

> **1. Be totally prepared.** Carry a hernia-causing pack of backup materials. Current, outside publications that praise your products are particularly effective. Letters of endorsement from satisfied consumers and happy retailers are excellent. Consumer reports, industry statistics, and copies of current ads and promotions should all be included in your materials. Show it all. Ignore their

protests, verbal or implied, that their day is too short and time is too limited. The fact is, they are interested and will be impressed by your preparation.

2. **Respect their schedule.** These buyers jealously guard their time and will consider the interview they have granted you as a gift. Your punctuality is expected, so don't disappoint. Be on time and keep the presentation as concise as possible.

3. **Be neat and businesslike.** Strong, silent types may personally be messy, but don't follow their example. Instead, be well groomed without being faddish.

4. **Rehearse your presentation.** Keep it as precise and compact as possible, without surrendering the power and passion.

5. **Try to start a dialogue.** As difficult as it may appear (and it will be), get them involved somehow. The best way of doing this is to ask for an opinion. For example: "Mr. Hardnose, I've been told the new, free-wheeling sprocket makes Monitor bicycle the easiest hill-climber available. Do you know anything about that?" This sort of inquiry will be a challenge to the storehouse of product knowledge that most strong, silent buyers have. They will be pleased to give you details you never dreamed about. It will open the door for a much better presentation on your part.

Of course, we have all learned in our first, water-testing sales days that asking questions is the best way to draw someone out. But be sure your questions require more than just a yes or no response. Think carefully about the questions you will ask and about your follow-up. If, for example, the buyer answers, "No, I don't know anything about the Monitor's free-wheeling sprocket," you either die on the spot or say, "Come to think of it, I have an article out of this month's edition of *Cycle Madness* about that new sprocket and the Monitor. Jon Warthan won the Seattle–Tacoma race with it last month." Then dig the article out of your mountain of backup material. You can be sure he will want to know because that trait is deeply ingrained in the strong, silent personality.

If that sort of opportunity is not available to you, ask about the buyer's successes. "I hear you exceeded your projections last quarter with that parking-lot sale idea. I've always thought security was such a problem that parking-lot sales were more trouble than they're worth. How did you overcome that?" Notice that the question was "how did *you* overcome that?" not "how did the *company* or how did *security* overcome that?" The buyer may be strong and silent, but he or she is not immune to praise and recognition.

THE "PROFESSIONAL" BUYERS

This is a name bestowed with tongue in cheek. I just don't know what else to call these buyers. I call them "professional" because they are typical of buyers found in large companies such as Kmart, the old Sears, JCPenney, and others. Receptionists, secretaries, and assistants insulate them from the sales cadres that assault their doors. Just getting an appointment is considered by some to be a great achievement. They are above us all — royalty in an egalitarian society. Their ego is bigger than Montana, and they accept and expect the homage given to them in a regal manner as befitting their exalted position. They know buying, and they know merchandise. They understand pricing and their competitors. They understand the market quite well, but they never let that interfere with their decisions. They remind me of some members of Congress who understand what is best for the country, but who vote for what is best for their personal fortunes. The professional buyers know the power of their pencil and will use it to their own advantage whenever they can. This is particularly true when they buy off-shore. Their favorite vendors are always overseas.

There are many reasons for this, but the primary one is that they are treated like royalty when they visit vendors and potential vendors overseas. They are wined and dined lavishly, and the "entertainment" is custom-tailored to their particular tastes. Then (or so I've heard) they will find envelopes stuffed with cash at the breakfast table.

American companies take a dim view of payoffs to their buyers. This practice is usually cause for the immediate dismissal of the buyer and banishment for the vendor. However, proving the case when the payoff is in cash and comes from a vendor located in Hong Kong or some other distant locale is just about impossible.

Professional buyers are usually introverts. Their training and job almost force introverted character traits on them. They are *so* smart that they *must* be right!

I once presented a line of goods to one of the buyers for a major, American retailer. I had first called on the regional office in California, and the regional manager was ecstatic about the line. He wanted these goods in his stores as soon as humanly possible. Explaining that his powers were limited, he urged me to travel to the eastern office. He even picked up his telephone and made an appointment for me. Things were looking good.

When I showed up at company headquarters, I was greeted by the national buyer with a deflating, "I hope you didn't travel all the way back here just to see me!" We were not getting off to a good start. He had a table in his office and invited me to display my line of goods, which I did. Now, this company had a "Buy America" program that was in full swing, and I was encouraged by the fact that I was the only American vendor for this kind of product. That was before I discovered their "Buy America" program was just a con game to fool consumers (for whom they had great contempt) into believing they were really buying American goods. Nothing could have been further from the truth.

My line was so obviously superior to the goods they were carrying, that I was mentally spending the commissions. I pointed out the excellent workmanship and the variety of models and colors, and I made comparisons as I worked through the line. To be honest, I violated my own rules of selling; I failed to get the buyer involved. He was silent, nodding his head and making little grunting sounds, but not really a part of the presentation. Still, I was offering him an opportunity to buy this line without a letter of credit (required by the off-shore vendor), in any quantity he wished (he had to buy large minimums from the off-shore vendor) delivered to his regional warehouses (foreign vendors offered one delivery point and required the retailer to break the goods off), 30-day terms (a letter of credit is, of course, posted in cash), full credit on returned goods (not offered by foreign vendors), and a price about 5 percent lower than his present vendor. Well, I thought I had a slam dunk!

He squirmed and avoided my eyes, pretending to examine my merchandise against the present stock. Finally, after an awkward period of silence, he informed me that he saw no difference! I was stunned! No difference? A blind person could have seen the difference, and an idiot could have understood that my offer was a gift by comparison. I dragged some women into his office and asked them to give us an "outside" opinion on which line they would buy. Not one person selected the line he was stocking — not one. Some even wanted to know if he was going to stock this line because they wanted to buy it for themselves.

Still, after lots of foot-shuffling and silence, he turned me down! I knew why, and he knew I knew why. He was ashamed and embarrassed, but he wasn't about to give up those trips to Taiwan and the delights of the Orient or those envelopes stuffed with cash. He had been bought and paid for. I wanted to tell him so, and I wanted to tell him what I thought of him, but I try never to burn bridges — not even the rotten ones.

Naturally, not all professional buyers are on the take, but a lot of them are. It is worthwhile knowing what kind of people they are: introverted almost all the time, smart, slow to commit, survivors, and definitely not "one of the gang." You will find a copy of *Barrons* on the desk. These buyers probably don't read it, but they want you to know or to think that they know all about the inner workings of Wall Street, as well as the thought processes of the movers and shakers. The general rules for selling to the professional buyers are as follows:

1. **Build up the image of your company.** Professional buyers are impressed with large "movers and shakers." Embossed business cards, impressive stationery, and similar shows of "class" will improve your chances.

2. **Let them know you are doing business with other prestigious companies.** You may drop a name or two of buyers you work with whom they would admire. If possible, have a buyer from one of your larger customers join you for lunch at an "in" restaurant or private club.

3. **Entertain the professional buyers in the daytime.** Invite them for golf at a private club or at an expensive public course, fishing on a private or chartered boat, or hunting (duck or pheasant) at a private reserve. This is going to cost you, so try to make sure in advance that it will pay off. It probably will.

4. **Emphasize marketing support.** These kinds of accounts usually require a line that has strong marketing support (big TV campaigns, national contests, and the like), a more or less proven seller so that consumers are asking for it in their stores.

Professional buyers will ask you to pay for shelf space, give larger than normal advertising allowances, a warehouse allowance, and then, on top of all that, a guaranteed sale. But they are for sale themselves, and if you are a smart seller, you may get them to waive some or even all of those requirements.

"I-CAN-GET-IT-CHEAPER" BUYERS

You may be inclined to think this really isn't a type of buyer, but merely an objection used by many buyers to find the bottom of your particular barrel. It is true that most buyers will haggle in one way or another because most of them have been lied to by salespeople in the past and their level of trust is low.

But some buyers — the ones I tag with this label — will never accept your price, no matter how low. More for fun that in the belief I would get an order (if I'd been given an order, I have no idea what I would have done), I have low-balled a buyer to a ridiculous extreme, far below our cost. He still insisted he could buy it for less!

Buyers like the one I just described usually work for small companies or own their own store. Obviously, they are very suspicious of sales people and harbor the notion that "the big guys" are buying the same goods for practically nothing. They lack foresight and are destined to remain small fish in a small tank.

They want "B" goods, close-out merchandise, or seconds. The only reason they are worth knowing is that one day you may want an outlet to dump discontinued models, returned goods, or tens (end-of-run merchandise). A few rules that will help you sell this type (if you really want their business) are:

1. **Find out what markup they take on retail.** From that you can determine what they have paid for various types of merchandise. This will give you an enormous advantage when you are haggling price with them.

2. **Make a deal with them.** Tell them that they will be your exclusive outlet at the best price, and that they will have no competition. In other words, other "I-can-get-it-cheaper" types won't be your customers.

3. **If you can get them extra billing, they are yours forever.** Never give them extra discounts or extra free goods, or they will nag you for them on all future sales.

4. **Use praise as a selling tool.** This type loves to hear that he or she is a great businessperson or an outstanding negotiator. Use praise to your advantage.

THE HAIL-FELLOW-WELL-MET BUYERS

These buyers are everyone's best pal. They are extreme extroverts and will welcome you into their circle of friends immediately. They avoid decision making because decisions might make people angry, and angry people won't be their friends. These buyers are courteous, thoughtful, and cowardly. They do everything they can — tell stories, swap jokes, let you into their confidence — all to dodge the bullet. In reality, they are putting up a front to keep you from selling. They have a host of friends because they know it is easier to say no to a friend. "Gee, Bob, I'd sure like to buy your stuff, you *know* I'd buy from you if I could, but my open-to-buy is flatter than my feet." In this way, the hail-fellow-well-met types can turn you down and still keep your friendship. "Sure, good old Harry would buy from me if he could. He just doesn't have any open-to-buy." Later you discover that he placed a huge order with the guy you passed in the reception room.

How did the other guy do it? He stuck to business. He laughed at Harry's jokes, but didn't give him any of his own until he had the order in hand. He listened to Harry's stories — often personal — and empathized, but quickly got back on track. He didn't play his game. These effusively friendly buyers are sidetracking you, trying to divert your attention from your purpose. They will cost you lots of lunches, greens fees, and football tickets, but they will not give you much business. How can they? They're trying to spread it around to all their "friends." Oh, you'll get an order here and there, but don't count on much.

There are just a few sales representatives getting the lion's share, and they usually aren't considered members of the buyer's "inner circle." These buyers will explain why your products weren't bought by passing the buck. "Fred (his boss) just insists I stock that line. Heck, if it was up to me ... " Yeah, sure. Follow these rules with the hail-fellow-well-met buyers:

1. **Stick to business.** Be friendly, open, and even jovial, but never allow yourself to be sidetracked from the reason you are there.

2. **Make their decision to buy easy.** Set out all the particulars of the sale and review them as you create the need for the product.

3. **Remember these buyers are extroverts, so don't neglect their friendship.** Let them know you appreciate their friendship, but stay in control.

4. **Restrict entertaining.** These buyers don't "wear well," and they usually are tiresome and somewhat boring. A lunch or group activities are best.

5. **Remember birthdays, anniversaries, and all holidays with a greeting card.** Most buyers of this type are highly sentimental, and a greeting card will make a great impression.

THE INTELLECTUALS

The intellectual buyers know it all. Naturally, we can quickly identify them as introverts. They want to be right. They are tight-lipped and generally difficult to be around. They usually limit an interview to a few minutes and will sometimes start by warning, "You have seven minutes," or some such nonsense. Don't fall for that approach, and don't allow it to happen. Never allow a buyer to restrict the time you need to give a concise, complete presentation. If you have pride in your product or service, you should have enough strength to tell the buyer, "Perhaps we could schedule this for another day. This product (service) will add significant black into to your bottom-line, and it deserves more than seven minutes. I know you will have questions and possibly suggestions, so I don't want to cheat either of us. Would Wednesday at nine o'clock fit your schedule?" Normally they will reply, "What have you got? I'll make some time for you." As they say in the infantry, "Take the high ground — and hold it."

Try not to disagree with any buyer. This is especially true in the case of the intellectuals. They will pontificate. (Why not? They know everything.) It's touchy to correct them, even if you know they are off-base. Nothing will inflame these buyers more than to be shown they are wrong. At the same time, you are confronted with a dilemma. If you point out the error, they will resent you and very likely reject you as a vendor. If you keep quiet, they will be making a decision based on faulty information.

One way of handling this is to agree and disagree at the same time. For example: Frank Intellect tells you that the Richman Monitor is rated as the finest lathe made in the United States, but you know that that's information from a report published three years ago. Your lathe is now rated the best. If you hit him with, "Wrong, you have three-year-old information," he will be wounded and resentful. Instead, you reply, "Frank, this industry is moving so fast, it is almost impossible to keep up with the new innovations and changes. The Monitor was rated number one just a short time ago, but look at this, an article that was published last week. As you can see, the Acme model 400 is now rated above all the others! Naturally, we are proud of this ranking, and that's why we offer an extended warranty with every model."

By switching from the correction to the sales presentation, you defuse possible anger Frank may have at being shown he is behind the times and faulty in his product knowledge. It goes against my grain to bow to this kind of buyer, but I would rather win the order than win an argument.

I am not suggesting a Uriah Heep approach to the know-it-all buyers; this is really an exercise in interpersonal relationships. You are dealing with a personality that is basically antisocial, introverts who have a strong self-confidence problem. In their minds, the only thing they have going for themselves is their knowledge. They will admire someone who is really on top of the game, someone who can educate them, someone who acknowledges and respects their intelligence. The intellectuals may be imposing and somewhat intimidating at first, but they probably are the easiest to sell. Follow these rules when you run across the intellectuals:

1. **Use praise cautiously.** Although intellectuals are almost always introverts, they also (almost always) have strong extrovert tendencies, but in a slightly different way. They need their intellect to be recognized, respected, appreciated, and praised. An apparent casual remark such as, "I was telling Bob Marks from Speedco that you would be the first to see the advantages of this new spring-loading feature," will normally lock in your sale. But be careful; an awkward or obvious attempt at making brownie points can be fatal.

2. **Ask for their help.** In general, people like to help other people. It makes us feel superior — even though we may not admit it, not even to ourselves. When we help a vision-impaired person across a busy street or give our subway seat to an elderly person, we bask in the imagined admiration of others who view us as a good person. The recipient's appreciation is icing on the cake. The same applies to intellectual buyers. If we ask for their help, they will eat it up. A sincere question such as, "Bob, where do you think we should price our new Model 225 to compete with the Morrison 116?" will result in a thoughtful answer and, believe me, it will puff up the buyer's chest, too. Moreover, the buyer will take a parent's pride in the Model 225 and in you.

3. **Be selective in entertaining.** Intellectuals will appreciate a tour of your facilities and a luncheon meeting with your company's brass. This is the best and probably the only way to "entertain" intellectual buyers. Sometimes tickets to lectures, the opera, the ballet, and similar cultural functions will be appreciated and repaid.

4. **Always avoid using street language when talking with the intellectuals.** Choose your words carefully, and whenever possible, let them do the talking. Be a good listener and guide the conversation with pointed observations and questions.

THE ARTFUL DODGERS

I used to classify one category of buyer as a "buck-passer." No more. There are now so many buyers who pass the buck to avoid having to turn aside salespeople or to avoid making decisions that this moniker could apply to *almost all* buyers. Remember, I said almost. The truly skilled buyers, the ones who really earn their paychecks, accept their responsibility and make decisions, are not buck-passers. They don't worry about the merchandise manager's reaction if their decisions are occasionally wrong. Truly skilled buyers have the confidence of the merchandise manager, and their track record speaks for itself, thus ensuring the buyers' and the merchandise managers' continued employment.

Today, the shortage of quality buyers (a shortage that grows daily and is recognized by most progressive companies) forces merchandise managers and other upper management people to devise methods of sheltering their weak members from the power of professional salespeople.

The "committee-buying method" of purchasing is probably the most popular way to prevent an individual buyer from being influenced by a powerful sales presentation. However, there are other ways to hide from sales professionals. Some buyers, after a powerful presentation, will tell the salesperson, "I like the product, but I have to talk to my boss about this to see if it fits in our product mix." This naturally forces the salesperson to follow up on the phone for an answer, which allows the buyers to hide behind the merchandise manager. "Well, I liked it, thought the line had real potential, but the boss says no." Or, "Well, I'd like to take this in, but if I do, I have to drop another vendor. Let me think about it. If I can drop someone, I'll buy your stuff." The follow-up on this excuse is usually, "Tried to get you in, but we're just too heavy with ABC's inventory. Next spring we should be in a position to do something."

Naturally, that is all hogwash. Any buyer worth his or her salt can place an order. If the buyers are low in the pecking order, they may have to run it by the boss, but if the presentation is strong and if they really want the line, they will do all that is necessary while you are there. If they suggest that they're going to see the merchandise manager for an approval, ask to go along and make the presentation. No buyers can convey your message as well as you can. Tell them you want to be available if the manager has any particular questions or wants any special treatment. You'll have a difficult time getting to see the merchandise manager, but it's worth the effort.

If buyers give you the story of having to drop another vendor, push for a decision then and there. "You like my line of merchandise, and you only need to decide if I should replace someone else. Isn't that so? Well, my job isn't complete unless I can help you make the decision that is best for your company. Let's compare the two lines together — my goods and the line you may have to drop. I can answer all your questions, and we can make an honest comparison. I want to show you how you will benefit by making that change." Put their feet to the fire and force a decision.

When you do that, you take control. You are in charge. If you get the opportunity to make those side-by-side comparisons, the competition's position will be weakened by their absence. Remember to ask questions and probe to discover why they bought the line to begin with and why they favor it now. You're sure to learn a lot, and very likely that information will help you to replace the entrenched product line.

If you represent a large, powerful company whose merchandise is supported by a massive advertising campaign, most of what I just stated will not apply to you. Buyers like the ones I am describing are docile and puppylike around representatives whom they consider important product sources.

2

THE CHANGING BUYER

In the preceding chapter, I may have given you the impression that buyers are inferior human beings and gutless wonders. Generally speaking, nothing could be further from the truth. As I said early on, buyers have a difficult job, stress-packed and loaded with responsibility. They are often underpaid and overworked, especially in today's business world.

Because of the way business is changing, buyers are sometimes forced to say no to the finest sales presentation and to products they would really like to carry. Many still have that adventuresome spirit and gambling instinct that makes business in general and selling in particular so much fun. But the rigid rules under which they work forbid much risk-taking.

Merchandise managers generally enforce a hard-and-fast rule: If the product is heavily advertised, it will sell. Their job is to make money by buying product lines the public will ask for. They want "presold" goods — namely, guaranteed sales, allowances, and proven, rapid-turn goods. The buyers will rarely depart from that rule. Why should they? It is safe and easy. To follow their own gut instincts can be dangerous.

Frankly, the buyer's *job* often hangs in the balance. Purchasing departments for major retailers still place orders worth millions of dollars each year, but it is the rare department that doesn't have a signed agreement on file that guarantees the sale of that merchandise, along with agreements for payment of shelf space, advertising allowances, freight allowances, warehouse allowances, repackaging charges,* and so on. Retailers have taken the risk (or so they believe) out of retailing, along with the excitement. The managers' rule works most of the time. Highly advertised goods do sell, customers do ask for them, and vendors do guarantee the sale, pay for shelf space, and buy their way into the stores. In spite of all these assurances and all these guarantees, some retailers still end up filing for protection from their creditors. Why?

See the end of this chapter for a complete explanation of what these payments mean.

There are many reasons, of course, some of which have little or nothing to do with the actual operation of the business. But much has to do with how the business is run, how the company views and values its employees, how it treats the vendors, and how it treats the customer.

If the company trusts its own decisions and its own employees, it will allow the buyer certain latitude in performing the job. The schematic will require a basic skeletal of product to be carried, but the buyer has the freedom to spot in other products and product lines to create a character, an atmosphere, a "feeling" in their stores. This buyer's latitude or "gamble" is sorely missing in many of today's mass merchandising retailers. Buyers are reduced to "order placers," monotonously placing the same orders for basically the same products, season after season. Naturally, a terrible sameness results. If you were blindfolded and led into a Kmart, Target, or Wal-Mart store or any other national chain, and if each were stripped of its company's colors and other identifying signs, you would be hard-pressed to tell any difference. The product mix and the pricing are virtually identical. The merchandising department tries to outguess what the competition is featuring that week and then drops its own prices for a product or group of products. (This is combated with: "We will meet or beat any price" proclamations.) That is their idea of merchandising! Some excitement. They remind me of those machines that pick up golf balls at a driving range, endlessly circling, picking up, and dropping off with no beginning and no end.

Just a few years ago, there were, perhaps, triple the number of national or regional retail chains as there are today. The big fish kept eating the little fish, and now we are left with just a handful of choices. The bottom-line guys — the bean counters, accountants, and lawyers — have caused this to come about. They buy the competition if they can't outperform them. They merge and acquire and lose all identity in the process. The merchandise manager's rule I mentioned earlier comes from executive row. Lacking in imagination and sales and marketing experience, the executives only look at the bottom line to judge how a business should be run.

It is true, of course, that consumers themselves have caused much of this to come about. By accepting a lower and lower standard of service and insisting on the lowest price, they have encouraged the growth and consolidation of mass merchandisers and the shrinking of full-service stores. When others saw the profits to be had in these "cattle-pen" operations, the concept spread, not just in retailing, but to other industries as well. We now pump our own gasoline, put condiments on our own hamburgers, pour our own drinks, select our own groceries (I even heard about a store that has the consumer scan the prices!), and soon we may be setting our own broken bones and taking out our own tonsils!

Until consumers stop believing that only price counts, the trend will continue and spread. But public tastes change with time; the pendulum swings back and forth. Some stores have already discovered a body of consumers who want better than just good quality and who demand retail salespeople who are trained and knowledgeable to wait on them. These stores are very successful, and others will, I believe, follow their trend.

Fortunately, there is more to the business picture than mass market retailing. Specialty stores of all kinds require good buyers and good salespeople to make them successful. Industrial goods and, in fact, all products that are used (consumed) by the buyer are still sold and bought by professionals. And we must not forget the direct sales business in which the finest salespeople and the best buyers (the direct consumers) carry on that age-old tradition of give and take, of selling and buying. Let's take a look at two additional types of buyers who best reflect that tradition.

THE VERY TOUGH BUYERS

Very tough buyers make you work for the order. They detest a lazy salesperson and demand a knowledgeable, involved representative. They will drive a hard bargain, but they will be fair and reasonable. They understand that every barrel has a bottom. Their job is to find merchandise that they can resell at a profit. They are buyers in the true sense of the word. Like all those who are good at what they do, they *want* to perform this function. They want to buy. That isn't to say they will roll over for every salesperson. On the contrary, they will listen, examine, compare, and finally give you an honest yes or no decision. Moreover, if the answer is no, they will give you a reason why — not some trumped-up nonsense, but a professional, business reason for why they have refused to buy. If you are successful in selling to them, they will expect follow-through from you that will assist them in implementing the product in the production system, home, or store.

Naturally, tough buyers expect honesty, and if you betray this trust, you will be finished forever in their eyes. Try never to make a promise to these buyers unless you are fairly confident you can keep it. They operate under the belief that "a promise made is a debt unpaid." But, from time to time, we all make promises we *think* we will be able to keep; however, conditions beyond our control prevent us from keeping them. If that happens, immediately face the buyer with the facts, apologize, and try to make it up in some other way. He or she will understand, but will remember what you owe.

Very tough buyers are the best of all customers. They are loyal to their vendors, but not to the point where they lose flexibility. Their door is always open to new vendors, new ideas, and new concepts, so you must always be on top of your game. Stay on your toes, or you can find yourself without an account. You can recognize these buyers by their openness and interest in knowing about new products and new vendors. Their product mix is on the cutting edge, rounded out with high-profile, proven sellers. Their stores are fun to shop in and always have surprises for the consumer.

If you lose a tough buyer because of some fault of your own, he or she may be difficult to regain. These buyers tend to have a long memory. At the same time, the honesty and fairness you demonstrated when you were a vendor is "banked" by them, and they will remember the positive things you did.

Unlike the timid, insecure, and frightened buyers who hide from salespeople to avoid having to make decisions, the very tough buyers will talk with any vendor representative who might have something that will add excitement, fun, depth, and, of course, profit to their product mix. They will accept telephone calls if they know the caller has something to say. And if they say they will get back to you, you can be sure they will be true to their word. Let me tell you a true story of a buyer who, to this day, ranks among my all-time heroes. He had honesty and honor, and he gained my respect and admiration. Together we earned big dollars for our companies and for ourselves and developed a lifelong friendship.

He was a buyer for a large and powerful West Coast general merchandise chain. I pounded on his door for months on end, had countless interviews, and tried my best to get even a trial order — all to no avail. He had good reasons for refusing me, but I had equally good reasons for believing my goods would sell well to his customers. Persistence is a big part of successful selling, so I kept him on my regular list of accounts. Every other week, I was at his door with a new approach or a reinforcement of my previous argument. The weeks added up to months. I got to know his receptionist well and had read the dog-eared magazines from cover to cover, but I never got an order. I was determined, but the frustration was mounting as weeks and then months slipped by.

At one interview he said to me, "I'm locked into the XYZ line just now. We have a lot of things pending — credits and so forth — but I will call you on August 4." This was in April or May. Naturally, I didn't believe a word of it, and discouraged, I nodded, shook his hand, and left. I admitted defeat; I was beat. I stopped calling on him.

You can imagine my surprise when my secretary told me he was on the telephone. As I picked up the receiver, I noticed the date was August 4! He called me to the day.

I had been prepared to accept what I thought was obvious: I wasn't going to get a dime's worth of business out of this account. Sometimes you have to take no for an answer. I was resigned to the fact that I gave it my best and that it just wasn't good enough. The first order he gave me was the largest my company had ever received from the western region. That account became my largest in California, and the business relationship lasted for years.

Salespeople, naturally, love these buyers and try to repay them for the fairness and honesty they exhibit. Salespeople will give them first refusal on goods, make sure every money-saving discount opportunity comes their way, and ensure that their orders are shipped on time and complete. They will rob another account's order, if necessary, to make sure that the very tough buyers get their merchandise.

The buyer and seller form a partnership. They become watchdogs for each other and a friendship often results outside the business environment. You can understand why it is so difficult to replace a vendor when that kind of relationship exists and has, perhaps, existed for years. Nonetheless, tough buyers will replace an existing vendor without a second thought if they are convinced another vendor can better serve the company, friendships notwithstanding. The salesperson should never feel that his or her task is impossible, merely because others appear to be entrenched.

THE CHANGING BUYER

My first full-time job taught me that anything can happen in sales. I was made district manager of a freight-forwarding company in St. Louis. The company was large nationally, but in St. Louis it had a succession of lazy and/or incompetent managers who were content with just getting by. After spending a week meeting the people I would be working with and getting to know the office routines, who the existing accounts were, where they were located, and what they were shipping by us, I examined the local freight market. St. Louis was (and still is) a fairly large city with old traditions and an "old boy network" business system. A few families dominated the business scene — breweries, shoes, and chemicals — with the exception of the aircraft and NASA hardware industries.

The largest freight account in town had made a name for itself in fighter aircraft, space vehicles, and related products. It was and still is worldwide in scope and was not only the largest, but also the fastest-growing account for freight service in the Midwest and certainly in the St. Louis market. I called and discovered that the traffic manager would see salespeople on Tuesdays — open hours! Promptly at nine o'clock on the following Tuesday, I was signing my name in the vendor book, nervous and excited.

I noticed an older man took particular interest in me, and after he checked the sign-in register, he came over and introduced himself. It turned out he was the district manager of my strongest competitor. With apparent sincerity, he told me, "I've been taking care of this company's shipping needs for years. You really don't have a chance here. Take my advice and call on some of the smaller companies. You're only wasting your time with this account."

I believed him! After all, he was experienced. I knew that his company handled this business, and my chances did appear slim. I thanked him for his advice and actually was about to leave when the receptionist called my name. "Well," I told my mentor, smiling somewhat sheepishly, "I might as well introduce myself, at least."

He grinned and nodded his approval as I was led to the traffic manager's office.

Remember now, I was an inexperienced kid, just out of college, and was very impressed with the trappings of this fancy lobby and spacious office. The traffic manager (let's call him Mr. Wilson) was a friendly fellow who could see I was as green as grass and nervous. He was kind and put me at ease as best he could with small talk, asking me about my background and education. I began to think that maybe I could get at least *some* business. After all, I knew my company's services and believed in them. Still, hovering in the back of my mind was the belief that the account was locked up tight.

In no time, we were on a first-name basis, but I knew he was a very busy man, and I didn't want to overstay my welcome. "Roy, I appreciate your seeing me this morning. I know I don't have much chance of handling any of your business, but if I can ever spot-in or ... "

Wilson stopped me in mid-sentence. "Why don't you think you have a chance at my business?" he asked, more amused than puzzled.

"Well, I met (I named my competitor) in the lobby, and he said he has this account locked up tight, and he told me not to waste my time here. He recommended I work with smaller accounts and not bother you." I was completely innocent. I didn't say this to nail my competitor or to get him in trouble or to sneak in the back door, and I think Mr. Wilson could tell that.

He was stunned. He sat there for a moment or so, with his mouth half-open. Then he stood up behind his desk. "Oh, he said that, did he?"

I nodded. "Bill, I run this department — not your competitor or anyone else. I think that point should be made clear. Can you read a tariff?" I admitted I could, and then we spent an hour together seeing if I really knew what I was doing. I passed the test.

Finally, he reached over and wrote out a freight order for about 80,000 pounds of freight headed to Los Angeles. I almost fell over myself, thanking him for the business. As I left his office, he told me, "Call me before the week is out. I'll have some other things for you."

My friendly competitor wasn't friendly for very long. He was sure I had sandbagged him somehow — and I had, but not on purpose. As his business tailed off and mine picked up (we used the same loading dock), he began to tell people that Mr. Wilson was my uncle, cousin, or brother-in-law. The fact was, of course, he had opened his mouth when he shouldn't have. His own smug, arrogant behavior put him in a tough spot. So I learned two things from that episode: (1) any account can be won, no matter how hopeless it may first appear; and (2) when you talk to strangers, restrict your conversation to the weather.

THE SMALL BUYERS

In small, sometimes emerging companies and in retail operations, the buyers are frequently promoted from the retail sales ranks. Retail salespeople are not normally big-time thinkers. They see things on a much smaller scale than do most wholesale people. They are notoriously tightfisted and take great pride in their responsibilities.

These buyers are busier than a one-armed paperhanger. They will usually retain the responsibility of selling on the floor and will accept the buyer's job as an extension of retail selling. They will now, of course, have to take inventory, arrange advertising, develop in-store promotions, hire and fire personnel, balance the cash registers, and God knows what else. Even with this backbreaking schedule of duties, they are normally underpaid and have few benefits and almost no security. Why they do it is beyond most reasoning.

Few have formal purchasing training, and many envy the freedom of the sales representatives who call on them. They will frequently approach the sales manager, regional manager, or anyone else who might accompany the sales representative with the suggestion that they would make excellent outside salespeople. This suggestion complicates the situation for the supervisor and the representative, especially since most, but by no means all, inside salespeople are terrible outside territory salespeople.

As buyers, I have found them to be among the finest I have ever met. First, they completely understand the wants and needs of their customers. They spot trends, fads, and hot products faster than anyone else. This often results in a shameful circumstance because when the big outfits pick up on the fads, the little retailer has a tough time getting the merchandise — another example of the big fish gobbling up the little fish.

Small buyers appreciate the salesperson who calls on them with measured regularity. They appreciate any favors, such as extended billing, free goods, or the first shot at "B" goods and close-outs — anything that will add a little profit. They will try to repay by placing a larger-than-normal order or by adding another product from the line. Like all buyers — in fact, like all people — they dislike salespeople who lie, and their distrust will freeze you out of the account for eternity.

Because they are so overloaded with work, they can't spend much time with anyone. The sales representative's job with these buyers is to help them, to evaluate new products, and to do some of the work for them. Write up the order in advance, for example, so that only a signature is needed. Take an inventory, or do something else that gives these poor wretches a little breather. Trying to nail down the small buyers can take more time than the sales representative wants or can afford to spend.

Some small buyers are reluctant to blaze a trail with a new product. Their imagination is limited, and they tend to stick to the tried and proven, but this really depends on the size and financial strength of the account. When you run into reluctance to try a new product, you will probably discover that the store is having money problems or that the buyer is restricted in buying what he or she really wants. Usually, the store owner still holds the decision-making reins in this instance.

The small buyers' way of dodging your strong sales presentation is to say, "I haven't had any calls for that item. When I do, I'll order it." The only way I know of getting around that is to sell to their competitors. The kiss of death in small retail operations is not having something their competitors have. They all suspect the competition has a magic method of stealing their customers, and having a product they don't have is simply not tolerable. Once you walk in with proof that the store down the block has your line, small buyers will fall like a ripe apple.

DEVELOPING A THICK SKIN

Being rejected is part of selling. It's a disagreeable part, but it's one that every salesperson confronts. No one ever gets accustomed to it, no matter what you might hear or read. All the talk about rejection not being personal (which is usually true) cannot take the sting out of being rejected, especially if you have worked hard and long to sell a particular account. That is one additional reason for appreciating a good buyer. If the reason is solidly based on business, you can understand the rejection and accept it.

What should you do if, in your opinion, the buyer is unfair, unreasonable, or just plain stupid? Should you go around him to his boss? That is a tough and tricky question. Generally, going over the buyer's head is a dangerous decision that rarely delivers a positive result. Remember, the buyer and his boss work side-by-side. They are probably friendly to each other (if not friends), and the boss will most likely have a protective attitude toward his buyers. At the same time, if he is a good manager, he wants his people to give every vendor a fair opportunity. After all, who knows where the next hot product line is going to come from? In spite of all that, you are still an outsider, a potential troublemaker, and an unknown. The manager and the buyer do not have a bunker mentality, but they probably do have a close working relationship. It is a tough nut to crack.

If you telephone the merchandise manager or write a letter, you can be sure he will talk with the buyer. He knows the weaknesses of his buyers, and he understands that they are not always fair. Your call or letter may be the method he will use to remind them of their responsibilities and what he expects from them. His reaction will, of course, only harden the buyer's attitude toward you.

"What's this all about, June? This salesperson says you aren't giving him a fair shot. Any truth to that?" June will screw up her face in disgust as she shakes her head. "What a jerk! I spent almost half an hour with him. The guy has a line that just doesn't make it in our chain. How fair can I be? I can't help it if he doesn't have a line we can sell, can I?"

The manager will nod understandingly, "OK, but call him and talk with him. If he insists, see him again, and I'll sit in on it. Then you can dismiss him." That will be that. You may have won a small victory, but your future chances will have been diminished significantly.

I have rarely seen an instance in which going over the buyer's head has paid off. It may happen, but not often.

When you take that big gamble, you burn a bridge that cannot be rebuilt. You are tagged with the label of whiner, complainer, or nonprofessional. That buyer, and any other buyer he or she may influence will be closed to you as a potential account. The smart thing to do, if you think you are being treated unfairly is to try to talk with the buyer, as one businessperson to another. Calmly explain why you think this person is being unfair. Ask him or her to walk through your presentation with you.

You may be surprised at the results when you honestly state your case: "Frank, I don't think you are being fair with my product line. I don't think you have honestly compared it with what's out there. I know how busy you are, but I'd like to make a side-by-side comparison of the Floogle line with you. If you still can't see what I see, I'll fold my tent. Could we meet for that purpose sometime next week?"

If, after the comparison meeting, the buyer still rejects you, or if the buyer refuses to meet, shake hands, say thank-you, and try another day. Remember, no single account will make or break your territory. Respect and appreciate all the business you secure, but never panic-react if you lose an account or can't dent a potential account. You will reach your goals with a little patience combined with hard, intelligent effort. By the way, a good sense of humor is highly recommended.

MINI-GLOSSARY OF TERMS

The following informal definitions are designed to help you understand the payments and practices that many buyers expect or demand.

PAYMENT FOR SHELF SPACE

Many, in fact most, grocery chains and many general merchandise chains now demand that the vendor pay a **slotting fee**. This is nothing short of larceny. It is very much like blackmail or extortion. It is unfair and should be a crime. Actually, there are some state and federal laws that make this practice a violation, but it is too widespread in many industries, especially in the grocery business. More important, the laws are almost never enforced by any legal agency. Usually, the buyer will tell the seller, point-blank, "If you want to be in our stores, the slotting fee is $XXXXX per item." Incredibly, the sum is often in the thousands of dollars, which effectively excludes small and medium-size vendors from being represented in important stores and fully sharing in the marketplace.

Some chains demand warehouse allowances or advertising allowances. These allowances also exclude small and medium-size vendors from the total marketing picture, especially in the grocery and general merchandise chains. This disturbing practice is now gaining favor in other industries that operate retail outlets. What is even more threatening is that smaller and smaller retailers are also demanding these tributes.

How can you beat this system? Frankly, I don't have a clue. I suppose you could try to get the Department of Commerce involved, but that would mean compiling hard evidence. It would probably mean that the aggrieved party would have to get deeply involved and maybe become responsible for gathering evidence (wearing a wire and all that). It would mean a long, long trial (if it ever came to that), which would represent a considerable investment of time and money. Few, if any, small companies would wish to take on that responsibility.

Something should be done, and I suppose that eventually something will be done. But, in my opinion, it will take a powerful vendor (or several powerful vendors) with courage and a strong sense of decency before any change will be made.

One last point. Some chains actually have their buyers on commission! These buyers get a percentage of the concession monies they are able to extort from vendors. It is clear how this distorts, twists, and muddies the buyer-seller relationship. The playing field isn't quite level.

WAREHOUSE FEES

Buyers will often ask if your company has a warehouse fee allowance. It is unspoken, but the implication is that if no warehouse fee is allowed, no order will be issued. The warehouse fee, I suppose, is to cover the retailer's cost of warehousing the vendor's merchandise before it is shipped to the stores for sale.

ADVERTISING ALLOWANCES

"Proof of performance," sometimes called "proof of publication," is the vendor's way to make certain the advertising allowance is spent to advertise the merchandise and not a disguised and stolen discount.

Proof of performance will require the customer to submit a tear sheet of the ad, and a copy of the publication's invoice usually before the allowance is given.

Most vendors are willing, even eager to grant an advertising allowance since it usually will guarantee a spot in the store where the product will be readily seen by the customers.

If a "proof of performance" is admitted, I have no argument with this allowance. If no proof is required, then it is another form of extortion.

REPACKAGING CHARGES

These charges are made if the retailer has to return merchandise. Supposedly, the account may have to repackage the goods, which costs them something. However, the charge is made regardless of whether or not merchandise is returned. I believe the retailer should have some responsibility and share in any such cost.

3

The Sales Profession — How Important Can It Be?

Patti Page used to sing a song called, "How Important Can It Be?" The song concluded that nothing is as important as it first seems. There is a lot of truth in that. Likewise, combat soldiers say, "Never sweat the small stuff — and almost everything is small stuff." Isn't that also true? You are never given something you can't handle. According to other words of wisdom, "Tough times don't last; tough people do."

We all have known people who almost worked themselves to death. They worried about everything in their business. Work affected their entire outlook on life: they not only never stopped to smell the roses, but they also never noticed the roses in the first place. Being a basically lazy fellow myself, I could never figure out why these people worked so hard. They almost never saw their families, and when they did, they never got along very well. They didn't spend much on themselves — maybe a fancy car they only drove back and forth to work and a big house they slept in for a few hours each night. Their business was their life.

Then sometimes God or fate or whatever powers you choose stepped in and scared the bejabbers out of them. Perhaps they found out they had a serious health condition, or perhaps a family member had an accident that jolted them back to reality, making them realize how much that family member really meant to them. After that, their lives changed, their priorities shifted, and their outlook broadened.

I imagine we all have asked ourselves from time to time, "Just what is so important about what I do? Is my life fulfilling? Am I happy?" These are simple questions, but tough ones to answer sometimes. How many of us really know ourselves? We spend most of our lives working or preparing for work. It seems that the rest of the time we spend thinking about work.

THE SALES PROFESSION — HOW IMPORTANT CAN IT BE?

Obviously, our work is important to us. It can and should be fulfilling, enjoyable, and satisfying. In order for that to be so, we must know that what we do has some importance. The drudgery of a job that has no impact on society soon leads us to a total lack of interest and inferior production. "If it doesn't matter, why should I care?" is the emerging attitude. If you think your job is only a way to exist or survive, then boredom will set in quickly, and right behind boredom is failure. Knowing that what you do is important is vital to your mental health and to your success. So let's consider what we do for a living. Is selling really important?

A LOOK BACK IN TIME

Selling, which was called "trading" in ancient times, is one of the world's oldest professions. The earliest traveling salespeople were merchants who opened trade routes in their search for new markets and new customers. Continents were discovered and settled, towns were established, and new and wondrous products were introduced to the world. These trade routes were jealously guarded and protected. Countless wars have been fought over trade routes.

America was discovered because of the quest for a new trade route to the East. Trading with the Native Americans became vital for the Pilgrims. Without it, they wouldn't have survived the terrible winters, the summer droughts, and other calamities. The trade of beaver, fox, and ermine was so profitable that it resulted in a nine-year-long war between France and England. Trade also figured greatly in the war that eventually produced the United States.

One of the primary causes of the Civil War centered on trade disputes between the industrial North and the agrarian South. The slave issue (in itself a trade, although a loathsome one) developed later, as a lightning rod and popular issue that inflamed the populace and "justified" the war.

American salesmanship has become part of our national lore and is renowned throughout the world. Anyone who travels overseas for the first time is always surprised to see so many United States products advertised on buses and billboards, in newspapers, and on television. Naturally, salesmanship made that possible, and it continues to expand our reach and influence throughout the world. The "Yankee Trader" tradition is ingrained in our national character. The United States is a nation of salesmen and saleswomen.

THE VALUE OF COMPETITION

If I were forced to pick the one thing that selling contributes to the good of all societies, I would have to say that it creates competition. Competition *forces* better products on the market, lowers prices, and provides choices. As salespeople, we may from time to time wish we were "the only game in town," but the truth is that the lack of competition would mean disaster. Honest and *open* competition is what builds a strong economy and a prosperous citizenry. Today, in some areas of our economy, we are seeing a restriction of competition. This is an issue with which we should all be concerned.

I always cringe when I hear someone say, "Oh, I'm *just* a salesperson." Just a salesperson! Egad! Selling is the *most* important activity in our society, or in any other free society! Your job, no matter what or even how much you sell, is critical, vital, and important to the general health of the economy.

I'm sure you've heard it said, "Nothing happens until someone sells something." It may be a cliché, but it's true. Nothing happens, no one is hired, no pay raises are given, no new machinery or equipment is bought, no improvements or inventions are introduced, and no new industries are created until someone makes a sale.

We should all bear this in mind when we make our calls. Selling is a proud profession with a rich history. Its importance that has never been fully appreciated or acknowledged. Before the recent collapse of the Soviet Union, politicians, media people, and political scientists constantly analyzed the differences between the free, Western nations (especially the United States) and the socialist nations. There were serious, conflicting differences between their economic and social systems and our own. Those differences were far ranging, but I believe they all are or were based on the lack of competition — a lack that only selling can cure. The pure theory of communism was "everyone according to his need." Not a bad idea, except that it forgot the one element that makes everything work — competition.

In the former Soviet Union, and other socialist societies, no salespeople existed. If a factory needed raw materials, a bureaucrat saw that a supplier was selected, and the supplier had a duty to fulfill the orders of the bureaucrat. There was no competition, no contract bidding, and no comparison of value. The supplier could care less if the material was of poor quality. What could happen? What would the bureaucrats do? Fire him? Find another source? No way; there was no other source. This "frozen" condition restricted, stifled, and eliminated competition. The ailing economy that resulted brought down the entire system. Under the communist system, if a citizen wanted a beefsteak, for example, he could only buy that steak at a government store (if he were lucky). If the steak was tough, loaded with fat, or in any other way unacceptable, the consumer had no recourse. The government store was the only place where the citizen could buy the beefsteak. To whom could he complain? Who cared?

I remember visiting Leningrad (now back to its original name, St. Petersburg). It was, in many ways, the showcase of the Soviet Union: a beautiful city with many fountains and parks and, of course, the celebrated Hermitage Museum. After a tiring walk around the city and a tour of the Hermitage, I was smoking a cigar and feeding the pigeons in a small park, enjoying the weather and watching the people stroll by. Suddenly, I realized that practically everyone I saw was wearing pinkish-red socks. The socks were garish and unbecoming, but I suppose the sock factory had received a shipment of raw goods dyed that hellish color. If you needed socks (and I later learned from friends that the socks didn't wear well, so the turnover was rapid), you bought what was offered. The selection and variety of goods were nonexistent. Prices were high for shoddy, inferior goods, yet there was no reason to improve or change. No salesperson was there to offer a challenge, to suggest a better way, to *force* a change.

In Leningrad, as elsewhere in that worker's paradise, food was frequently in short supply and expensive (measured in terms of local incomes). People lined up for the opportunity to buy bread, meat, cabbage, and potatoes. Whenever it was possible, many hoarded foods that could be stored, because the frequent shortages would mean going hungry.

At the same time it was reported that food rotted in the fields and on the trees, while people went hungry in the cities, because no adequate roads or transportation systems existed. Wheat, oats, and other grains were piled high on farms and in rural communities, feasted on by hordes of rats and left to rot on the ground, exposed to the elements. Why was this allowed to happen? No competition existed and no sales pressure forced better transportation systems, better roads, more silos, and a more effective, efficient method of distribution. No marketing system existed.

As I learned of these conditions, I constantly compared them to the system in the United States. If a salesperson in America (or in any progressive, free society) represents a farmer and finds that the farmer can't deliver products to the customer, the salesperson soon finds someone who can. The left-out farmer would be in immediate contact with the local division of highways and demand that he be given a way to get his products to market.

Recognizing grain as wealth, the farmer would borrow money from the bank (that would be issuing loans) to build the silos to safely store the harvest to be sold when the market was right. Little would be wasted. The politicians would push the necessary buttons, and the roads would be built. Soon an improved road network would develop, new markets would spring up, housing developments would stretch out from the city, and the cause of it all would be, as it always has been, a salesperson.

Competition, prodded by salespeople, causes new products to be invented. When McCormick saw that grain was wasted due to slow, manual harvesting, he invented the harvester. Thompson recognized the need for a rapid, transatlantic communication system and invented the telegraph; Bell invented the telephone; and all of these inventors worked to improve a system, to increase sales. In a way, these great inventors were salespeople, because they created competition along with their inventions. Frequently, their ideas were not readily accepted; they met resistance, argument, and challenge. Sometimes those challenges forced them to reexamine their inventions, to make changes, to improve. That's what competition does.

CREATING A NEED

I like to remind salespeople that selling is creating a need. That is worth thinking about. What is meant by "creating a need"? I give the example of the first person to sell soup in a can. Just consider what a job he had! Prior to canned soup, all soups were made from scratch in the home. It might have taken most of a day to make a pot of soup. Usually the soup was great, but sometimes it didn't turn out too well. Perhaps, busy with other chores, the cook would burn the meat or chicken, overcook the vegetables, or overseason the mixture. If that happened, the family ate the soup uncomplaining, knowing that the cook did her best. At worst, they tossed out the entire afternoon's effort. But the savory smell and wonderful taste of the homemade soup seemed worth the effort. Besides, what else could you do? If you wanted soup, you made it in your own kitchen.

Then, along came a salesperson who said, "Here is soup in a can. Just open the can, add a little water and heat, and then sit down to a wonderful, satisfying, delicious bowl of soup. You can stock several kinds: vegetable beef, chicken noodle, clam chowder . . . and all are ready when you are." What a convenience! This innovative concept freed the homemaker from being tied to the kitchen all day just to make soup for dinner. The salesperson created a need.

I'm sure the new idea was met with stiff resistance. After all, who had ever heard of soup in a can? The idea was revolutionary. Perhaps some considered soup in a can as an attack on the family itself. Surely the grocer must have narrowed his eyes and shook his head. Who would buy soup in a can? How could it be as tasty and nourishing as homemade soup? But eventually, some bold soul took it on and stocked soup in a can, and some overworked homemaker bought it. The rest, as they say, is history.

Today, there isn't a store in the United States or in most of the world that doesn't stock and sell soup in a can. The people who sell soup are no longer truly salespeople. That first tough, brave trailblazer was a true sales professional, an innovator who was in competition with tradition. He saw a need when no one else did.

And so it is with any new product, service, or concept. Expect resistance and welcome it. Never fear it. If you know your product, you will be eager to hear an argument and a challenge. When buyers complain, attack your product, and ask questions, they really want to buy! If you are prepared, you will eventually overcome their arguments. As one song says, "You gotta have heart."

Remember, you are doing the most important job in commerce. The buyer is nothing without the salesperson. Without salespeople, no business can grow — indeed, no business can exist — and our entire society would eventually collapse without the salespeople who create competition, force improvement, and challenge old ideas.

GETTING STARTED

As boring as it sounds, and usually is, organization is nonetheless vital to sales success. An organized salesperson is a good salesperson. In today's business world, in particular, salespeople must have all their tools at hand. They have to know what an account has bought, when the account placed its last order, the rate of inventory turn around, advertisement placement, what was sold as a result of that ad, what the competitive pricing is, and what the PSF (per square foot) margin was.

All this information and more can be recorded on simple index cards or in an account book, along with the name of the buyer, name and address of the store, buying hours, telephone numbers, fax numbers, and even personal notes about the likes and dislikes of the buyer.

Today's technology provides even greater information capabilities. Laptop computers and new inventory counting systems make available more information than an entire statistical department formerly provided. This is an enormous advantage to selling, and the person who refuses to maintain either a written or computerized file on every account is at a distinct disadvantage and will surely fall behind the competition.

Successful salespeople have always known the importance of record-keeping to their success. Although they may not have enjoyed keeping records, they understood that the information provided was well worth the tedium. In this chapter we'll cover some important steps to getting organized and enhancing your success in sales.

STEP ONE: GRADING THE ACCOUNTS

Depending on the company you represent and the territory you inherit, the best approach to getting organized will vary. In general, the first step in organizing a sales territory is to know which of your accounts are active and which of the existing accounts you would like to have as customers.

Project what the territory is presently producing, and compare that projection to your quota or personal goal. Account by account, you should make a projection of what the account is capable of producing, regardless of whether it is presently a customer or merely a potential account.

Next, you should place a coded grade alongside each account. That grade should determine what, in your opinion, is your realistic chance of getting at least some business from each account. You should be optimistic, along with being realistic, as you code/grade the accounts. Grading will encourage you to design plans that enable you to improve or land each account. It is a focusing method that makes you work on tough accounts and face unfriendly buyers.

You should also know what your predecessor was working on, what advances he made, what work was in progress, and details that he noted (which you should accept with question) about the buyers and other issues. Was he doing the things you would do? Was he off the scent? Had he done any damage, or do things look promising? Once you have completed this listing of accounts, you can begin to create your daily, weekly, and monthly itinerary.

STEP TWO: CREATING AN ITINERARY

A daily itinerary is a list of the accounts you must see on a regular cycle, every week (or more than once a week). Not all accounts require this kind of attention, of course, and some only need to be seen every two weeks or once a month. This is why I separate itineraries into daily, weekly, and monthly divisions. Actually, there is only one itinerary, but I sandwich in accounts that should be seen on an irregular basis, along with the accounts I hope to land. Without a daily, weekly, and monthly guide that regularly puts you in front of buyers, you will overlook accounts that you should be working, and you will find yourself avoiding difficult, but potentially lucrative, accounts.

An itinerary will save you time and money, make you more efficient, make your job easier and more fun, and give you more time to investigate selling opportunities that lie right under your feet. If you change jobs, you will be able to carry with you a complete, blanket knowledge of the territory, which will give you a jump-start with your new company. You cannot expect to carry that information in your head, even though many believe they can and try unsuccessfully to do so.

I would like a penny — heck, make that a million dollars — for every hour salespeople waste looking for accounts. I have worked with salespeople who spent most of a day in the car looking for addresses! I never interrupted their wanderings, believing they would learn more from being frustrated and embarrassed than from any suggestion I could make. At the end of such a day, I would have coffee with the offending salesperson and ask him how much time he felt he had wasted that day. Amazingly, many thought the time lost was not worth mentioning! I can only assume they were so accustomed to this sort of daily behavior that they considered it as business as usual. Wasting time had become part of their regular workday! The underlying reason could be (and it has occurred to me) that they harbor some fear of facing the accounts, of making a presentation, and of having to ask for business. In short, they are afraid of doing what they are being paid to do!

The fear of closing is an irrational fear experienced by many salespeople. It is irrational because closing is the whole reason we salespeople are out there. But more on that in a later chapter. For now, being organized, prepared, and ready to act is one big step toward eliminating that fear.

Obviously, the simplest way to avoid driving around in circles is to buy an up-to-date street guide or map book. When the address is located in the map book, mark the page number in the book and note the cross streets on your card files or in the laptop. Highlight the location of the account in the map book as well. Naturally, after a short time, you will know where all of your current and potential accounts are located. Nevertheless, things will change: companies move, hire new buyers, establish new buying hours, and so forth. The itinerary must be updated and corrected frequently.

This all sounds easy to do, but, unfortunately, the accounts never cooperate. Call A is located next door to call B, but the buyer at call B only sees salespeople on Mondays, and the buyer at call A only sees people on Tuesdays. The buyer at call C interviews in the mornings, and the buyer at call D interviews in the afternoon. Arranging your itinerary can be a maddening and time-consuming exercise. Just when you get it into some kind of reasonable order, call A will change buyers, and the new guy will only see salespeople on Thursdays.

In spite of the adjustments necessary, maintaining an updated itinerary is worth it. Once you become expected at a particular account, at a particular time, and on a particular day, you become part of the buyer's business week. She looks forward to your visit, with pleasure or with dread. Then, perhaps in spite of herself, you soon are included in her buying plans. You are in the forefront of her mind when she designs a product mix.

I consider an itinerary extremely important and an absolute, proven sales booster. Nonetheless, it is one of the toughest things to convince a salesperson to organize, follow, and maintain, simply because many salespeople are not properly organized. These unorganized salespeople spend much of their time looking for excuses, rather than looking for sales opportunities by taking an aggressive, attack-oriented approach which often results in rejection (their greatest fear). They drive around, complaining about the high cost of working their territory and about the poorly organized and "unfair" territory boundaries their manager has drawn. They are like water spiders that skitter about on the face of stagnant ponds — seemingly without purpose — speeding from one spot to another, accomplishing nothing, and never getting beneath the surface.

As stated, an itinerary cuts down on wasted time and permits you to make more calls per day, sell more orders per week, and earn more commissions per month. To the territory salesperson, a properly organized and maintained itinerary can increase sales by as much as 35 percent! And that means thousands of dollars in extra commissions.

STEP THREE: ORGANIZING THE ACCOUNT BOOK

Step three involves organizing an account book. Most good stationery stores have a variety of account books that require few or no changes to adapt to your business. Or, if you like, you can design your own account book. The form I suggest (see Figure 4.1 at the end of this chapter) is as good as any and has worked well. However, you may wish to store your information in a computer. I can't recommend any particular software, but any good computer store will be able to suggest the proper program for you. The important thing is that you do it.

On the back of each account page is a "Post-Call Notes" page (see Figure 4.2). I can't stress too strongly how important these notes are. No one can remember precisely what took place with every call. What was said? What was the mood? What did you promise? When should you follow up? All this information and more should be noted immediately after every call, and the notes should be reviewed before the next visit.

Buyers are impressed when you show up with the samples or the support literature that you promised during your previous call. They are gratified when you recall exactly what they said or promised and when a complaint they had has been handled to their satisfaction. Your stock rises sharply in their opinion of you and your company.

With records like these, you never miss a selling opportunity. I recall a prospective account located in northern California. It was medium-size company, growing by leaps and bounds, but we couldn't break in, no matter how hard we tried. When working with salespeople, I always asked to see the toughest accounts they had. After all, if they were doing well with an account, they didn't need me. Anyway, the sales representative and I had made several calls on this account without any success. But on this day, the representative was confident and gleeful and assured me that today was our day.

My ideas about recordkeeping had been pounded home and were showing results. This early success fueled the flames of enthusiasm, and I had a fanatical recordkeeping disciple. I often received memos and phone calls reporting the steady growth in the territory, thanks in large measure to excellent records and organization.

Before our call, the salesperson once again reviewed the post-call notes from the last visit and plucked a file from a well-organized case. We met the buyer-owner in her office a few minutes later.

"I remember your telling me you had some problems with XYZ's top camera model, their auto-focus 35mm," the representative began. "In fact, you said you had had some customer returns and more than a few complaints, right?"

The buyer acknowledged that was true, especially when the camera was used in cold or wet weather. But, she added, it was a really nice camera, except for those few problems, and she went on to note that those were not major concerns in California.

"I guess you've seen this article from last month's issue of *Modern Photography*? (*Handing her a copy.*) *Modern* points out that the shutter mechanism is lubricated with a new synthetic that is too heavy for the delicate shutter blades. As a result, you often get shutters that freeze or are slow in closing. Not too great for good photos!" The last statement he said good naturedly and with a smile. "They noted this was especially a problem in cold or wet weather, but suggested it might be a long-term concern as the camera is used over the years.

"Our auto-focus 35mm never needs lubrication, thanks to a design normally found only on cameras selling for three or four times more than our retail. In the upcoming issue of *Consumer Digest*, our AF-35 will enjoy the 'Best Buy' recommendation. If you place your order today, I can promise you delivery for the upcoming Labor Day holiday. Frankly, we expect a rush of orders when *Consumer Digest* hits the newsstands."

Naturally, the buyer was impressed, and the salesperson landed that account as promised. It developed into one of the largest in that region.

Would he have landed that choice piece of business anyway? Maybe, but maybe not. Other competitors were after that business, too. We could have ended up in a race with the other suitors. Instead, my sales representative got the order because, although he was not the first to call on the buyer that week, he was by far the best prepared. The representative was alert to the article and immediately connected its significance with the account.

This was a busy salesperson with a large, active territory. While working on, perhaps, twenty other potential customers and while serving his established accounts, could the representative have remembered what that buyer had said a month before, without the post-call notes? I doubt it.

This system works equally well with existing accounts. You know what the stock position is, what the hot selling items are, and you can determine from your notes what should be featured and advertised and what should be dropped or added to the product mix. That sort of take-charge selling puts you above the average, run-of-the-mill salesperson. You become a partner with your customer. You avoid missing stock orders and reduce or eliminate rush orders. The buyer, who will blame you when things go wrong, no matter who is at fault, will depend on your input and your information, because he or she knows you are organized, and errors will be held to a minimum.

STEP FOUR: USING A BRIEFCASE

Lately, some sales managers have drifted away from requiring their people to carry a briefcase. They say that a briefcase is intimidating, creates a stiff image, and looks like a close before you ever open. "It reminds me of the old IBM guys, you know, all wearing banker-gray suits and solid blue ties — like male versions of *The Stepford Wives*."

I suppose there is some truth in that, but selling is a serious business (with the emphasis on business). In order to conduct it properly, a salesperson must have certain information at hand. A briefcase is the only sensible method to transport that material. I have no problem with carrying only a catalog into the account's place of business, but the briefcase should be readily available and always carried when introducing a new product or product line.

What should a briefcase contain? Every well-stocked briefcase should contain business cards, extra pens, a small notepad, order forms, credit applications, product or service catalogs, support materials, copies of current advertising and promotional offers, an address book, and extra "The salesperson you leave behind" materials, such as product brochures.

HOW BEING ORGANIZED PAYS OFF

Frankly, I hate to work at organizing a territory. It is boring work, tedious and tiresome, but it pays off big-time. Let me tell you about a sales situation I witnessed a few years ago. Two salespeople, calling on the same account, arrived within minutes of each other. Salesperson X was a handsome, glib, clever, and capable man who enjoyed a friendly relationship with the buyer, who was a tough and demanding professional. Salesperson X arrived first and so was the first to be interviewed. He presented his new promotion with excitement and enthusiasm, showed his samples, outlined his program, and used support materials to bolster his presentation. It was a good presentation, and the buyer placed an order. Before leaving, Mr. X asked, "Do you need anything else?"

"Yes, I need two dozen of your model 776 and maybe a dozen of model 777," the buyer answered. Salesperson X added these items to the order, thanked the buyer, winked at his colleague, and left. All in all, he wasn't there more than thirty minutes. As far as he was concerned, he had done a good job. But had he? Could he have done more? Could he have done better? Think about that. Would you have done anything differently? If so, what and how? Now read what Salesperson Y did.

Salesperson Y was not very glib; in fact, she was a bit on the shy side and had a slight stutter that sometimes worsened with tension. But she made her impediment work for her; she listened more and talked much less (which, over a period of time, made her one of the best salespeople I ever knew). She was knowledgeable and well organized. This was only her second or third call on this tough buyer, and I could see she was a little apprehensive. On the previous call to this account, she had taken a careful inventory of our products, and while she waited for X to finish his visit, she updated the inventory, compared it to the old one and discovered some interesting things.

"OK," the buyer called out, "what do you have for me?"

"I have some great, new products to present," she replied. "But before I do, I wonder if you realize just how much money you are losing with us?"

I blinked, and the buyer was shocked. "What do you mean?" he asked, suddenly very interested.

"On my last visit I took an inventory, and while I was waiting to see you this morning, I took another and discovered you are again out of stock on Models 441, 445, 450, and 611. The inventories show that you were out of stock on those same items last month, too. Since you normally order two dozen of each per month, that means you are selling out of stock sometime in mid-month. If you double your order, you won't be missing sales and losing dollars. Your customers won't be going elsewhere. I'm sure you want that, so I've drawn up this proposed order and I've tripled the quantities. The reason for that is so we can gauge just how fast each model is selling and what the proper inventory level should be. I want to protect you from vacant shelves, lost sales, and empty cash registers."

I could see the buyer looking at my salesperson with a new respect. This young woman was really on top of her job. In fact, she knew more about some parts of his operation than he did. She had touched on a strong emotion in him — the fear of losing sales to competitors.

"Yes," he said, "but your suggested order has many more models listed than the ones I'm out of stock on."

She nodded, "Right. I took a complete inventory and compared it with the earlier one from last month. I brought your stock up to your mini-max inventory levels, making some adjustments where necessary. I'm sure you want to add those to your order as well, right?"

"Right," he smiled in appreciation. You could see he admired her reasonable and strong approach and her terrific organization. He glanced at me and shook his head slightly in admiration of this dynamic salesperson.

"Now, about our new products, I'm sure you've heard . . . "

"Stop it!" the buyer laughed. "I surrender, add what you think I'll need. Chances are you're as good a buyer as you are a seller."

She laughed too and beamed as she thanked him for the order, which was easily five or six times bigger than Salesperson X's order.

I was bowled over by her excellent presentation, by her entire demeanor. But what really was the "cherry atop the sundae," was her carefully recording in the "Post-Call Notes" page what had transpired, and reminding herself of what she would present on her next visit.

This is a classic example of how organization assists a salesperson to gain larger orders, and how it develops in the buyer's mind the impression that the salesperson is a helper, an extra employee, or a partner who will contribute to building and strengthening the business.

Being organized does something else, too. It gives you confidence and a sense of sureness. When you are prepared and ready for anything that comes your way, you can't wait to get to the buying decision. Closing is something you look forward to, because you know in your heart and mind that your close will be successful.

One of the surest ways to damage your sales presentation is by running out to your car to retrieve something or having to call your office. Anything that distracts from the focus of your presentation or that separates you from the buyer should be avoided. Such interruptions open the doors for telephone calls, employees asking questions, and fires to be extinguished — all of which break the continuity of the presentation and the concentration of the buyer.

STEP FIVE: FINDING FOLLOW-UP METHODS

Finally, you must establish a way to follow up on your sales call. If the account is new and perhaps as yet unsold by you, you may find it difficult or awkward to recontact the buyer. What do you say? How do you open? What can you say or do that will have some meaning? There are many different ways of following up.

Some salespeople find it effective to send a brief note, thanking the buyer for the time and reviewing the high points of the interview. Others will telephone in a day or two, and still others will send samples, product surveys, and other support materials with a note and their business card, thus jogging the buyer's memory.

Recently, I received a charming gift delivered to my home. Beautifully packaged, it included chocolates, fruit, and cheeses. I was confused. Who was sending me gifts and why? The tasteful card read simply, "Thank you for the business," and was signed by a company I represent. I was very pleased at this thoughtful gesture. Never before had I received anything like this. The companies I worked for always considered my commissions pay enough, and they were right. But this small, kind, and thoughtful extra made me want to work even harder for that company. I was, for the first time, able to experience firsthand how a buyer might react to this sort of follow-up.

Some average salespeople don't believe that recordkeeping is important in their particular business. Direct sales, for example. "Why bother? I sell them once and never see them again!" Mind you, I said *average* salespeople, but you don't want to be average, do you?

One of the most powerful direct salespeople I ever knew kept careful records of all the accounts he sold. After three or sometimes six months, he would contact his customers again and ask if they were happy with their purchases. If there was a problem, he tried hard to solve it. Most people were surprised to hear from him. (Think about it. Have you ever had a direct salesperson call you again to see if you were happy or had problems with which he or she could help?)

Most of the time, he told me, his customers had no problems and were happy with their purchase. He would enjoy a few minutes on the telephone and then, just before ringing off, he would ask if they knew anyone who might also be interested in his product, such as neighbors, relatives, coworkers, friends, or anyone else to whom they might refer him.

This was a rich source of leads for him, and the percentage of sales from those leads was very high. The referred people were highly qualified, because he came highly recommended by his former customers, who were the referrals' trusted relatives, friends, and coworkers. He told me that often he never had to ask for referrals; the names of potential customers were simply volunteered.

NOTES AND CARDS

I'm sure we have all received birthday, anniversary, and holiday cards from insurance, real estate, and automobile salespeople. It is their way of staying in touch, and I think a nice way, albeit an ineffective way. The weakness in this approach is simply this: It leaves the recontact in the hands of the recipient who has no particular reason for making the contact. In fact, he or she may want to call, but feels awkward.

How much better it would be to have that card followed up by a brief, friendly personal telephone call. "I remember today is your birthday, and I wanted to add my best wishes on this special day." Wow! You have to feel some obligation to that kind of call. From there, it is an easy step to asking for and getting referrals.

As you went through this chapter, you may have thought that some or all of the information was pretty obvious, and you'd be right. But, like Poe's "The Purloined Letter," the obvious is often overlooked. If you sit down and honestly analyze the time you spend each week in front of a decision maker, you will be amazed to find that it only amounts to 5.2 hours! Think of that! The average salesperson only spends 5.2 hours a week doing the most important activity of all. The rest of the time is spent driving, waiting, eating, phoning, merchandising, doing paperwork, looking for addresses, missing appointments (or having them miss you), and more waiting. Mind, I said the average salesperson. I hope this book will help to make you a better-than-average salesperson and increase the time you spend before the decision makers. That will mean more satisfaction for you, more time to yourself, and more money in the bank.

Figure 4.1. Account Page

STORE NAME: _____ BUYER'S NAME: _____
ADDRESS: _____ DAYS OFF: _____
CITY & STATE: _____ BEST CALL DAYS: _____
TELEPHONE: ( ) _____ BEST TIME: _____
LABEL: _____

PRODUCT	DATE	INV.	ORD.	INV.	ORD.	INV.	ORD.	INV.	ORD.	INV.	ORD.	INV.	ORD.	INV.	ORD.	INV.	ORD.	INV.	ORD.	INV.	ORD.	INV.	ORD.

Figure 4.2. Post-Call Notes

POST-CALL NOTES

IMPORTANT: SALESPERSON SHOULD CHECK NOTES BEFORE CALLING ON THIS ACCOUNT.

DATE							
DATE							
DATE							
DATE							
DATE							
DATE							
DATE							

5

THE PERFECT PRESENTATION

Sales managers are "now people." They want business *now*. They want their people to write orders *now*. No excuses are accepted. "On every sales call, either you sell the buyer, or the buyer sells you" is a familiar refrain from many managers. They have quotas to meet, bosses to satisfy, and overrides to earn. Naturally, they want things to happen *now!*

However, buyers often do not cooperate. They want to "think it over," they have no open-to-buy, they can't program you into the computer system yet, or they have adjustments to complete with their present vendors or advertising plans that cannot be changed. The list is endless. So, sometimes you have to accept their excuses or their reasons and regroup for an attack on another day.

When managers ask a salesperson about a certain account, the questions are often confrontational. "Rogers, what is happening with the Morgan account? I expected an order in here by now. What's going on?" The salesperson may feel that he is making headway with the account and that he has done some good things that will result in significant business in the future, but he can't put that in a sales report or in the bank. An experienced and proven salesperson might tell the manager, "Relax, the account is coming around. She's got inventory she has to dump and some returns for which she wants cash credit. After that, we get the account."

The manager may accept the explanation because the track record of the salesperson is good, and his or her skills and judgment are excellent. However, managers can't have that attitude with all their people or they would never do any business. They must push to get orders *now, today, this week*. And the salespeople should develop that attitude, too. They must try to nail the order at the moment they see the buyer. They must look past the excuses and design a close around expected stalls. Nonetheless, sometimes it is wise to accept no for an answer.

There are legitimate reasons for not buying. The trick is to get on an honest give-and-take footing with buyers. Develop their trust and ask for straight answers. Tell them, in a subtle but frank way, "I'd rather know where I stand than be waiting for the phone to ring, hoping for an order. Just give me a simple yes or no. If I'm going to be of value to you, I need that honesty." Then, of course, should they say no, you can dig, ask questions, and discover the real reason for the negative answer.

Building a territory takes a lot of effort and a lot of time. Some accounts will fall quickly; others will take time. Often the difficult accounts, the ones that are tough to land, become the best customers, and the easy-to-get accounts will prove to be a bit flaky, switching from vendor to vendor.

But, if you can sell *all* the people *some* of the time, and *some* of the people *all* of the time, you will have an outrageously successful career. Depending on your product and marketing support, you can achieve your short-term and long-term goals more quickly than you might imagine, if you develop a selling method that is proven, powerful, and nonadversarial.

OLD AND NEW SALES METHODS

The old saw, "People want to buy, but they don't want to be sold," is rubbish. This bumper sticker cliché ignores the basic character of people. People do want to be sold, but they don't want to be shoved. So, what is selling?

Remember the last time you looked at an automobile with the possible intention of buying? Probably the salesperson walked up and offered to help. He pointed out the features, answered your questions, and finally offered you a test drive. So far, so good. When you returned to the showroom, he practically dragged you into his office — a tiny cubicle that gave you the feeling of being a prisoner (which in effect you were). Perhaps you began to sweat a bit and felt uncomfortable, and from that you consciously or unconsciously raised a wall of resistance. Then came the heavy-duty arm-twisting. He asked a leading question, "If I could deliver this car to you today, at $18,000, would you buy it? Right now? Today?" This question is meant to qualify you. Many customers will either answer vaguely, "Well, maybe," or state positively, "You bet!", or offer a counterproposal, "No, but if you can make it $16,500, you have a deal." Most balk, not because they don't want to buy, but because they feel squeezed, pushed into making a decision they aren't quite ready to make. The salesperson feels he has "culled the lookie-loos"; in fact, he has thrown out the baby with the bathwater.

Auto dealers are learning that such high-pressure methods simply don't work very well. Today, you may still be confined to a tiny office, but now the salesperson uses a more civilized way to try to sell you: "Mr. Smith, did you like the car?" "Do you have any questions I haven't addressed?" These and similar probes are meant to put you at ease — no arm-twisting, just accommodating questions as though you both were two old friends talking. If you admit you liked the car, the salesperson will advance another probing question, "There are several options on that model. Have you decided which package best meets your needs?" This is an early closing question. If you have decided on the package, you have bought the car. If you answer that you haven't selected a package, he will offer to help you with your decision. Eventually, you will have to say that you want the car or you don't. This is exactly what the salesperson wants; he has forced the decision without being obvious or applying pressure. The dealer keeps that friendly, helpful salesperson from even discussing price. That is left to an unseen power — namely, the sales manager. Your offer will be conveyed to the decision maker by your trusted friend, the salesperson. There is a good reason for this strategy. The salesperson never becomes adversarial; he's on your side. He will be the voice of reason representing both sides of the situation.

The persistent salesperson will not accept your not wanting the car. Why would you take the trouble to visit the showroom, take a test drive, and spend your time unless you had a strong interest in the car? Immediately, he will probe for the *real* reasons that changed your mind: "Are you suffering sticker shock? Was there something about the vehicle you didn't like, but didn't talk about? Is there something about the dealership you dislike?" There has to be a reason, and if he can find that reason, he can turn your negative answer into a sale. Automobile salespeople believe that financial concerns negate most sales. Money is a touchy subject, so they will approach it in an oblique way.

They may show you a different, more expensive model. If you show interest in the more expensive model, money probably isn't your concern. Likewise, a casual remark about a feature you like in the more expensive model, which is lacking in the cheaper model, may indicate something that you want. Alert salespeople will latch onto that feature and sell it rather than the automobile itself.

The strongest selling method automobile salespeople use to close is the emotional appeal to your ego. They know, in spite of yourself, you care what the neighbors think, what your coworkers think, and what *you* think about yourself. An automobile is an expression and a manifestation of that opinion, and it is a public declaration of your worldly worth. The salespeople will weave words, such as *prestigious, elegant, exclusive, limited,* and *sleek,* throughout their conversation to condition your thought processes. I had one clever huckster say, "You'll be the envy of your club when you pull up in. . . " Wow! My club! He thinks I'm a successful guy and I belong to a country club. All those other rich guys will envy me! Dyno-mite! Of course, this was a blatant appeal to my extroverted personality, which didn't work.

In order for a presentation to go smoothly, you must first establish a need for what you are selling. The car salesperson mentioned above never tried to determine or establish a need for buying the car. He never asked, "Have you decided it is time for new wheels?" Or, "I've always liked that model you're driving. Why have you decided to trade?" He didn't because he *assumed* the need was there. I would advise all automobile salespeople to correct that in their sales approach immediately. Simply because someone is looking does not automatically translate into a need to own. The salesperson must distill, refine, define, and present that need.

CONCEPT SELLING

In a manner of speaking, a successful salesperson *never* sells a product or service! Does that surprise you? Well, it is true. The creative salesperson sells a product by filling a need. When you enter into a "show-and-tell" or a "me-too" world of selling, three negatives can and often do happen:

1. **You immediately increase the stature of your competition.** When you show and tell, you force a comparison between your merchandise and the goods your customer has in stock. Now, ask yourself what he is going to do. Will the customer admit that she made a mistake in selecting the goods she bought? Not likely. She knows the goods in inventory and has faith in them. That merchandise has been producing profit for her. If it hadn't, she would have called you

long ago. Trying to replace another vendor is a major task. Unless, as occasionally happens, your line is the darling of the buying public, you can figure on an uphill battle. Your every argument will be met with a skeptical look, and every point you make will be questioned and doubted. In addition, the buyer knows and probably likes the salesperson she is currently dealing with. You, on the other hand, are a question mark.

Change is painful, troublesome, and scary. When you try to sell your item by the show-and-tell method, the buyer will counter with a feature your products don't have. Her defense can often lead to argumentative confrontations. Does it make any sense to create this kind of selling atmosphere? Of course not.

2. **You question and challenge the buyer's previous decisions.** In addition to challenging the in-stock product or service, you challenge the buying intelligence of the buyer. She bought the stock, made the decisions, and will defend those decisions until hell freezes over. When she bought the goods, she was convinced that she did the right thing, and her sales may have supported that decision. So no frontal attacks, please.

The most natural thing for the buyer to do is to immediately compare what you are presenting to what she has already bought. As difficult as it may be, try to forestall any comparisons. Present your line and emphasize its features, especially the features that her present inventory doesn't have, but don't draw a comparison. Ignore the competition as much as possible, and if forced to make a comparison, you may cleverly "damn with faint praise." Most buyers take an immediate dislike to salespeople who knock the competition. Whenever you do that, you strengthen their resolve not to buy.

Trying not to bruise the ego of the buyer is difficult because she will almost always try to force you to make a comparison. She is, after all, proud of her merchandise and the product mix she has selected. When you are forced to compare, do so with a kind word for the competition: "This (the competitor's goods) has been the standard for the industry, no question about it, but recent design breakthroughs have allowed an even more versatile product. I'm sure you can appreciate the improvements, right?"

You may also refer to changing consumer tastes: "For several years, the consumer has been enamored of heavier, bigger models. Since late last year, however, a decided trend toward lighter, more fuel-efficient models has captured the market. Naturally, there is a continuing need for the heavy models, but we are betting that the future will belong to these quick, efficient models, like our XZ-55, and our sales support that contention."

3. **You allow the buyer to say no.** When you try show-and-tell selling, you offer the buyer many ways to reject your products. You load the gun with reasons to maintain the status quo. She can point to successful sales results, customer satisfaction, and excellent vendor-buyer relations. You must remember that she considers changing vendors a difficult and sometimes complicated job, as well as an attack on her good judgment.

Instead, if you create a need for your product, you take away all those bullets. You create a need for your goods, and once that is done and the buyer starts stocking your merchandise, she will accept the reduction, or elimination, of the competition as her idea. In this way, the customer isn't being pushed; she is doing the pushing.

Selling a product instead of creating a need is called *front-loading*. It means that you are placing all your chips on your presentation. You're betting that your product will, on its own, sell over the competition. This is a dangerous gamble and one that you will usually lose. Why? Because unless the buyer accepts the *need* for the product, she will not support it with merchandise aid, marketing help, or advertising. She is still defending her previous purchases (consciously or unconsciously) and will let the new goods sink or float on their own. That is not a good situation for you.

COMPARING SALES METHODS

Suppose you were trying to sell bicycles to a store with many different, established brands already available and in stock. Your product is good, but it has no consumer awareness, no dramatic price appeal, no outstanding advertising campaign, no snob appeal, no market advantage, and nothing to separate you from the competition except a single feature — your bicycle can also be used as a stationary exercise unit. This is a controversial feature. Some consumers believe a bicycle that can be converted into a stationary exercise unit cannot be a good street or trail bike. Others endorse the dual feature with enthusiasm. Suppose you are making a cold call on a bicycle shop, and the buyer and you are strangers. First, we'll try product selling; then we will sell by creating a need.

PRODUCT SELLING

SELLER: Good morning! My name is Scott Smith, and I represent The World Is Neat Cycle Company. I'd like to present to you our latest model, the XK-5. This is the only bicycle available that is both a first-class trail bike and an excellent stationary exercise unit. It costs just $250 retail and comes in six exciting colors. You'll be happy to know that we have stock locally, and terms are available.

BUYER: That's interesting, but my customers are vigorous, active people. They want to be out-of-doors, on the bike trails. I don't think a stationary exercise feature would be appealing to them. Leave some literature about the XK-5. I'll look it over and show it to some of my regular customers. Maybe on your next visit we can do something. If my customers show any interest, I'll be in touch.

Note: You may try to rebound, but the table has been set, and the buyer isn't about to change his mind. He has, in effect, convinced himself that his customers have no interest in this special feature. The standard procedure, at this point, is to try to argue the merits of your product and compare it with goods already in stock (we already know that won't work), or offer an introductory deal, lower the price, or make some other concession — all of which continue to weaken your position. What the salesperson has failed to do is show the customer *why* he must have the product. The salesperson must demonstrate the *need*, and he hasn't done that.

SELLING BY CREATING A NEED

SELLER: Good morning. My name is Scott Smith, and I represent The World Is Neat Cycle Company. Do you have a few minutes for me?

BUYER: Sure, what do you have to show me?

SELLER: Some really interesting things, but first I'd like to ask if you've seen this month's copy of *Cycle World*, and the survey they took?

THE PERFECT PRESENTATION

BUYER: This month's issue? No I haven't had time. What was it about?

(You have started a dialogue and have somewhat piqued his interest!)

SELLER: It is a real eye-opener. They surveyed over 11,000 cyclists in Texas and in two adjoining states. As you know, *Cycle World* is the most widely read magazine of the avid cyclists — people like the ones who shop in your store. The surveys in *Cycle World* really take the pulse of the cycling public. This survey addressed the question of how to enjoy the benefits of cycling regardless of the lateness of the hour, the weather, and crowded, busy schedules. I'm sure you've heard that a few times, huh?"

BUYER: Sure have. So, what did *Cycle World*'s survey show?

SELLER: It showed that cyclists are always looking for a way to enjoy their favorite sport to stay in shape. It can't be done sometimes with rain, snow, darkness, and busy schedules. So thousands told *Cycle World* they wanted a bicycle-type exercise that they can use anytime, indoors or out. Now, stationary bikes are nothing new. The problem is that they really don't give you true cycle motion, and they are expensive. Plus, of course, they are only good for one thing: indoor stationary exercise.

BUYER: Yes, I know I stocked a few units a couple years ago. I thought I'd never get rid of them.

SELLER: I'm not surprised, but wouldn't you agree that a unit that could serve both functions as an outstanding trail bike and a stationary exercise unit would be a big seller in your store?

BUYER: Well, I don't know. I suppose it might.

(He is weakening.)

SELLER: An overwhelming number of the 11,000 cyclists surveyed think so. Did you know that 70 percent of all stationary cycles are bought by people who have and use a recreational bike? It's true. Now, isn't it also true that most of your customers are serious about their sport?

(The salesperson waits for agreement to that last statement. A positive answer here nails the close.)

BUYER: Well, yes, that is true.

(He's in the bag.)

SELLER: After a tough day at the office, nothing feels better than a good cycle workout, wouldn't you agree?

(Be patient and wait for a reply. Every yes answer brings you closer to a sale.)

BUYER: Oh, yeah. There's nothing like it.

(Now he is smiling and nodding. You've connected.)

SELLER: You bet. So this survey tells us two things. First, cyclists prefer this kind of exercise. Second, there is a hot and ready market among cyclists for a stationary cycle. Cyclists want this kind of feature, isn't that right?

BUYER: It appears that way.

SELLER: Wouldn't you agree that a world-class trail bike that is easily converted into a sturdy, stationary exercise station would be an outstanding seller in your store?

(Wait for the positive answer.)

BUYER: Maybe. I suppose you have such a unit?

SELLER: The World Is Neat's Model XK-5. It's a sleek overachiever that sells for just $250 retail. It is an outstanding performer on the trail, and anyone can convert it into a sturdy indoor exercise station in just minutes — actually, in seconds. Now your customers can enjoy the benefits of cycling all the time, year-round, indoors or out, regardless of the weather or the time of day!

BUYER: Hmm, I guess it would appeal to some of my customers.

SELLER: I'll even tell you how to sell it. Don't tell them about the stationary feature. Sell it like a regular trail bike, and then show them how quickly it sets up as an indoor workout unit. It knocks 'em over! You'll find it to be the fastest seller in your store and a favorite of beginners and pros alike. We can deliver before the weekend out of local stock, so you can have them on sale this coming three-day weekend!

BUYER: Do any other stores have it?

SELLER: Not in this area. Buckley's and Owens have a complete stock, but for now, you've got the market all to yourself!

(Use an emotional appeal.)

BUYER: Hmmm. Well, guess I better get some in stock. I'll try six bikes.

SELLER: Let me save you some money. Our introductory package is eighteen units in all the hot colors. Since the bikes come in male and female models, we know what sells fastest. Our intro pack gives you eight female models and ten male models in the colors most people prefer, OK?

BUYER: Yeah, OK.

SELLER: Here is my card, if you need more before my next visit — and considering this marketing area and the popularity of these models, I think you will — just give me a call. Otherwise, I'll be back in two weeks to write a reorder. Is morning or afternoon the best time to call?

BUYER: Mornings and early in the week, if possible.

SELLER: Fits fine. I'll see you two weeks from Tuesday in the morning. Thanks again.

ANALYZING THE DIFFERENCES

I'm sure you can see the marked differences in the presentations. Product selling opens the door to refusal. Unconsciously, buyers are placed in the position of having to defend existing stock and previous decisions. You present them with more inventory and only marginal differences and remind them of existing stock that may or may not be selling well. By product selling, you pit yourself against established vendors and the salespeople with whom buyers probably have long-standing friendships or at least good relations. Product selling gives buyers nothing to consider except additional inventory (of which they have more than enough). You become an interruption or an annoyance that they will want to eliminate as quickly as possible.

Conversely, by creating a need, you ignore the competition and all the arguments engendered by comparisons. You present buyers with an entire new set of circumstances they must consider: "Do I dare not stock an item that so many cyclists say they want? Am I missing a profitable market by not having a product my customers will want? What if my competition stocks this product first? Will I lose the market forever?" These questions and similar concerns are what the concept buyers will be considering, instead of the negatives: "I have too much inventory now, and we are coming into a slow time of year. Maybe this product won't sell. I'll wait for customers to ask me to carry the line. Or, I'll wait until my present vendors come out with their own models."

When you have created a need, the close is almost secondary. By encouraging buyers to agree all along, what are they going to do at the close? Suddenly disagree? Of course not. They would appear stupid. Even though they may not have examined the results of a favorable survey or read the latest endorsement, they cannot deny the results, nor can they reasonably suggest that their customers are different from the others. Logically, after the buyers have responded positively to supporting evidence and have agreed that their customers will want the product, will they refuse to order it? Hardly.

When creating a need, take care not to rush through your presentation. Some buyers, by their actions and words, threaten to cut the interview short, although most won't. It is a way of rushing you forward, and it is a trap you must avoid.

Be enthusiastic about the backup source that helps you create the need. This is the keystone of your entire presentation, so treat it as such. Some buyers may try to trivialize the source. Anticipate this possibility and be ready to support your source.

BUYER: *Cycle World* is a rag. My customers don't read that garbage magazine.

SELLER: It really doesn't matter if they do or don't read *Cycle World*. The publication is only reporting the wishes and desires of cyclists in our area. Your customers have the same needs and wishes as the 11,000 people who took part in the survey. *Cycle World* is simply telling us there is a market out there. It's a market you will miss without the XK-5 in your store.

The salesperson's simple, honest, and logical response effectively deals with the objection (real or false), without having to argue or bicker. What does it matter if his customers did or didn't take part in the survey? They, like others who love cycling, want a stationary cycle when they can't be out-of-doors. The buyer doesn't have any in stock, and the salesperson is there to fill the *need*. Realize that no single sales presentation will sell everyone, and some customers will resist the finest presentation no matter what. People buy for emotional reasons, not logical ones, and they *fail* to buy for emotional reasons, too.

When you create a need, you create emotional responses to that need. These emotions may include fear, pride, anger, self-satisfaction, and even love or hate. Your enthusiasm for the proof you present (that a market awaits and that buyers will be missing out), will stir emotions. The buyers may hate the competition and will go to great lengths to outdo them. They love their store and don't want customers going elsewhere. They may be prideful and want to be the "first on the block" with a cutting-edge product (if they are any good). All of these emotional darts will stir them to buy.

On the flip side, they may not buy because they are timid and insecure. They fear tying up money in inventory that may not sell. A whole series of emotions can crop up during your presentation. Most of the negative emotions will be overcome by the positive emotions, *if you properly create the need*. Few sales are made without the buyers understanding how they will benefit from the sale. Creating a need defines and clarifies how buyers will benefit from purchasing whatever it is you're selling.

Of course, you are not always going to have a convenient survey or endorsement to rely on. But remember that the product you are trying to sell was manufactured, packaged, and advertised because there was a perceived need for it. No one invests money and time in product development unless there is a need for that product.

Many times, sales managers will send their people out to sell something without giving them the ammunition to succeed. Do they assume the "troops" instinctively know? Do they themselves know? I really can't say. But most of the time, salespeople must discover the utility of the product all by themselves. They must recognize the need, simplify it, and present it in a clear-cut way that stimulates emotions and triggers the sale.

There are many ways to discover product needs. In the next chapter we will look at some of those ways, and we'll also present a few other examples of selling by creating a need rather than selling a product or service.

6

WHO NEEDS IT?

The title of this chapter poses a good question, and it's one that all buyers ask themselves, "Who needs this (*fill in the blank*)?" They will then compare existing stock with the newly introduced merchandise and consider what this new offering has that the present stock doesn't have. They will then analyze if the degree of difference is enough to make the investment in inventory worthwhile.

There is only one way to ensure (or at least better the odds) that the result of their analysis will also result in a sale for you. That way is to create in the buyers' mind a need for your product.

It is not always easy to do this. It takes concentration and study to determine what the need is. Most salespeople hope that the benefits and features will do the selling for them. They won't. The benefits and features of a product will confuse the best of salespeople into believing that the benefits and features are the same as the need. They aren't.

Let's take the previous chapter's bicycle-exercise station, for example. It would be easy and tempting to present the benefits: The XK-5 allows the user to exercise on a cycle regardless of the time of day or weather conditions. It costs less than having to buy both a trail bike and a stationary exercise cycle. It assembles quickly and easily. It is a first-class trail bike. It is a sturdy, efficient exercise unit. All those benefits and features may be true, but if buyers do not recognize a need to add this product to their stock, you will not ring up the sale.

If you fail to establish the need for the XK-5, buyers will ask you (and themselves), "What value does this product have for me and my customers? So what if they can use the XK-5 at anytime, regardless of weather conditions or time of day? My customers wouldn't be interested. So what if it is cheaper than buying a stationary exercise cycling unit and a trail bike? My customers wouldn't use it anyway. They want outdoor cycle exercise."

By creating the need, you are answering the *why* questions: "Why should I stock this new product?" (Because most stationary exercise bikes are purchased by avid cyclists.) "Why should I buy this product?" (Because cyclists — your customers — want a cycling method of exercise they can use when outdoor biking is unwise or impossible.) "Why should I invest inventory money in this product?" (Because your customers will want this, and there is nothing to compare with it presently in stock.) "Why will this product sell and produce profit for my store?" (Because 11,000 cyclists have said it will — cyclists from your market area.) By satisfactorily answering all the *why* questions, buyers can more easily make a decision to buy: "I need this product. If I don't buy it now, my competition will, and I will lose sales and customers."

ANOTHER LOOK AT CREATING A NEED

Let's consider another example of creating a need. Suppose you are selling vitamins, and you know the buyer. The product you want to place today is the Sublingual B-12 — not a new concept, but still unique enough that you can supply new information and be creative in your presentation. You've sold the buyer many things over several years. You enjoy a good rapport, but you're not quite buddies. Although not everything you have sold him in the past have been sales winners, overall you are an accepted vendor. This buyer is tough and smart, and his credit is A-1.

PRODUCT SELLING

SELLER: Good morning, Bob. It's nice to see you again.

BUYER: Thanks, Mary, it's nice to see you, too.

SELLER: (After a short warm-up) Bob, we have a new promotion that everyone is selling like crazy. It's our Sublingual B-12 promotion, and it is hot!

BUYER: Mary, you're a day late and a dollar short, as they say. Frank Newhouser was in yesterday. He has a promotion on the same product, and I've got Sub-B comin' out my ears!

SELLER: Oh really? What strength? Ours is 2,000 micrograms and ...

BUYER: Their stuff is 2,000 micrograms, too, and their deal is unbelievable.

SELLER: Yes, but our product is cherry-flavored, and ...

BUYER: Theirs is sour apple. My customers seem to prefer that flavor. Maybe on reorder, Mary; I'm set for now.

End of interview. You are finished and nothing you can say or do will bring this one back to life. Now let's see how it works when you create a need.

SELLING BY CREATING A NEED

SELLER: Morning, Bob, good to see you again.

BUYER: Same here, Mary.

SELLER: I notice you carry a heavy stock of vitamin B-12.

BUYER: It's one of our constant big sellers.

SELLER: Do any of your customers ever complain about the high cost of B-12 vitamins?

BUYER: Complain? No, can't say that they do. No, not at all. Why do you ask?

SELLER: The Vitamin Research Council's study last month shows that B-12, although popular with the buying public, is losing in sales because it is so expensive.

BUYER: No more expensive than any number of other vitamins I stock and sell.

SELLER: Because B-12 doesn't assimilate well, the actual cost of B-12 doubles or triples the shelf cost.

BUYER: Yeah? Well, no one around here has complained, and my sales of B-12 have been steady — maybe even growing.

SELLER: Well, that's good to hear. But you and I know that poor assimilation means disappointing results; that is why so many customers shop around for their B-12. (*Note: Mary moves ahead with her presentation and ignores his remarks for the most part.*) When I say they shop around, I mean they shop for price. You may have seen this ad (*producing the ad*) from Goliath Drugstores. They're selling B-12 for less than half your retail. You know, Bob, once customers start shopping for vitamins in supermarkets and drugstores, we stand a real chance of losing them forever. (*Note: Mary uses "we" instead of "you"; she is his partner.*) They don't have the quality, but they do have the low prices.

BUYER: Well, I don't know about that (*getting defensive*). My customers are loyal, and they know that B-12 doesn't assimilate well. They don't expect more.

WHO NEEDS IT?

SELLER: The point is, Bob, why tempt them? Why shouldn't they expect more? Why pay for 5,000 micrograms of B-12 and only get 50 micrograms in actual vitamin benefit? You know and I know that customers expect more from specialty vitamin stores. They pay more — and they expect more. Isn't that right?

BUYER: Well, yes, that's true. What else can we offer?

SELLER: Exactly. If you could guarantee as much as a 145 percent increase in B-12 blood serum content with a special type of B-12, wouldn't you feature it in your store?

BUYER: Sure, who wouldn't? What have you got up your sleeve, Mary?

SELLER: Sublingual B-12. Studies show this kind of delivery system provides the user with an amazing increase of B-12 blood serum content.

BUYER: Oh heck, Mary, I thought you had something special. We have that in stock. In fact, Frank Newhouser was in yesterday and loaded me up. I've got plenty of B-12.

SELLER: I'm glad you recognize the value of Sublingual B-12, but remember according to the Vitamin Research Council's study, your customers are starting to shop for lower prices. And the Goliath Drugstore advertisement supports that study. We can't match the supermarkets and super drugstores in price, but we sure can outperform them. With our promotion on Sublingual B-12, we can come close to their price levels, and easily outperform them. That's a win-win situation, right?

BUYER: Well ...

SELLER: Can you give me this counter space for at least the first thirty days? If customers shopping for B-12 bargains know you have our product in stock at a price they consider fair, you'll want to reorder in ten days or less. Mark my words. How about it? Right here next to the register, OK?

(Mary is doing an end run on the buyer. She is assuming the sale, and she avoids a long-winded, time-consuming discussion by drawing his attention away from his already substantial stock on hand, and works for a merchandising advantage instead. If he gives her the counter space, he has bought her promotion.)

BUYER: Well, yes, I guess thirty days would be OK.

SELLER: Great. I'll have your order shipped at once so we can have them on hand for this weekend's rush. Are 200 pieces of point-of-sale literature enough?

BUYER: Better make it 300.

SELLER: Three hundred it is. Thanks, I'll try to get back to help you set up the display.

BUYER: Thanks, Mary, I appreciate your help.

As you see, Mary didn't "close" in the true sense of the word. She assumed the sale and diverted the buyer's focus from making a buying decision to giving a concession for shelf space. She asked no closing questions, she ignored the competition, and she loaded the buyer with facts that would help him accept additional inventory. In short, Mary showed the buyer the need for Sublingual B-12. If she had pushed the features and benefits of B-12, she would have crashed and burned.

Read the presentation again and note the emotional appeal that Mary interweaves throughout. She is planting fear in the buyer's mind. Sure, he has similar (maybe identical) product in stock, but he is missing the price point. Of course, the in-stock product is already selling well, but Mary has programmed the buyer. Thanks to the Vitamin Research Council's study and the advertisement from Goliath Drugstores, he is now aware that price is going to be a major factor when customers shop for Sublingual B-12. If he doesn't meet or come close to the mass merchandiser's prices, he will lose sales, and more important, his customers may develop the habit of shopping for their vitamins in super drugstores and supermarkets!

I make a point of ignoring the competition whenever I can. But sometimes buyers will force you into making comparisons, mainly because they are comparing products while you speak. If forced, agree that the competition's product line is worthwhile, but develop a niche for your merchandise. In the example, Mary created a price niche. You can create a special niche market for your products in any number of ways: higher quality, better selection, special or unique features, excellent service after the sale, durability, lower prices, and even higher prices, which is surprising to many people.

Higher prices as a selling feature? Absolutely! Higher prices appeal to many consumers. Higher prices convey the perception of worth or better value in their mind. Higher prices have snob appeal. Is there really that much difference between a Lexus and a Rolls Royce? Actually, no — but the Rolls sells for much more than the Lexus, and the Rolls dealers have no trouble selling them, no matter how high the price. Why? The answer is obvious. When you drive a Rolls Royce, you are telling the world that you are different and (at least in your mind) better or more successful than others. You have arrived. In addition to all the consumer appeals, higher-ticketed items have an even stronger appeal to the seller because they produce more profit.

HOW TO HANDLE THE PROBLEM BUYER

When I give examples, I mean to create a sales situation that reflects the "real world." Naturally, not all buyers are going to be cooperative or follow a script. Some are going to give you problems. I believe the previous examples are reasonable and true to life. But, what do you do if the buyer gives you a tussle? Let's suppose, in the above example, that the buyer balked when Mary attempted her end run by asking for shelf space.

SELLER: Can I have this shelf space for the next thirty days? If your customers are going to be price shopping for Sublingual B-12, they must know you have our product in stock.

BUYER: No, Mary, the idea of featuring Sublingual B-12 is a good one and one I will steal from you, but I have too much stock from Newhouser. I think I'll whittle away at that stock, and when I'm ready for a reorder, we'll do business. OK?

SELLER: Bob, you missed my point. Newhouser's stuff is priced too high to connect with this market. Our promotion allows you to offer high quality at a reasonable price — a price that will be acceptable to your customers. You know I never knock the competition, and I'm not going to start now, but I'm obligated to you. You must understand that we are in an important battle with the "Big Boys." If we lose your customers because we can't give them a reasonably priced Sublingual B-12, what are the chances that they will start buying all their vitamins at these cut-rate places?

BUYER: Yeah, I guess you're right.

SELLER: Bob, you know I'm right. Since you only placed your order yesterday with Frank, why not call and cancel? Save him and yourself some time and hassle. I personally hate to get a cancellation, and ordinarily I would never suggest you cancel, but this is just too important to you — to the entire industry.

By this kind of emotional reaction to his refusal, Mary is demonstrating how strongly she feels about placing a reasonably priced product in Bob's store. Notice she makes the return suggestions *after* she has a positive response from Bob. He is going to buy her promotion anyway, so what has she got to gain by her suggestion? People have been telling me for years that competition is great (and it is), but getting rid of it from time to time sure adds to the commission checks. And that is exactly what Mary has done.

When you create a need, you follow three steps:

1. **Identify the need.** Ask yourself, "What is the need for my product or service?"

2. **Separate the benefits and features from the need.** Needs and features are often confused with each other. Ask yourself the question, "Is this a need or a feature?"

3. **Determine if any other competing product fills the need.** If so, know why your product fills the need more completely.

Let's consider this book. I hope this book is easy to read and somewhat entertaining. It is also educational, reasonably priced, a tax write-off, nicely printed, and available to you in most bookstores. Are any of those things needs? No. So, who needs it? You do, as do many practicing and would-be salespeople. Why? Because it teaches, it demonstrates, and it allows you to relate to real-world situations. It tells you how to handle yourself and the buyer under actual sales conditions. You are (or were) looking for a manual that would be a ready reference guide, a teacher, something you did not have before your purchase. It fills a need.

If I were to sell you this book, one-on-one, I would probably ask a number of questions to gain the information I required in order to create the need: "Are you happy with your sales production? Do you enjoy selling? If not, what part of selling do you enjoy and what part do you dislike?" Let's assume you are not happy with your present level of income. You want to earn more money; therefore, you must make more sales. Let's further assume you like people, you like to visit with them and show your product, but you "just can't close."

With that intelligence, I would say to you, "Mr. Reader, self-help books are the biggest sellers in the publishing business. That tells you something, doesn't it? It tells you that they work. I have been in sales for more than thirty-five years. I have managed and trained salespeople for more than twenty years.

"When I was training salespeople, I was constantly searching for a good, down-to-earth, honest-to-goodness manual that would teach my salespeople when I couldn't be with them. I couldn't find what I needed. I scoured the bookstores and all I could find were books written by and for direct salespeople: insurance agents, investment counselors, siding salespeople, or real estate promoters. We all know the names; most of us have heard their tapes and attended their sales seminars. I did, and I must admit I admire many of them. But I also saw that their approach was not realistic and their logic was flawed. Their sales situations were setups. Not one of them had ever built a territory.

"Direct sales and street sales are two very different things. This sales manual will tell you how to sell the buyer you will see again and again — not the same as the 'sell 'em once and never see them again' salespeople and that type of sales trainer.

"This is why you should have this book available to you every day. So you can refer to it as situations arise. You will recall those situations, and you will know what to do because you bought this book. You will recognize buyer types, and you will understand what an extroverted or introverted buyer is really telling you about himself. Your approach will be different than it was in the past; it will be powerful, effective, and successful. You'll have more fun — even when you fail to sell — because you will understand why you failed, and you'll know how you can recover. The power of selling will be yours. You will have no fear of any buyer. Closing will be as natural and ordinary as brushing your hair. In short, this will help to make you a professional."

The title of this chapter is "Who Needs It?" That is, perhaps, the best question you can ask yourself before every sales call. Who needs my product? Why does the buyer need it? How does my product satisfy the need? If you know those answers, you will have made the sale.

7

The Mechanics of Selling

Like most things, selling has definite and specific parts. Like the nuts, bolts, gears, springs, and gaskets of a complicated machine, the mechanics of a sale is also complicated. But you can, by understanding the mechanics of selling, make them less complicated. Obviously, some parts of the machine are more important than other parts, but all have their function, and all should be present and in good working order if the sale is to be made.

This chapter will deal with the step-by-step procedures of making a sale. It will help you to better organize the way you approach every customer and potential customer. Most experienced salespeople know about these mechanics, but not every experienced salesperson follows the script. Why?

The road to Hades, it is said, is paved with good intentions. All of us have made New Year's resolutions. We are going to eat a more sensible diet and exercise regularly. We are going to cut back or eliminate some bad habits: smoking, drinking, overeating, and so on.

Few of us are strong enough or determined enough to rid ourselves of our old, bad habits for long. By the end of January, we are doing fairly well. By the first of March, we have slipped a little. Our good intentions have taken a beating by April Fool's Day, and by Memorial Day, we are not doing at all well. When summer is upon us, we are back to our old, destructive habits.

That is the way with salespeople, too. They read a how-to book, attend a lecture or seminar, watch or listen to a tape, and promise themselves they are going to change, they are going to make calls "by the book." To their surprise, they discover the seminar was right-on, the book's suggestions actually work, and the tape contained a world of information.

A week goes by; then a month. Slowly, they slip back into their old ways of selling — the ways that don't work very well. As their sales and earnings dip toward the basement, they cast about for reasons or, more often, excuses: "My territory doesn't have any good accounts." "The sales manager set my quota too high." "Our products just can't compete." These and a hundred or more variations will be heard from the unsuccessful salesperson, when all he or she really must do is get back to basics.

Oh, I know that sounds simplistic, but too many salespeople make calls without a clear agenda. They really don't know how they will operate when they are in front of the decision maker. When you lack a clear agenda, a clear road map of where you want to go and how you are going to get there, you develop poor selling techniques.

There are four parts to every good sales presentation: (1) the warm-up, (2) the qualification, (3) the presentation, and (4) the close. There is also an after-close, which is not always used, but which is vital to some situations, especially direct sales. If you pay attention to each mechanical part of a sale before every call, you will discover your sales growing steadily. Your ratio of sales to calls made will improve, and you will enjoy selling much more.

Let's take a closer look at each part of a sale and discover just how each affects the presentation's conclusion.

THE WARM-UP

The parts of a sale are nothing more than common sense, and the sequence of those parts is logical and obvious. The warm-up is important because it "melts" the frost that most people experience when they first meet a stranger. Even if you know the buyer well, a reminder of your previous visit will be useful.

Buyers see many salespeople during the course of the average day. All of them have something to sell. They may remember you well or not at all. They may confuse you with another salesperson (which may be good or bad). Obviously, the purpose of the warm-up is to warm the atmosphere in a sales situation. But it can have other purposes as well. During a warm-up you may discover intelligence regarding a buyer's attitudes toward a competitor, plans that the company has developed that directly affect your product line, or what the buyer wants or needs at this particular time (extended billing or guaranteed sales).

A warm-up should be brief, but I have seen some warm-ups last a very long time. When that happens, the salesperson has lost control of the situation. As in all contacts with a buyer, the salesperson must have control. This is not always easy, especially if the buyer falls in the "hail-fellow-well-met" category. Be careful about how you move from the warm-up to the second stage of selling. Being too abrupt may be offensive or even insulting to the buyer. Allowing the warm-up to drag on may determine the length of your entire visit. I have witnessed a warm-up that took so long, the buyer considered it the entire interview, shook the salesperson's hand, and returned to his office without any sort of presentation being made! Remember, you are there to sell, not to socialize, and the warm-up is only one part of the entire process.

WHY THE WARM-UP?

Why is a warm-up so important? Well, we already know its purpose, and that in itself is critical, but consider what you gain from it. Suppose you are invited to a party, and you are anxious to meet new people and make new friends. We can assume you would smile at everyone, show that you were friendly, and introduce yourself to one and all. To start a conversation, you might compliment a new acquaintance, ask questions about him or her or an interest that he or she has, and then you would listen. We know that people like to talk about themselves or their families or their hobbies. So we feed them ammunition, and we listen. The same general rules apply to the warm-up part of a sale. Remember that you must *earn* the right to hear the buyer's personal information, and you do that by asking questions.

Now suppose you are calling on a new account. You've heard that the buyer is tough. He has been getting along without you or your company just fine and is reluctant to even consider changes that will upset the status quo. If you immediately plunged ahead with your presentation, it would be the same as meeting someone for the first time and assuming that he or she is fascinated with your work or your private interests. That would be presumptuous, of course. Probably, when first meeting someone, you would engage in small talk. But when meeting a buyer, be careful how small the small talk gets. If it is too trivial, he or she may judge you to be a lightweight, and that, too, will affect the outcome of your sales presentation. Warm-up topics and any questions should have substance.

SMALL TALK

Intelligent salespeople recognize the need for an icebreaker. They will build a cordial relationship and shape the buyer's opinion of them. They may know something or nothing at all about the buyer's interests.

They may know the buyer is a dedicated fisherman, golfer, hunter, or sports fan, for example. If so, a comment about the new golf course opening or the hottest trout stream will probably start the ball rolling. If the representative knows nothing about the buyer, a quick look around the office may reveal some tips on where his or her interests lie. Tennis? Family man/woman? Runner? Introvert? Extrovert?

It goes without saying, I hope, never to discuss politics, religion, or controversial topics in the news. Stick to positive topics. We all know that people respond well to flattery, but you must be careful how you flatter. An obvious, overt attempt at gaining the buyer's favor in this way can be disastrous.

If you try to break the ice with flattery, choose your words well. For instance, noticing a mounted marlin on the wall can be the source of good warm-up material, as well as a compliment, or it can be a dead end, an obvious effort at ingratiating yourself. "That is a beautiful fish! You must be a great fisherman," may be viewed as an obvious effort to gain favor, or even as a wisecrack. The same comment will be well received if the remark is made in this manner: "What a beauty (*indicating the fish*)! I caught a smaller one off Cabo just last September." The latter statement may encourage the buyer to ask where you stay in Cabo, if you fish a lot, or what the circumstances of your catch were. Once that conversation is going, the frost is melted and a friendly tone is set.

Telling jokes can be effective in opening a conversation. Most people like a good joke and the person who tells them. Nevertheless, telling jokes can be like walking across a frozen lake during the spring thaw. All it takes is one misstep to turn you into a statistic. Be very careful about the kind of joke you are telling. An ethnic joke or a joke with religious, racial, or gender slights can be insulting and seriously damage your efforts.

The safest opening is one that requires the buyer to respond in some way: "Mr. Harding, Harry Coulee told me to make sure I extend congratulations on the recent addition to your family. Boy or girl?" Unfortunately, that sort of opportunity doesn't happen every day, but if you can bring in the name of one of the buyer's friends or acquaintances, a good warm-up segment is assured.

As stated earlier, the good representative will control the length and content of the warm-up and will segue smoothly to the qualification.

THE QUALIFICATION

Nothing is more disquieting or wasteful than to spend your valuable time with someone you think is the buyer/decision maker, only to discover that he or she is completely out of the loop and has no authority to buy your product or service. You not only have wasted time, but also you have diluted your presentation when you do get to see the real buyer (if you get to see him or her at all). Your second presentation will be flat, unemotional, and anticlimactic. In addition, you will feel foolish and unprofessional.

Talking with clerks, retail salespeople, secretaries, and receptionists may have value, but usually these people have little or no authority to place orders. You should cultivate their goodwill, teach them (especially the retail salespeople) about the value of your products, but understand their limitations. In some instances, a secretary or a clerk can authorize a sale, and that is why it makes sense to qualify them to determine just where their authority kicks in.

There are several types of qualifications. One is qualifying for creditworthiness, and another is qualifying for authority/responsibility. Qualification is not difficult and is expected by the account. "Mr. Jackson, could you supply me with credit information for my accounting department?" This question is not considered blunt or rude. Mr. Jackson is in business and seeks accounts whose credit is strong; he understands the need to verify the creditworthiness of accounts.

"Mr. Jackson, are you the buyer for sprockets?" This is a direct and perfectly acceptable way of determining if you are talking to a decision maker or just a nosy office assistant. But suppose that Jackson always discusses anticipated purchases with his production manager. When you close, he'll tell you, "Bob Fabersham, our production chief, likes to interview new vendors, and, in fact, he likes to discuss any anticipated changes before we move forward. If Bob likes these new designs, I'll be in touch." Now what do you do? Well, you learn that you must qualify more thoroughly.

"Yes, I am the buyer of sprockets."

"Excellent. Is there anyone else who might benefit by sitting in on our conversation? Or is there anyone with whom you consult before placing an order? The reason I ask is that Fuller & Company always asks their production managers to review new products, and I think that is a pretty good idea." If you get a no to that, you can be pretty sure you are talking with the person who can make a decision. But not always.

Never ask questions that set you up for rejection, such as: "Do you have any open-to-buy this quarter?" "Are you happy with your present supplier?" If the buyer has a full calendar and wants to get rid of you, all he must say is, "I have no open-to-buy until January," or "Yes, our vendor for sprockets has been supplying us for over twenty years. We are very happy with him." With that latter answer, the buyer dulls your presentation and partially slams the door.

Instead, you might try an oblique approach. "If your tests of our new sprocket meet your qualifications, can you schedule us to be included in the Washington Day Expo?" By asking this kind of question, you qualify that the buyer does or does not have open-to-buy monies, and you force him to tell you if he has an interest in your product. If he tells you he has no interest, you can then dig and determine what his objections are. If he has no open-to-buy, and you are pretty sure he is telling you the truth, you are then free to go to a more qualified account and stop wasting your time. There is no reason I can think of for making a presentation to a buyer who cannot buy. Salespeople who do that are wasting their time, because subconsciously, they are trying to avoid the true decision maker. They want to hear yes, but they want to avoid hearing no even more.

Qualification is important, no matter what you sell or to whom you sell. However, it takes on a special importance when the sale is to the end user. Direct sales of insurance, real estate, investments, automobiles, books, cutlery, and many other products, demand that the sales representatives carefully qualify their target customer. These salespeople know that they have only one chance at making the sale, so they are frugal with every prospect and rarely waste an opportunity. They discover early on if the prospect will buy *right then*, and if he or she is *able* to buy. Sometimes they get a bit too blunt, and I think that loses them many sales and gains them a reputation for being "pushy."

"If I can put you in this car for $18,000, would you buy it tonight?" Sound familiar? Of course it does. Anyone who ever bought a car or shopped for one has heard that many times. Although this is meant to separate the real buyers from the tire-kickers, I believe it paints people into corners, making them uncomfortable and actually rendering them *unable* to make a decision. A friendlier and less threatening qualification would take more time, but I think it would result in more sales. Perhaps a better, more palatable question is, "If I could save you about $1500 tonight, could you afford just $13.75 a week?" If the prospect has credit or assets, and if he or she really wants the car, it would be difficult to say no to that question.

Qualification is a time-saver and a sales maker. The qualification can also be part — or even all — of a presentation! It can contain promises and guarantees. "Mr. Rio, if I can show you, to your *complete satisfaction* and *beyond a shadow of a doubt*, how you can increase the value of your home at a budget price, could you afford just $400 down and only $45 dollars a month?" Mr. Rio would be an idiot if he says no to the offer of improving his home, unless he is broke. If that is the case, he will tell the salesperson immediately. That can either save precious time or set up the close. Either way, the salesperson has done the job well.

By making or hinting at a guarantee, the salesperson has made a powerful thrust toward the customer's pocketbook. What prospects are going to say no when they think the real power is in their hands? The phrases, *beyond a shadow of a doubt* and *to your complete satisfaction*, seemingly allow the prospect take control over the sale. Actually, they do no such thing. If the prospect answers positively, the salesperson has actually closed the sale. The prospect has qualified himself; he can afford the down payment and the weekly or monthly payments. The rest, the guarantee, is cut and dried in the presentation — a presentation that has been field-tested a catrillion times and over which the prospect has no control. The qualification phase can also be used to shame the prospect into buying or considering the purchase. "Mrs. Clinton, your brother-in-law has chosen our two-year, no-interest financing plan for his driveway refinishing. The payments are just $45 per month. Is that a plan that appeals to you, or would you want to make a larger down payment?" The buyer, if she cares what her brother-in-law thinks, will be put in a position where she must admit that she is not as well-heeled as the in-law, or that she doesn't have the same pride in her home.

THE MECHANICS OF SELLING

"Ms. Lincoln, your neighbors, the Smiths, have redone their home with our new all-weather siding, and they have chosen our extended finance plan. After a small, $450 down payment, their payments are only $50 a month. (*Notice, the representative didn't specify how many months.*) Mrs. Smith told me you were interested in having your siding replaced with an all-weather product, too. Would that payment plan fit your budget?" The representative assumes the sale, and here again, the Smiths apply the peer pressure *forcing* Ms. Lincoln to make a positive decision and to select a method of payment. This is qualifying at its oblique best.

You may notice that in some of these scenarios the salesperson doesn't follow the script I suggest when making a "perfect presentation." There are two primary reasons for this: (1) expediency and (2) if the opportunity to close presents itself at any time, or if the representative feels he or she can "cut to the chase" immediately, I advise that it be done.

As I've said and will continue to emphasize, direct salespeople never squander their one chance at selling. They give it everything they've got and will push and push until it is obvious to all that no sale will be made. These sales professionals know that they normally have only one shot at selling the prospect, and they make the most of it. There is a danger in this. Many prospects are discarded too quickly and are never contacted again. In fact, many of them could be sold if only the salesperson would apply a little patience.

When qualifying, try not to ask for too much at one time. "Mr. Reynolds, would $450 down and just $50 a month fit your budget for that new roof you've been wanting? A roof that will increase the value of your home by at least twice what it will cost?" These two questions qualify ("would this fit your budget?"), create a need ("increase the value of your home"), and assume the sale.

If you try for the hat trick and attempt to sell a driveway repaving, for example, you may be pushing too hard. You are filling the plate too full and are giving the customer too much to think about. This may result in a negative response for everything: "I want to think it over."

THE PRESENTATION

We have looked at the importance of the warm-up and the qualification phases. Now we will look at the presentation. This phase is often considered the most important of the four steps in making a sale. Actually, in my opinion, it is equal but not superior to the warm-up and the qualification.

You might call the presentation a test. It is a test of your product knowledge, for it is normally at this stage that the prospect will ask questions, present objections, make comparisons, and either accept or reject the product.

Salespeople are usually schooled in their product's benefits and features. They become enamored of these things, and as a result, they can't wait to tell all about them. Consequently, they lose many sales. Why? Because they forget that there are four parts to a sale, and concentration on one part at the expense of another weakens the entire sales effort. This isn't meant to suggest that the presentation phase isn't important. It is, of course, but it is just one part of a four-step process. If you have broken the ice with a good warm-up and carefully qualified the prospect, the presentation will flow naturally. It is a natural progression and will move with smooth precision.

We will assume that the salesperson has performed the warm-up and qualification properly. The prospect is relaxed and friendly. He or she is the person who makes the buying decision and has the wherewithal to pay. If that is true, the presentation is nothing more than "dotting the i's and crossing the t's." The sale is already made. But, not in all circumstances. The prospect is certainly interested or else he or she would have terminated the interview. Now, however, the prospect wants to compare what you have with what he or she has before making a buying decision.

It is in the presentation phase that salespeople have the most problems. The argumentative buyer, for instance, flourishes in this phase. During the warm-up and qualification, the prospect may appear calm and docile. But if this person is an intellectual, a professional, an I-can-get-it-cheaper, or a strong, silent buyer, you can expect to be questioned on every statement you make and to walk through a mine field. This is when the customer challenges you to establish why your merchandise is needed and demands that you list features not available in existing stock. You can be certain these buyers know a lot about products on the market, and that they feel sure they have the finest and best-priced merchandise in stock. You must be well prepared to reprogram their thinking, and the presentation phase gives you that opportunity.

During the presentation phase, the buyer may disrupt the thoughts of the salesperson and siphon away the power and energy of the presentation. Some buyers will ask about products that are months or even years away from the market. It is their way of showing how informed they are, and it is a method of putting off having to make a decision.

I cannot stress too strongly the importance of knowing your product or service. You should study it until you know everything there is to know about it. You should question the product development people, your sales manager, the order desk personnel, even the shipping and receiving employees. When you are ready to sell the product, you should know all about it: what need it fills; how it compares with what's on the market; where it fits in terms of price; how it is shipped; what the master pack dimensions are; what the unit, carton, and master carton weights are; and even the cost of shipping. Knowing all this will imbue you with a confidence you cannot get in any other way.

HANDLING GLITCHES

Buyers who lay traps, try to disrupt your thoughts and ask silly, pointless questions, will likely be the ones who ask about future models that you know nothing about. Never try to con your way through this mine field. Instead, be frank and admit you don't know. Say that you are not always informed about products your company may be marketing in future years. If you get hung up on some technical point, suggest that the buyers talk with your technical people. "Mr. Washington, I must admit I've never met anyone who understands our products better. I can't answer your questions, but I can get you the answers. If I could use your phone, I'll call our technical chief, Terry Hodkins. I know he'd enjoy talking with someone as informed as you, and he'll be able to supply the information you need."

This sort of reply accomplishes two things. First, you get the buyer off your back and provide another target for the stupid, pointless questions. Second, it ties the buyer to the company network and soothes his or her ego. Because this person is an introvert, your answer will be considered the ultimate compliment.

During presentations, you may also come across know-it-all buyers. They don't know everything they should know about existing products, but they know how they all should have been designed — and your product doesn't even come close. These buyers are frustrated engineers. The switch should have been placed on the left side of the handle; the power cord shouldn't be coiled; the unit should use less plastic and more stainless steel, and so on.

Respond to these questions and comments the best you can — honestly and as you understand the design. "We placed the switch on the right so that it is easily accessible to right-handed people. As for the power cord, that is a UL requirement. Plastic is used because is doesn't conduct electricity." If your responses satisfy the know-it-all, then he or she will use your products as a standard for all. Your competitors will be tasting your dust.

In any case, it makes no sense to belittle a buyer's ideas and suggestions or to ignore questions. Don't argue, no matter how dumb the ideas may appear to you. Know-it-all buyers will be easy to recognize, and you should be able to defang them before they start the redesign. "Betty, we placed that switch on the right-hand side to eliminate or, at least, reduce accidents. Don't you agree that is a good idea?" The buyer will likely answer: "Yes, that is where I would have put it." But you're not out of the woods. This buyer is sure to have other corrective changes to make. There is one important thing to remember about know-it-all and argumentative buyers — from time to time they come up with sensational ideas.

Normally, the representative doesn't discuss prices, terms, guarantees, or return policy during the presentation, but if those things are particularly favorable and attractive, there is no hard-and-fast rule against it.

Always start the presentation phase by establishing a need for your product or service.

SELLER: Mr. Jenkins, industry figures and research statistics show that failed widgets cost our industry over $12,000,000 last year alone. I've talked with your production manager, and he tells me that you had as high as a 60-percent rejection rate from existing suppliers. Does that figure agree with your records?

BUYER: Well, yes, the failure rate was high last year. But we've switched to ALCOM, and we believe they will hold up better.

SELLER: Your production manager also tells me that most of the failed widgets resulted from faulty O-rings, right?

BUYER: Yes, that continues to plague us.

SELLER: If you could buy a widget with a six-month or three-hundred-million turn guarantee, wouldn't that allow you to sleep better at night?

Creating a need during the presentation stage is vital (unless it is created during the warm-up or qualification stage), and your opportunity to *fill* that need comes during the presentation as well. Don't be shy about establishing the need. Consider the frontal approach: "We all agree on the *need* for a low-cost, lifetime battery, right? Well, let me demonstrate how we have filled that *need*."

Often during the presentation, buyers will indicate their willingness to buy. Stay alert for those signals (buyers may not verbalize this willingness), and as soon as you see them, shut up and start writing the order. The only talk permitted at this point is to determine how many units you can sell.

THE CLOSE

As you have seen, every part of the selling process logically follows the preceding one. The warm-up is followed naturally by the qualification. The qualification is followed by the presentation, which leads to the close.

I could never understand the difficulty that so many salespeople experience with closing. They fear the close, and I've often been told: "I just can't close. It isn't me. It feels so unnatural, so forced, so pushy!" Well, if it isn't you, I recommend you get into some other kind of work. But before you do that, let's consider what closing is all about, and let's discover how simple, easy, and even pleasant it is when someone has followed the mechanics of selling.

Exactly what is *closing*? *Closing*, the dictionary tells us, is "bringing to an end," and "reaching an agreement." Exactly. When we close, we are bringing to an end the entire selling process. We are reaching an agreement with our prospect. So, what's so scary? Isn't that what we want as salespeople? A decision? An agreement? We work hard at setting a comfortable and friendly atmosphere during our warm-up. We continue that when we qualify and discover if we have a decision maker. If we aren't going to close, why does the setting have to be friendly and comfortable? If we aren't going to close, why do we care if the prospect is a decision maker? Just considering those two aspects, the fear of closing seems like nonsense. The fear is not of closing itself, but of refusal. The fear of rejection is fed by sales managers who make such a big deal out of closing. "Did you close him, Alice?" "Why didn't you close, Martin?" These and similar questions blow the closing phase completely out of proportion. Closing is just another part of the selling process — the best part.

The entire idea of selling is getting an answer. If that answer is positive, we have made a sale. If the answer is negative, we begin to ask questions and dig for the "real" reasons for refusal, and after we have dispensed with them, we close again.

Closing doesn't have to be a blunt, "can we do business" question. In fact, if you taped many sales presentations, you may have difficulty isolating the close from the rest of the presentation.

Many salespeople consider the close as the "moment of truth." The bullfighter's moment of truth comes when he either dispatches the bull, or the bull dispatches him. So it is with closing. Either you get the order or you don't. Unlike bullfighting, though, the salesperson gets a second, third, fourth, and fifth chance. The close isn't a life-and-death situation. The only time that closing is difficult or awkward is when we have failed to follow the preceding steps in selling.

When should you close? How soon? How often? The answer is difficult to give because every sales situation is different. Generally speaking, you should close as soon as you think the buyer may be ready to make a decision. This readiness takes the form of signals that, over time and with experience, you will pick up on your "sales radar." These signals may come as early as the first stage, the warm-up. "Jim, you said you wanted a corner lot near the lake. I've got a listing that fits right in with your budget, and if we hurry, we can lock it up for you today."

Or the signals may not appear until after the presentation. "Aaron, I think I've shown you the need for our Roll-a-Lot skates. The market is ripe, the price is right, and the terms are outstanding. How many pairs will you need this month?" Is that so scary? If you answered yes, then you haven't prepared the ground by following the steps. Each of the steps in the selling process makes the close a natural progression and encourages you to strive for a yes or no answer.

You should only have to close once, but if you get a negative reply, you retrench, back up, and review. Then you close again. "Ms. Atkins, I'm surprised at your answer. From the beginning you agreed with me that Skate-a-Lot fills a need in the market, a need your customers have verbalized to you. Isn't that so? (*Wait for an answer. She must answer.*) You also agreed that the retail price isn't out of line and, in fact, meets a price point you have been trying to establish. Right? (*Wait for a positive answer.*) Well, then, I cannot understand your reasons for not wanting stock as soon as we can ship. Is there something I haven't explained? Do you have some questions I haven't answered?" These sorts of questions may dislodge the real reasons for her not writing an order then and there.

LISTEN TO SELL

Many salespeople do not pick up on their customers' buying signals. They rattle on about features or benefits, oversell, talk too much, and give buyers reasons not to buy. Learn to listen. I've heard prospects (actually buyers), say something such as, "If I could find one of these in forest green, I'd buy it." Sitting in the warehouse were many forest green models, but the salesperson continued on about features and benefits and lost the sale entirely.

Especially during the early stages of a sale, learn to ask the *if* questions. *If* questions can also be used during the qualification or the presentation, and definitely during the close. Asking *if* questions is a form of assuming the sale, and using them is an early closing method: "If I could get you a forest green model … " "If I can prove to your complete satisfaction … " "If I can arrange the kinds of terms … " "If I can show you how this can fit into virtually any household budget … " All these and many other *if* questions demand an answer; they qualify and they close. When prospects are asked an *if* question, they must answer yes or no: "Yes, if you can get me a forest green model, I will buy it." "No, I don't think I'd buy it even if you can get me the forest green model." What has this done for you? It has shown that the prospects aren't qualified to buy or are concerned about something else. At that point, you start selling again, until you sell or until you are convinced there is no chance of selling.

Be careful when making judgments that your prospects can't be sold. In other words, don't give up too quickly. During the presentation, for example, the buyer may tell you what will prevent him from making a buying decision.

SELLER: The Titan forklift has a lift capacity of over five tons; other forklifts can't match that, and our price is a surprisingly low $25,000!

BUYER: Yes, but I noticed the operator doesn't have full protection. The Yale has a wraparound screen that really protects the operator and his helper.

SELLER: Is that what you want on your forklift?

BUYER: We want our people protected, and our insurance man tells us we can reduce injuries and claims by 22 percent with the wraparound screen installed.

SELLER: Congratulations! We've added the wraparound safety screen to all models effective immediately! I can arrange to have your new Titan delivered by Tuesday. Is that soon enough, or should I arrange for a weekend delivery?

This not too subtle close nails the prospect rather well. He wanted a screen, and you got him one. He saw a need; you filled it. Tagging on a delivery time cements the sale.

Just to illustrate how pieces of each sale are intertwined, let's look at an example of a closing opportunity that shows itself during the qualification.

SELLER: Bob, I assume you are the buyer of conveyor equipment, is that correct?

BUYER: Yes, I buy all production and shipping equipment and supplies.

SELLER: Is there anyone else who might benefit by sitting in on our meeting? A production manager, for instance?

BUYER: Good idea, I'll see if Mark Franklin, our production manager, can sit in. He asked to be included when I consider automatic conveyors.

Terrific! If you can get the production manager into the meeting, you can talk with him about all the concerns he has and answer his technical questions. Probably you are the only salesperson who has ever bothered to meet with the production manager, and he'll be flattered by your attention. *This is your closing opportunity: all the decision makers are in one spot at one time. So close!* Moreover, meeting with all the decision makers will eliminate having to come back to the account a second or third time, and it will prevent your presentation from being given to the production manager by a less-informed, less passionate buyer.

THE MECHANICS OF SELLING

I listened to a self-promoter tell an audience that closing was fun. Well, I don't agree. If the four steps of selling are followed, you hardly know you are closing. So how can it be fun? I believe he may have meant that we strive to close — to bring our meeting to a successful ending — and that is fun. I agree with that. But why the fear of closing? I recall one rookie salesperson who looked me in the eyes and said, "I'm terrified to close. I can't force myself to ask for the order. My closes sound so phony, so false and contrived. *And*," she continued, "I suppose I'm afraid of the answer I'm going to get." She was suffering from a massive lack of self-confidence, and she didn't believe a word of her presentation. That's why she sounded contrived when she tried to close. You must believe.

People say, "I can't sell anything unless I believe in it." That is usually true for most. But there are those who can sell anything to anybody, anywhere, and at anytime, without the slightest belief in what they are selling. Aren't con artists great salespeople? Of course they are. They create a need, play on emotions, and close. That's selling! Do they believe in what they are selling? Of course not. They sell dreams that turn into nightmares.

Most of us are honest, and that honesty forces us to see the need for what we are selling and to accept that our product or service is a value for payment received. In today's market, consumers are smarter than they have ever been. The old snake-oil huckster has a tougher job than ever. Nevertheless, the hucksters are still with us, selling everything you can imagine. We read about companies — protected (so it seems) by accountants, lawyers, and corporate structure — being taken for millions of dollars, or about investors being swindled out of their life's savings, and about old people, confused and lonely, being cheated out of thousands. In all these cases "salespeople" successfully closed the sale and didn't believe a word of what they were saying. Naturally, as a professional salesperson who is proud of my profession, I hesitate to lump con artists in with the honest, hard-working salespeople who serve people. Nonetheless, the con artist *does* sell. We can't escape that fact.

Since it is possible to sell without believing in what you sell, can we conclude that believing in your product or service isn't necessary? Absolutely not. Unless your soul is bare and your heart cold, you must honestly serve the needs of your customers. Having that belief will give you self-confidence and make your closing tasks easy.

THE ASSUMPTIVE CLOSE

There are many ways of closing. Some have cute names, such as the Columbo close or the Stutter close. Some take devious routes to the sale. Of them all, assuming the sale, or the assumptive close, is the one most often used, and it is the one rookie salespeople fear using the most. They fear it only because they are not following the four steps just outlined.

Should you use the assumptive close? It's up to you. The important thing is to use the close that you like best, the one that fits the situation and works for you.

For all closes, however, there is one unbending rule: Once you ask a closing question, shut up. Wait for an answer even if it takes all day. Those few minutes (if it takes that long) will be well worth the wait. You have brought the buyer to the point of making a decision. Don't let him or her off the hook by more talk. As the old saying goes, "If you talk, they walk." Or as many have said before me, "The first one to speak loses."

THE SOFT ASSUMPTIVE CLOSE

Your job is to write orders and obtain as much business as possible. That can mean you will have to push from time to time. But I know many salespeople do not like even the thought of being pushy. And, many buyers resist being pushed as well. So what do you do? You disguise the push: "Mr. Nubar, I know you like our gauges, and we agreed they will do a better job for you than your present gauges. I understand you want to hold off installation until you examine the Holman gauge, but at the same time, I need to get this order in house before the price increase. Tell you what, I'm going to place your order for sixty gauges at the old price. After you examine the Holman gauge, if you decide their product is better, simply call me to cancel. I can easily sell them to Franklin Foundry at that price, with no problem. You are under no obligation, of course."

Now that push is about as soft as you'll ever want to get. You are applying pressure, but it is subtle and disguised. The buyer will feel an obligation for the gauges set aside for him at the old prices. He will, despite himself, have a feeling of ownership, and that will figure in his examination of the competing gauges. He probably will feel obligated to the salesperson as well. After all, the salesperson is doing a special favor for him, reserving the gauges at the old prices and taking the product off the market when Franklin Foundry is just sitting there waiting to buy. His thoughts may run even deeper. "This salesperson isn't at all pushy, in fact, just the opposite. I'm under no obligation. Maybe I should get some backup stock at this old price." With a deep feeling of ownership and influenced by the rapport the buyer now has with the representative, chances are he will ask that the gauges be shipped at once. After all, he doesn't want his competitor, the Franklin Foundry, to get the deal.

There are many ways to push without being pushy. The easiest, fastest, and best way is to follow the mechanics of selling. Practice this method; make it part of your professional being. Don't divert yourself from the formula. As it becomes a part of your everyday selling methods, it will help to make your presentations logical, smooth, and successful.

THE CLOSE AFTER THE CLOSE

In some sales situations, especially in direct sales, the "close after the close" is used to cement the deal. We all have heard of "buyers' remorse," a condition that begins sometime after prospects have agreed to buy a product or service, signed an order, and written a check. The salesperson leaves, happy that she has made a sale. But now the prospect begins to examine the consequences of the decision. He checks his bank balance and compares it against his outstanding bills and fixed expenses. His brother-in-law assures him he has made a bad deal. His wife warns him about his gullibility, and his coworkers guarantee he could have bought it at a better price. He wonders if he really needs his recent purchase and, finally, decides that he doesn't. The telephone rings as he starts to pick up the receiver to call the representative.

"Ralph, I've got good news for you. First of all, your credit has been approved, and we got the exact shade of blue that you and Marge wanted. It took some doing, but I reserved it for you, and I'm having it expressed in this afternoon." The first thing this call accomplishes for the salesperson is that it creates a feeling of obligation in the buyer. "Gee, the poor salesperson, went to all that trouble. How am I going to cancel now?" he wonders.

But our prospect is determined. "Well, that's great, Liz, but Marge and I have been talking it over, and we want to hold off for now." How do you handle that?

Allow a few moments to pass without dialogue. Then say, "Ralph, I'll need to meet with you and Marge. Will you both be available this afternoon around 2:00?" Notice, Liz didn't say why she had to meet with the couple, just that she had to see them. An eyeball-to-eyeball meeting makes a cancellation difficult (as opposed to a telephone conversation in which only one buying party is confronted).

When the couple meets with Liz, she will review all the selling steps and all the needs they have for the product or service. She will subtly remind them of why they agreed to buy in the first place. She will not, however, offer a better price or give any other concession. To do that would imply that she had taken advantage of them in their first meeting. Once the deal is reestablished, Liz will nail it down by making a securing statement or asking a securing question. This is called an "immediate after close," and it eliminates the need for calling the prospect again. It secures the sale and makes cancellation difficult and awkward. Ralph and Marge would look foolish if they tried to cancel a second time. "Ralph, Marge, you guys aren't going to back out on me again now, are you?" (*All said with a smile, and with an implication that the very idea of this happening a second time is absurd.*) The couple will laugh and assure Liz that the deal is firm. But, just to make very sure, Liz might make a telephone call to the office and verify that the blue model is being reserved (never *held*) for Ralph and Marge.

Naturally, most sales stay sold. But it still makes good business sense to close after the sale. "Ms. Tagett, I wanted to call this morning and tell you we do have that power unit in stock. It should be shipped in plenty of time for Christmas. Please call me if you have any questions, but I'm pretty sure you won't have any trouble in assembling it. With your experience in electronics, it should be a snap." What does that accomplish? First, if the prospect has any doubts or questions, they will come out then. Second, it "holds the buyer's hand" and lets the customer know that he or she has not been abandoned. You are there if the buyer experiences problems or has questions.

Because many states have passed laws requiring the seller to cancel any agreement without prejudice within a specific period following the sale, the close after the close is particularly important. This cancellation opportunity is written into the agreement, and many buyers find it after the salesperson has left. I believe it is smart to bring this clause to the attention of the buyer after he or she has signed the agreement. Many disagree with me, believing it opens the door to cancellations and actually suggests the buyer exercise that option. I feel it shows your confidence in the efficacy of the product and cements the sale.

"Mr. Williams, as you know, state laws provide an exit for any agreement, such as this one, within twenty days. This will give you additional time to compare our policy with any other available. I bring this to your attention because I am proud of our company and the policies I sell. Frankly, there are no better deals, but I welcome a comparison." That should seal the agreement. In fact, that might be included in the close. It surely is an assurance, a statement that you believe in your product. I'd use it.

8

WHAT IT TAKES TO SELL

A commonly asked question of sales applicants is, "What do you think is the single most important quality a person must have to be successful in selling?" The answer most interviewers want is "Attitude" or "Enthusiasm." Neither answer is correct. In fact, no single answer is correct because there is no single quality that will spell success in selling. Selling is a complex, involved endeavor. The salesperson will meet and contend with many different people, all with wildly different personalities, in the course of a single day. He will try to bridge the personality gap between himself and the buyer. He may be struggling against an unseen and unknown problem in the customer's business or personal life. Regardless, the salesperson must find some common ground to establish rapport.

What single quality can overcome those obstacles? There is none. Complex, involved endeavors require a combination of skills, talents, and qualities that are forged into a single presentation. So, we have to consider not one but many qualities that make a salesperson successful. What does it take to be successful in selling?

Not long ago, I was asked to give a speech before a group of small business owners. These people sold advertising space in what is normally referred to as "throw-away" newspapers (a term they detest and avoid). I was told to fashion my talk in "bottom-line" terms. By that, my employers meant I should tell them how they could increase their personal sales production and how they could train their salespeople to be more productive. Since that is my "bag," I anticipated no problems.

My aim was to provide a working seminar in which members of the audience could discuss specific problems they were having, and I would attempt to solve those problems on the spot. I would give examples and set up role-playing situations. As each situation would be revealed, I would apply the methods that my years of experience had taught me. The idea, as I sat in my office putting thoughts to paper, sounded like a slam-dunk. I imagined a spirited give-and-take session with vigorous participation from the audience. What actually happened was very different from my imaginings, and the seminar was an extremely difficult experience for me.

First, the group was too large for the kind of give-and-take symposium I had planned. In addition, although the room had an excellent sound system, the system was what is called a single-station system. I was unable to go into the audience, and it was cumbersome having people come to me. It was also difficult to get volunteers to take part, and my attempts to relate to this large group weren't going well. But, if the truth were known, my problems really compounded before I ever took over the rostrum.

Preceding me was a motivational speaker of considerable charm. He was an animated, exciting speaker who knew how to get people involved in his subject. His theme was *enthusiasm*, and it was well suited to his nature. According to him, enthusiasm was the one and (he implied) only ingredient salespeople needed to reach success. He went on to give example after example to illustrate his belief that enthusiasm was the key to sales success. That one factor was all that anyone needed to reach the promised land of sales — the top of the sales chart.

He was a smash. As I walked down the hallway toward the meeting room, I could hear the shouts and screams from the audience. As I entered, I saw women standing on chairs, cheering as if they were at the Super Bowl and their team had just won in a thrilling come-from-behind victory. Men were applauding vigorously, many whistling and stomping their feet! What an act to follow! The place was bedlam; the noise level, deafening.

After he finished his talk, he tossed little furry doll-like things to the crowd; he called them "warm fuzzies." People fought over them — actually fought over them! The women in the audience embraced and kissed him after his presentation. Men pumped his hand with gusto. He had clearly won the day. I admired him. He was a great speaker, entertaining, interesting, and fun. There was just one problem: He either didn't know what he was talking about or didn't care what he was teaching. He was entertaining, but he was wrong.

As you might imagine, my dull-by-comparison talk was a flop. I tried my best, but having heard my predecessor speak, I had to make some corrections, and that was my blueprint for failure. I couldn't let these good people walk out of that hall believing that all they needed was enthusiasm in order to attain success. I just couldn't.

My blasphemy was met with hostile stares, disapproving grimaces, and silence. I flopped, big-time; I was humiliated, and worse I felt I had cheated my employers (the organizers of the seminar). I won't embarrass myself with a further recounting, but in spite of it all, I learned some valuable lessons.

I learned two important things: (1) People will believe — at least, until experience shows otherwise — almost anything a powerful speaker says if it is said with passion and humor and if it is supported by examples (no matter how unrelated and questionable those examples might be). (2) Salespeople want to know the "secret" of selling. Many actually believe there is some magical word or key that can turn a plowhorse into a Kentucky Derby winner. *There are no secrets.* Many believe that a single characteristic can propel them to success. *No such single characteristic exists.*

I can't tell you how many times I've been asked, "What does it take to be successful in sales?" People who ask this question want a one-word reply. That is simply not possible, and I refuse to entertain that nonsensical idea.

From this book, I'm certain you know that the mechanics of a sale is complex and has many parts. Is one part stronger or more important than another? Perhaps, but that single part cannot stand alone. With very rare exceptions, all the parts must function for the entire machine to work.

I have walked you through the four stages of selling and some after-the-sale techniques. We have looked at the types of buyers we must face everyday. We've seen how buyers are changing and how their duties and authority are being affected by a changing marketplace. We've examined how important it is to be organized and prepared, and we've discovered the importance of selling a need instead of a product. We have discovered new meanings of the terms *introvert* and *extrovert*.

We still have much to discover and discuss, but at this point, with what we have already learned, does it make any sense to assume that a single quality or a single trait can propel you to success in selling? Of course not.

So, when I am asked that question and know that time and circumstances do not allow me to answer it truthfully, I usually say, "Product knowledge, honesty, and hard work." That's as close as I can come to a one-word answer. Fortunately, in this book I am allowed all the space and time I need to spell out what it takes — and it takes a lot.

PRODUCT KNOWLEDGE

Every structure must have a foundation, and the same is true with sales. The foundation of any sale is product knowledge. If you don't know your product, you are quickly found out. You appear foolish and untrustworthy. I admit that customers are at a disadvantage in this confrontation, because they probably know even less than the uninformed salesperson. But not always. Moreover, customers today are often well informed or will take the time to educate themselves. Some enjoy crossing swords with a salesperson and delight in destroying the uninformed.

Having a thorough understanding of your product and its position in the market will give you great self-confidence. You will welcome questions and challenges. You will defy anyone to make a comparison, and you will close eagerly because you understand how valuable your product is and how it will benefit the customer. You will be perplexed that anyone could say no to your presentation. Price objections will be handled easily. If a product is priced higher, you'll know why; if it is priced lower, you'll understand that as well.

In my opinion, one of the major problems in today's business world is the lack of product and sales training, especially in small and medium-size companies. It is a great temptation to send salespeople out to solicit orders, regardless of their product knowledge. "Get them in front of a buyer," is the message that sales managers receive from their CEO. This message usually costs much more than it returns in sales revenues.

Most uninformed and untrained salespeople are slaughtered by knowledgeable buyers, and the product line suffers. Not only does the prospect distrust the salesperson, but also that distrust transfers quickly to the product itself! Once buyers question the salesperson's product knowledge, you can be sure they will stay with the "tried and true" products they know. In addition, other products presented by the suspected or proven "know-nothing" salesperson will usually be scorned.

I have witnessed how much buyers truly appreciate the salesperson with solid product knowledge, and I've understood the power of knowledge since the early days of my sales career. I have analyzed the sales production of those who make it a point to be knowledgeable. You might be surprised how often I discover that salespeople have misconceptions or even a complete misunderstanding of their product. I often wonder where these people were during the product meetings, when they had a chance to learn and ask questions, to develop that all-important knowledge.

You've probably been told that if you are asked a question you can't answer, admit you don't know, and promise to get the information. That is, I suppose, the wisest course. But it is infinitely better when you are armed with all the information you need — even if it is in a notebook, written in longhand, or in a company catalog with the pertinent information highlighted.

If I were to take on a territory today, before I ever dared to make a call, I would first learn everything I could about the products I would be selling. When I say *everything*, I mean *everything*. I would learn about the materials used in manufacturing; how the parts are assembled; how safety features have been incorporated and tested; various applications of the products, and where my products rank in terms of quality, price, and sales. I would learn how the products are packaged and how many units are shipped in a carton and in a master carton. I would know the weight of the unit, the weight of the master carton, and the dimensions of the master cartons, as well as the guarantee or warranty provisions, the return policy, the terms of sale, and any existing or planned promotions or advertising.

If, while I was learning, I found that my product wasn't perfect, I would try to learn if those flaws were known to the company and what the company planned to do about them. I would know how serious the imperfections were to the user and how the guarantees or warranties were affected by this shortcoming. I would want to know if others in the industry had similar or more faults than my product.

If I determined the products were so imperfect that they would cause me difficulties in selling, or if I felt my products would not serve the customers, I would either refuse to sell them, or change companies. In order to live with myself, I must believe I am serving my customers. I must believe my customers are getting true value for their dollars. If I don't believe that, how am I different from the con artist who takes money under false pretenses?

Yes, knowing your product is vital to successful selling because you can't sell what you don't know. Product knowledge fits in with the other elements of a sale. It is important — darn important — but it is only one of the things you need to succeed in sales.

PERSISTENCE

A few years ago, a poster proclaiming the value of persistence was selling like hotcakes. You could hardly find an office without this poster stuck to the wall or hung in a fancy frame. "Nothing in the world takes the place of persistence," it began, and continued with how persistence alone succeeds where education, genius, and talent fail. It didn't, of course, point out where persistence alone has failed.

Have you ever been annoyed by a pesky, persistent salesperson? Of course you have; we all have known the insurance agent who insists we buy a policy we don't want and can't afford, and the car salesperson who won't leave us alone in the showroom. And probably no one has escaped the annoying telemarketing salesperson who usually calls at dinnertime.

All of these and many other salespeople are persistent. They have been trained to believe that persistence will pave the road to their personal success. There is some truth to that, of course. Sales is a "numbers" game, and if the salesperson persists, someone will buy eventually. I suppose you could call that success. I once worked for a sales manager who truly believed that if you walked into enough businesses — whether or not the business used your product — and asked for an order, someone, somewhere, would buy whatever it is you were selling. That may be so, but I am not that salesperson, nor have I ever met anyone who wanted to follow that route to success.

Persistence has its place. You must be determined and you must persist. You can't afford to take no for an answer, at least not the first five times.

Persistence means developing a thick skin. Your persistence will sometimes invite buyers to be rude or even insulting. Personally, I never allow any buyer to insult me, but I have accepted rude behavior from time to time, in the belief that I could overcome the rudeness and gain the sale. It usually worked out that way. Persistence is viewed by many buyers as rude in itself; so, perhaps, what goes around comes around, as they say.

MOTIVATION

Motivation is something we all must have in order to succeed in sales or in any other endeavor. If there is no reason to go to work, why do we go? Certainly we can all think of things we would rather do than work. Work is and should be enjoyable, but other things surely have more appeal: travel, golf, fishing, hobbies, or just being able to do what we want whenever we want. We've all read newspaper stories and books about members of incredibly wealthy families who turn into wastrels, alcoholics, or drug addicts. We shake our heads in bewilderment. They have every material thing a person might want, yet they live a life of despair and misery. But they lacked the one thing their money couldn't buy — a feeling of self-worth, of being useful and valuable to society. Many wealthy individuals suffer from massive guilt; they see others in desperate need, and they feel unworthy of the wealth that was given to them. Equally strange to some of us is to witness rich men or women, with all the material things surrounding them, working harder than any of their employees. We wonder what their motivation could possibly be. Certainly not money, no one could be that greedy, we think. And we are right. Money is the thing that's least important to these men and women. Their motivation is to compete with others, to have a feeling of social value, and to help others by providing jobs and opportunities.

Money itself, contrary to popular belief, is not always a motivator. People work and strive to succeed for many reasons: the admiration of their peers, prestige, titles, power, and God knows what else. Napoleon said, "Men will die for a piece of ribbon." The truth is, they won't die for a medal itself, but for what it represents: valor, conviction, loyalty, and dedication. And, perhaps above all, that medal will demand the esteem and respect of everyone. That is worth dying for, or at least many brave people have believed so.

Your personal motivation may be to get your kids through college or provide for retirement or just have money in the bank. If you can find that motivator (it isn't easy) and stay focused on it, your success is assured.

ORGANIZATION

If by now you doubt the importance and value of being organized, reread Chapter 4. Nothing can replace organization in the formula for success in sales.

APPEARANCE

Entire books have been devoted to the importance of being well groomed and tailored. I have no quarrel with them. If you want to be successful, you must dress properly and, of course, be clean and neat. Salespeople (especially those just starting out) may have wardrobe budget problems and make the mistake of thinking that a good wardrobe is an extensive one. Not so. Turn yourself over to a good specialty clothing store. Explain to the manager just what your situation is and ask for help. You will be amazed and delighted to learn these good people will go overboard to make certain you look great. As your income grows, so will your wardrobe.

At the risk of stating the obvious, always have clean fingernails and hair, and be conscious of your breath and personal hygiene. Women should avoid overpowering perfumes, and men should use understated colognes. Your dress may be fashionable, but never foppish.

TRUTHFULNESS

Certain businesses and professions have gained a murky image for themselves: politicians, used-car salespeople, trial attorneys, auto mechanics, and television evangelists, to name a few. These people and the businesses they work in have a particularly difficult time getting people to believe them. Not all have that problem, because there are exceptions — the Billy Grahams of this world — but some occupations can't rid themselves of the stigma. This is a terrible burden to bear. If people suspect your truthfulness, how can you expect to sell anything?

Telling the truth can be a difficult thing to do. It is seductive to cut corners or lie by omission. You can get away with it for a time, even for a long time. I've known a few first-class liars who did extremely well for a long time. But, eventually and inevitably, they were found out. Then, it seems, everyone found out at once, and they were finished with their company. One was even washed up with an entire industry.

HONESTY

Honesty and truthfulness are closely related, but they are actually different. You can be truthful and still withhold harmful information. You may remember that, not too many years ago, an automobile manufacturer marketed one of its cars that had a faulty fuel tank. The company realized the danger this fuel tank posed to the consumer, but it resisted recalling the automobile because of the massive costs involved, as well as the loss of image. Some managers of the company, I've been told, vigorously protested; some even resigned. However, the decision makers sold the car without disclosure.

Thousands of people bought the cars and were served well by them. Several years went by without incident and, I imagine, the executives breathed easier. But then, one summer afternoon, a teenage girl and three of her friends were involved in a minor accident: a rear-end collision when they were stopped for a traffic light. Normally, such a fender-bender would have resulted in little damage. But in this case, the faulty fuel tank exploded, and the four young girls were incinerated.

Obviously, the decision not to admit the manufacturing mistake and recall the cars was devastating. Four young people, just starting their lives, died because of a lack of honesty and, perhaps, a lack of courage as well.

If the executives of that automobile company had been asked about the fuel tank before the accident, what do you imagine they might have answered? Would they have been truthful? I believe at least some of them would have. These were probably truthful people. Whether they were truthful *and* honest is something else again. Telling the truth and offering the truth without being asked are two very different things.

Even though the implications of the auto executives' decision were deadly, most lies told in sales situations are relatively harmless in the grand scheme of things. Yet, lacking truthfulness and honesty can be as inflammable and damaging to your sales career as that tragic crash many summers ago. Being honest and truthful are two extremely important characteristics every successful salesperson must have.

COURAGE

As I said, those auto executives lacked courage. Their jobs, their position in the company, and their entire future were probably on the line. The willingness to hide the facts from consumers may have meant a bonus, a promotion, stock options, or just job security. But what a price they paid for that cowardice. As I suggested, some of these people, perhaps all of them, were considered honest, decent people. They didn't lack truthfulness or, in most instances, honesty. They lacked the *courage* to risk their careers by being honest and truthful.

Your job may not hold life-threatening implications, but your truthfulness and honesty could have serious effects on the career of your buyers. If the buyers accept what you say as truth even when it is a lie, their company could lose money and image, and the buyers could lose their jobs. This is why buyers demand truth and honesty from salespeople. They can't afford to deal with liars, and they won't. Even a small fib is a risk to your reputation and to your standing in the buyer's eyes. Moreover, you are climbing a slippery slope. Little lies lead to bigger lies and to the beginning of a terrible habit. Successful salespeople have the courage to be honest and truthful.

ENDURANCE

Endurance is the quality of hanging in there, doing a full day's work every day, and never giving up. Selling is hard work; persistence is separate from endurance. I've known salespeople who set their sights on a particular account. They do whatever is needed to nail that account and neglect the rest of the territory in the balance. They persist with one account, but they lack the endurance to work the entire territory. There is no substitute for hard work. It may take some time to reach your goals, but remember that every account is important; none can be neglected or ignored.

Did you ever watch someone make pudding? If you did, you know that in the beginning, the pudding mixture is thin, like water or milk. The cook stirs and stirs, and nothing seems to change. Then, in the blink of an eye, almost magically, the compound "gels." Suddenly, the thin, watery mixture becomes a thick, tasty pudding. I always thought of building a territory in the same way. You work and work and work, and nothing seems to change. Then, almost overnight, good things start happening. First one key account topples, and then another follows suit. The buyer you couldn't get to first base with calls and places an order. Everything gels, and you have a "tasty pudding."

WHAT IT TAKES — THE BOTTOM LINE

We can assume that most salespeople will be neat, clean, well groomed, and careful about personal hygiene. Being organized and prepared, knowing the product and why it is needed, and having persistence are all things we can work to develop in ourselves. Truthfulness, honesty, and courage are qualities we are taught in childhood and work to strengthen throughout our lives. Character traits are almost singular. If you're truthful, you usually will be honest. If you have honesty and truthfulness as a part of your character, you will have the courage to exercise those traits. This is why I put *product knowledge* first, not because I rank it over *honesty* and *truthfulness*, but because it must be sought and learned. *Persistence* is another developed trait, as is *endurance* (as defined here). You can discover what *motivates* you, but motivation requires honesty ("to thine own self be true"). Some people are born *persistent*, but most develop dogged persistence as they gain experience and motivation.

Finally, I don't wish to eliminate or reduce the importance of enthusiasm and attitude. Enthusiasm about what you are doing helps make you want to work hard (motivation), to share your knowledge with others (product knowledge), and to be persistent and *organized*. But the enthusiasm has to be *genuine,* and that can only be achieved by knowing your product completely and understanding how it helps others.

All these things *together* are what it takes to be an outstanding, successful salesperson. And a little sprinkling of good luck helps, too.

9

Magic Words and the Magic in Words

In the preceding chapter, I identified the most important elements in the selling "machine." I indicated that there is no secret formula that will change a bookkeeper into a salesperson, nor are there any special, heretofore unrevealed tricks or magic words that will transform an average salesperson into a top sales producer.

Although there are no magic words, there is magic in certain words and phrases. These words cause us to react in a predictable way. You don't believe it? Think about this: We listen to beautiful song lyrics or an enchanting poem, and we remember a romantic interlude in our lives. We relax and perhaps even close our eyes and smile as the memories flow over us. Couples adopt "their song," which simply means that something special happened in their lives when that song was playing. It became part of their relationship. The music is the trigger that recalls the pleasant intimacy.

THE POWER OF WORDS

During political campaigns or on patriotic holidays, we might hear a stirring speech that dredges up personal memories of our own military experiences or of the sacrifices of a relative or close friend. Our emotions will overflow, and we may be brought to tears. Speakers will recall for us the bravery and courage of our military and use descriptive words to depict our flag. The flag will be called "Old Glory," and the speech will be seasoned with words such as *sacrifice, courageous, selflessness, sentinel, guardian,* and *brave*. All these words create immediate mental pictures for the audience. We see our sons and daughters or even ourselves keeping watch at some desolate post, alone and in harm's way. An instant bunker mentality is evoked — America against her enemies. These words generate emotions, recall memories, and stir our souls.

What is it about certain words and phases that can affect almost everyone in the same way? How can mere words have that almost mystical power?

We've all heard that the pen (and the spoken word) is mightier than the sword. It's true. Written words have changed the world. The Bible is an outstanding and perfect example of that. Many other books and documents have had a profound effect on society. The *Torah*, the United States Constitution, the Bill of Rights, *Das Kapital* — *The Communist Manifesto*, the sayings of Chairman Mao, *Mein Kampf*, and thousands of other writings have stirred ideas, strongly influenced human behavior, and changed the course of history.

Are there certain words with special powers, words that encourage certain responses in everyone? According to the studies of social scientists, there are words with special power over us — words that trigger certain predictable responses. Authors, playwrights, and journalists know that there are phrases and words that conjure up mental pictures that will frighten, repulse, amuse, anger, or sadden their target audience. Experienced salespeople will automatically, perhaps subconsciously, weave certain words throughout their presentations — words that add power and emotional strength.

Charitable groups understand that certain words will touch our hearts and compel us to reach for our wallets. Words such as *betterment*, *fellowship*, and *voluntary* are used by these groups because they convey the idea of community, recovery, and generosity. People give money to charities to help not just the recipient, but the community as a whole. Although most contributors are kind and want to do something for their fellow human beings, they also want recognition and acknowledgment. The use of the word *voluntary* somehow projects that notion. When people hear evocative words, they may consciously be deaf to them, but subconsciously the words register in their minds and satisfy the message the charity wishes to send.

Words such as *coalition, international, foundation,* and *center* all paint a picture of unity and strength. The phrase, "a coalition of charities under the umbrella of the Community Chest," projects power, strength, and unity. Using the word *foundation* gives the reader an image of a solid, sturdy, conservative, and substantial organization. A "united front against poverty" is a phrase that gives the contributor a feeling of belonging to a special fraternity — a strong, united group with a single purpose, a group that is powerful enough to do something about the problem. It says, "We all know there is a problem we must deal with, and together we can solve it."

Adding *international* — as in the International Red Cross, promotes an image of strength, size, and sturdiness and lets us feel we have joined hands with people all over the world against a common foe.

Charities and other nonprofit organizations will shun words that might be interpreted to suggest a profit motive or personal gain. Rarely, if ever, will you see words such as *invest* in a solicitation letter. "Invest in your community" is replaced by "Help the needy in your community," or "Solve the problem of hunger."

In the commercial world of selling, there are specific power words, too. According to researchers, these words are the most pleasing to the American ear. Tested against thousands of other words, in hundreds of situations, these words and phrases were judged best able to change the attitudes of the listener/reader. A list of the top twenty power words is provided later in this chapter.

PUTTING POWER WORDS TO WORK

What you say and how you say it is important. As we have seen, closing does not necessarily occur after your presentation; it may and can occur at any time, even during the warm-up. Therefore, our selection of the words we use during our contact with buyers is important. Consider the following statements:

"Ms. Jenkins, we have found the answer to acne with Blemish Begone."

"Ms. Jenkins, our discovery, Blemish Begone, has banished acne forever!"

Can you find the power word in either of these statements? The word is *discovery*. What is it about that word that makes it so powerful? *Discovery* suggests a breakthrough, something that is fresh, new, and previously unknown. The word is associated with exploration, treasure, adventure, and secrets. The discovery of America, the discovery of Dr. Livingston, the discovery of the Salk vaccine, the discovery of a cure for the common cold or for AIDS or for cancer — all of these discoveries are thrilling, exciting, and important to society.

"Mr. Ford, an easy and proven method to improve your game is explained in this book."

"Mr. Ford, a positive way to improve your game is explained in this book."

Both statements say the same thing, and both are perfectly acceptable. However, one statement is more powerful, and if it is used, will sell more books than the other. Can you detect the two words that set one statement apart from the other? The two words are *easy* and *proven*. In the United States, we are well known for wanting things to be easy and uncomplicated. And we want guarantees or proof. We don't want to struggle with complicated instructions or untested equipment.

Japanese camera makers could never accept the fact that statistically there were fewer than one 35mm camera in the average family in the United States. In the average Japanese family, there were more than four! Why? The answer was simple. People in the United States neither wanted nor enjoyed dealing with F-stops, lens speeds and film speeds. Nor did they want to concern themselves with composition, balance, and depth of field when taking photos. They wanted a simple, fast, and effective way to shoot pictures of the family. The Japanese finally listened to their American market advisors, and after much urging, produced easy-to-operate, 35mm point-and-shoot cameras. The phrase *point and shoot* tells you how simple these cameras are and what the Japanese think about the technological grasp and interest of the average consumer in the United States. Consequently, advertisements and sales presentations stressed the ease with which one could "point and shoot" — just aim and press the shutter release.

The word *proven* is a guarantee, and consumers love guarantees. "Mrs. Jones, if you take this vitamin, I guarantee you'll feel more energetic in just thirty days." Now, how can the salesperson or anyone else make that guarantee? Mrs. Jones may be suffering from a serious medical condition; she may be suffering from low blood pressure or worse. That "guarantee" can't be honestly made, but Mrs. Jones will buy if the product is *proven* — that is, it has been tested and judged against competitors — and reasonably delivers the features and benefits "as advertised."

"This washer-dryer will cut your washday time in half!"

"This washer-dryer will save you an entire morning of work."

Once more we have two power words. Which are they? At first glance, you may see no particular differences between the two statements. But two words, *save* and *you*, pack a power punch. Subconsciously these words convey many meanings. Saving is important, whether saving time or money, hassle, grief, or trouble. We *save* things we value. Using the word in an advertisement (it is probably the most-used word in advertising) will draw attention to the ad and motivate the consumer to at least investigate the buying opportunity. Using *save* also hints that you are gaining an edge over other consumers. You buy and you save; the poor chump who doesn't buy, doesn't save. It's a one-upmanship game.

Inserting the word *you* into a sales presentation or advertisement personalizes and focuses the message. The statement, "This washer-dryer will save the average homemaker an entire morning's hard work," depersonalizes the message and separates the product benefits from the person for whom they are intended.

When we read an advertisement or listen to a sales presentation, we ask ourselves how we might benefit if we buy, even if we are buying for someone else. For example, a husband buys his wife a labor-saving device in the form of a vacuum cleaner. Does he buy because he feels his wife is working too hard? Does he believe that the old vacuum is too heavy and cumbersome? Or does he wish to stop her constant requests for a new, lightweight machine? Like most consumers, he considers how the vacuum will benefit *him*. Will the new unit be so quiet that he can watch Monday night football without turning up the volume to its highest setting? Will buying the vacuum release him from the obligation of buying another, more personal, more expensive gift? He never considers the vacuum a gift at all. His wife will be happy to get the new appliance, but it isn't really a gift for her. It's something for the household that will benefit him in some way.

Traditionally, the gender of the consumer has greatly influenced word selection. Words such as *rugged, powerful, tough, electronic,* and *scientific* have been directed to the male buyer and have been interspersed with words that appeal to the female buyer, words such as *fresh, simple, light,* and *color*.

Although the picture is rapidly changing, men still pay most of the bills while women make most of the buying decisions. We are beginning to see a change in the thrust of major advertising campaigns as the gender image continues to blur. What I'm trying to say is that the roles of the man and the woman are becoming more alike with each passing day. As that happens, sales and marketing people must make considerable adjustments to their approaches and avoid making offensive references.

"This wide-angle lens will permit you to take pictures of the entire group."

"With this wide-angle lens, you can shoot the entire group at once."

Which is the power word here? Actually there are no power words in either statement. There is, however, a negative word that you might call a *reverse* power word. That word is *permit*. *Permit* is an authoritative word. It suggests that there is a higher authority that allows us to act.

"This annuity will return to you 7 percent in annual interest compounded!"

"This annuity will reward you with a healthy 7-percent annual compounded interest!"

I guess this is the easiest one so far. The power words are *reward* and *healthy*. Who among us hasn't daydreamed about getting an enormous reward for some brilliant act or brave deed? Rewards are associated with doing admirable things. Even as children, Mom gave us a cookie as a reward for being good or quiet. Whatever our background may be, *reward* carries powerful, positive connotations..

Healthy is also a very forceful word. *Healthy* means soundness, sturdiness, and strength. The most important thing in our life is our health and the health of those we care about. When we hear the words *health* or *healthy*, we create "mind-pictures" of happiness — a smiling, wind-blown, athletic young person with a healthy color and not a care in the world. This is why we often see the word *healthy* used in advertising to sell everything from lifestyles to alarm systems.

Words reflect perceptions. *Sexy*, for example, is rarely used when trying to reach older citizens, because the perception is that older people have no need or desire to be sexy. Senior citizens, it has been decided, are more concerned with safety and security. Therefore, advertisements or sales presentations aimed at older people will emphasize words with that projected image.

"This Certificate of Deposit is guaranteed by the strength and integrity of the U.S. Government" is a recognizable pitch aimed at the elderly.

Nothing is said about return on investment. The perception behind this is that seniors are not as concerned with the *return on investment* as they are with the *safety of investments*.

"Live at Crotchety Commons. Relax in the safe, secure, and friendly atmosphere created especially for active seniors." This statement pushes the safety feature, but it also appeals to the extroverted senior with the words *friendly* and *active*. Because many retirees are physically active and want to stay that way, using *active* in the statement conveys the appropriate image. Loneliness is also a condition many seniors face; hence the word *friendly* is used to suggest that new friends with similar interests live in Crotchety Commons.

"Protect those you love with a Gottcha Home Security System."

"Protect yourself and your family with a Gottcha Home Security System."

In both statements, the name of the product itself contains a power word — *security*, which conveys the notion of safety. However, the first statement has two additional zingers — *you* and *love*. "Protect those you *love*," brings home the need for a home security system without assaulting the ego of the masculine breadwinner. Men feel or like to think they can protect their families from whatever may threaten. To suggest otherwise attacks the male ego. That is why television ads for home security systems usually depict the home empty when an intruder appears. The ads are saying, "Sure, if you are home, you can handle any situation, but you're not always there!"

If the advertisement read "Gottcha Home Security Systems, the ultimate in alarm systems," the idea would still be there, but the personalization would be lost. Let me cite an amusing example of personalizing. Willie Sutton, the infamous bank robber, wrote that when threatening someone, he always directed his threat to a specific part of the body. He never said, "Do what I say, or I'll shoot you." That, according to Willie, may not register in the mind of a would-be hero. Instead, he would say, "Do what I say, or I'll blow your kneecaps off." Willie knew his trade well and probably would have been a good salesman. He knew that when you direct someone's attention to a specific body part, it personalizes the threat. The potential victim "feels" the pain, visualizes the injury, and then usually decides to act with prudence. (No, I don't recommend using Willie's presentation-at-gunpoint technique!)

Another example further illustrates my point. In a recent sales situation a salesperson was having difficulty developing interest in a product that helped correct memory loss. The customer, a woman in her forties, seemed about ready to terminate the interview, when the salesperson asked, "Do you have a mother or grandmother, someone *you love*, who is suffering forgetfulness? You know, forgets where he or she left the keys, shows up on the wrong days for appointments — that sort of thing?" Immediately the customer started to show interest. "Why yes," she answered. "My favorite aunt has us all concerned. The poor dear tries to hide her forgetfulness, She's ashamed, I suppose. You know, with all this talk about Alzheimer's, she is worried to death."

The salesperson drew the customer's attention to the product by personalizing the need. The customer may have eventually recognized the need in her own family, but maybe not. Perhaps the salesperson would have made the sale anyway, but by using the two power words, *you* and *love*, she personalized the sale and got the order immediately.

New and variations of that word carry terrific power to the consumer. The world is built on change, and *new* epitomizes change. People, especially in the United States, are rarely satisfied with the status quo. They want new things, new ideas, new challenges, and new opportunities. Newness drives the nation forward and makes us reach, and, as Americans, we like to stretch as far as we can. Compared to the charming old cities of Europe, the United States has few buildings with historical significance. As soon as a building loses its utility, we tear it down and build a glass and steel box over it. Businesses flock in, and we rarely hear a voice raised to defend a part of history, which has been lost forever. With that in mind, we can see the power of the word *new* and better understand how it affects us.

Advertisers have long known the importance of the word *new*, and they use it even to describe products that have existed for decades.

"Try the *new, improved*, sodium-*free*, Bambell's soup!"

Now that statement is loaded with power words! *New, improved*, and sodium-*free*! What more could a consumer want? Sodium is a no-no ingredient in today's health-conscious society. However, *new, improved,* and *free* are the power words. As used, *free* doesn't necessarily connect in the consumer's mind with sodium. In other words, if that statement had said, "Try the new, improved Bambell's Soup," and elsewhere noted "no sodium," the message would not have been as powerful. *Free* is the magic word in selling. Everyone wants something that is free, as long as a value is perceived and the giver is considered legitimate.

Volunteers who hand out flyers (free, of course) find it difficult to get everyone to take one. There is no perceived value. Solicitations for "free" gifts that require sitting through a time-share presentation are also difficult to give away because the giver is asking for something in return (your time), and the recipient of this largess may believe the giver represents an arm-twisting, hard-sell, somewhat sleazy real estate operation.

The list of power words is long and varies with the situation. Advertisers use one set of power words (that often change with the times), while salespeople usually stay with the tried and proven. Words or phrases that we know will be short-lived or those that are in vogue, carry a danger with them. If they are used in a presentation, they may not be understood. Even worse, the buyer may be offended because the words make him or her appear "out of the loop," and a bit square.

As we know, language and word meanings change constantly. In our lifetime we have seen the meaning of *square* change from "honest and fair," to "dull" or "unfashionable." Words go in and out of fashion. *Dude* has come to mean someone who is very much in style, someone who is "with it." Not very long ago, *dude* referred a greenhorn, someone very much "out of it." The name "Dude Ranch" meant a ranch where city folks went to experience the joys of the out-of-doors and savor the Western lifestyle. Today it still serves that purpose, but it has lost the negative connotation.

Some old-fashioned words and phases are completely lost in the mists of time. Phrases our parents used in their youth may have no meaning today. It is peculiar how many old-time phrases do come back — but with totally different meanings. "She's a dandy," meant that the person referred to was terrific, wonderful, or stylish. Today, that same expression is usually said in a derogatory way and means that the individual is a problem.

New words, formed because of some modern happenings, didn't exist just a few years, months, or even weeks ago. "He's in orbit," or "she went ballistic" are two examples of new phrases that use old words whose meanings have changed. And, of course, we are always coming up with new words, such as *teflon*, *internet*, *cyberspace*, and *floppy disk*.

Our founding fathers would have difficulty communicating with us, and we with them. But, I suspect that somehow we would manage to communicate with each other. I further suspect that the twenty power words recognized by specialists today would have been powerful back then as well.

As we've seen, power words are successfully used in advertising and in sales presentations to convey, in the strongest possible way, the message the advertiser or salesperson wishes to send. We also know that many power words have strength and can nudge us toward making certain predictable decisions.

Twenty Power Words

So what are the most powerful words in the English language? Although you will get an argument from some advertising people and others in the "convincing" business, according to leading social scientists and etymologists, the twenty most powerful and most influential words in the English language are as follows:

discovery	love	results	easy	money
safety	new	save	you	health(y)
guarantee	proven	power(ful)	swift	skilled
wise	free	simple	shrewd	safe

I think you can see why these words are considered to be very powerful. They are positive words; there are no negatives to be found. People want to hear the positive and shun the negative. Remember these words and try to weave them into your presentations. Remember, too, if you start to find yourself getting negative, that no one wants to hear negative input. It is, to use a contemporary expression, a "downer."

Don't take my word for it. Prove the power of these words to yourself. Give two presentations to similar customers. In one, sprinkle the power words throughout your presentation, and in the other, make a conscious effort to use no power words at all. I am confident you will notice a difference in your customers' responses.

10

PROMOTING SALES

One of the biggest problems any salesperson has today is taking fear away from the buyer. After all, fear prevents most customers from placing an order in the first place. The fear of making a mistake, of buying something that will not sell and turn a profit, can be debilitating. If a mistake has been made, the buyer will get "heat" from the merchandise manager. "Why," he will be asked, "didn't you get a guaranteed sale on this merchandise? If you had bought it from GE we could have returned it!" The buyer will try to explain his reasons for buying the goods and will then try to remedy the problem. He will call the vendor and try to return the goods (a delicate situation for the salesperson, who must say no). He may take a markdown and blow out the goods at little profit. Or he may (and this is rare with most buyers today) "merchandise" his way out of the situation.

Buyers often go a bit bonkers when they discover they will not be allowed to return goods. They will usually threaten the seller with: "That is the last order you'll ever get from me!" Some accounts will attempt to return goods (especially if they haven't yet been paid for), without authorization to do so. To counter that move, vendors usually require a RAN (return authorization number). Without a RAN on every returned carton, the receiving clerk will refuse to accept the shipment. This results in a ping-pong game in which the shipment bounces back and forth, and only the trucking company makes money. Obviously, buyers and their companies are responsible for the merchandise — paid for or not. However, in recent years, the consolidation of retailing power has emasculated the vendors (especially the medium-size and small vendors), and they often surrender to virtually any demand made of them. Still, some vendors are hard-nosed and determined to stick with their policies. If that is the case, the buyers have two other choices: taking a markdown or merchandising.

The option of taking a markdown affects the bottom line of a department's profit-and-loss statement. This, in turn, affects the bonus payments the buyers might make, which affects the bonus the merchandise manager can make, and all of this brings down HFOH (heat from on high). This domino effect is a major reason why there are so many timid buyers and so many companies with strict buying rules determined by the merchandise manager or even higher authorities. If buyers have too many product markdowns, heads will roll (theirs, in particular).

Markdowns, many believe, give the retail chain an "image." They make the stores look like pawnshops (or so it is said), and they tie up important funds that could be used to buy profit-making merchandise. Although shoppers love markdowns, and it has been proven that markdowns increase store traffic, those facts are usually ignored or scorned.

Picture this. Your merchandise isn't selling very well. The merchandise manager is breathing down the buyer's neck. The buying seasons are changing, so the goods have to be moved. Your company absolutely refuses to accept the goods back, and the buyer is threatening you with banishment unless you do something for him. What do you do?

You do what good merchants always have done — you merchandise your way out of the predicament. Buyers love salespeople with merchandising ideas. In today's bland retail world in which "everyone has the same goods at the same price," trying to add zest to the product mix is a constant struggle. Yet, that struggle must be won; otherwise, the consumer has no particular reason to shop in one store instead of another. In a way, retailing is show business with its glitz, glamour, and staging.

Generally speaking, retail salespeople are minimum-wage, part-time people who really could care less about the store in which they work. They follow directions, and that is about the extent of their involvement. They usually won't take the initiative to help sell the slow-moving goods. Why should they? Throughout the chain of command, no one will step up to the bat, except the buyers (and they are forced to do so). It falls to them to merchandise the "distressed" goods, which means that they will have to figure out a way to make "distressed" goods, "undistressed." Naturally, they look for help, and the vendor is the most logical person to give it. Buyers are desperate for new ideas and new methods of selling in their stores. They cater to vendors who can create fresh, exciting promotions that attract shoppers and sell merchandise, especially if the goods start to back up.

Some time ago I had a good account located in a terrible neighborhood. The account was part of a national chain, but because the store was located where it was, the managers had certain leeway to do what they thought would work outside the strict rules that other stores in the chain had to follow. Security was a prime objective of the store's manager because shrinkage (shoplifting elevated to a fine art) was a big problem, but he was also somewhat of a retail gambler.

One day at lunch he mentioned how bored he was. "The same thing, day after day," he lamented. "Do you have any ideas? I'll bite on anything." I don't know why I blurted out what I blurted out, but I immediately said, "Let's have a truckload sale right in the parking lot!" Now understand, a parking-lot sale is an open invitation to shoplifters. If the day is sunny, the glare hides all sorts of activities. Fewer clerks are working outdoors, employees are carting goods back and forth, problems are always developing with power cords to the cash registers, and scads of people are browsing about the makeshift aisles and merchandise tables. It is a nightmare, but it's a profitable nightmare. Although many stores had held truckload sales prior to my idea, no one in our industry had tried one up to that time.

"No," he answered, "even I'm not that nutty. In this neighborhood a truckload sale would be a disaster. Besides, we don't know how to run one."

"I mean a *real* truck load," I replied. "We'll sell goods right out of a tractor-trailer. That will help with the security problem. We can have a few secured tables with samples of what is for sale, and the retail salespeople can demonstrate the merchandise and answer questions. The customers can pick out what they want from the secured tables, and take delivery out of the trucks by presenting a paid receipt. I'll get you a deeper discount — say an extra 10 percent — if you promise to buy a preset amount and agree to keep at least 50 percent after the sale." He thought for a few minutes, and I was sure he was going to turn me down. "So what?" I thought. "I gave it a shot."

"If you get the trailer and the parking-lot decorations and arrange for some promotional stuff, like balloons for the kids, maybe free ice cream and soft drinks, I'll do it!" We did it right. The parking lot looked like Disneyland. I hired a couple of clowns to entertain the kids while the parents shopped. We had a huge popcorn machine dispensing free popcorn, alongside a "bar" where free sodas were available. A cotton candy machine made big, sticky treats for everyone. It was a gas! The kids screamed bloody murder when the exhausted (and usually broke) parents finally dragged them home. People thanked us for a terrific day. Everyone had a great time, and we almost doubled our best day in sales!

The headquarters learned about the sale and — I couldn't believe it — ordered it never to happen again! They cited some nonsense about insurance or something, but we had had our day! It was one I'll never forget. The manager and I were good friends and held several other ambitious promotions. Some did well, but none came close to our famous Truckload Sale.

I later discovered that promotions such as ours were specifically forbidden in that chain due to concerns about personal injury and liability. The legal department and insurance department had issued bulletins several months before, outlining the reasons for prohibiting such promotions. The manager knew that, but he was bored and had more latitude than most, so he could hide behind that. Also, like most store managers, he was crazy for a fresh idea and a little excitement.

You don't need to face a crisis before you think up a promotion that will boost your sales and make you a champ in the eyes of the buyer. A successful promotion is one that will snag new customers, hold on to old customers, accelerate the sale of goods, invigorate the retail sales staff, educate the consumer, and alter the attitude of the entire store personnel.

All too often, the buyer or a so-called promotional aide will hold a sale and lose money. This is because many believe a promotion is only based on lower prices. Nonsense. Hard-to-get items, special credit terms, or companion bargains (that is, buy unit A and get unit B at half price) can all be used to accelerate sales, increase revenues, generate excitement, blow out slow-selling goods, and supply the store with more consumer traffic.

Promotions that are unusual in their very nature, such as midnight sales, sidewalk sales, truckload sales, and the like, are often successful because the consumers are drawn to their uniqueness. Shopping becomes an outing, an amusement for the consumer.

In general, retailers lack imagination and are terrified of the unknown. If the promotion has proven itself and if the risks are minimal (better yet, nonexistent), they might try it. This is not true of all retailers, of course. Someone had to take a chance at some point in time, or nothing would be a "proven success."

STEPS TO PROBLEM-SOLVING PROMOTIONS

Let's return to our scenario of your customer stuck with goods at season's end, with your company's strict policy of refusing to accept return goods, with his management raising heck, and the buyer threatening to kill your firstborn and burn your house. What do you do?

Step one: You meet with the buyer and the store's merchandiser (not to be confused with a merchandise manager) to outline a promotion that will move the goods *without* taking a markdown. You should stand by the value of your merchandise. "It isn't selling because it wasn't understood or merchandised properly," is your position.

Step two: With the approval of your company — who is anxious to keep as much of the chain's goodwill as possible — you "spiff" the retail salespeople. A *spiff* is a small commission paid to the retail clerk who sells specific merchandise.

Step three: You secure as much advertising money as possible from the chain and try to get your company to match it on a 50-50 basis — all to be used to promote this "special" sale.

Step four: With the approval of the merchandiser, get "hot spots" in which to feature the distressed goods and get the strongest retail salespeople to handle the sale of that merchandise. A meeting before the sale with all salespeople is encouraged. It is particularly important to meet with the strongest sales clerks and, perhaps arrange for a contest with special prizes for the top two or three producers. Use theater tickets, sports tickets or some other relatively inexpensive but highly prized reward as the additional incentive. Place the distressed goods in several places throughout the store, especially at entry and exit ways.

Step five: If possible, get a tie-in promotion. For example, if you're trying to sell shoes, meet with a hosiery vendor who will be interested in promoting his goods, and tie the two promotions together. If you're trying to sell water skis, tie in wetsuits, safety vests, or swimwear.

Step six: Enlist the aid of the store manager, merchandiser, or window designer to decorate the store. The purpose is to create an air of excitement and to set your promotional goods apart from "regular" merchandise.

Step seven: Limit the promotion. A weekend or, at the very most, a week is all that is needed to move the goods. Most promotions lose energy after a few days.

Step eight: Visit during the promotion. Stay out of the way, but make sure you are seen. If possible, talk with the salespeople, encourage them, praise them, and help them.

After the promotion, have a careful inventory taken. If the eight steps have been followed, the bulk of the goods will be sold, and the buyer will be delighted. He or she will happily keep the residue merchandise, and you will be a hero. If the promotion flops, the buyer will know that you did your very best and that your company cooperated. He or she will respect your no-return rule in the future. At the very worst, the buyer will have to take a markdown to move the goods. What will you have gained?

1. You now know the retail salespeople, who will give your products special attention.

2. The buyer will consider you an "idea" person and will look to you for future promotional ideas.

3. During the promotional period, your goods will have been prominently displayed, featured, and sold.

4. Even if the promotion is not successful, you will have reduced the distressed goods inventory somewhat and will have gained at least that advantage for your buyer.

Naturally, when the buyer is desperate, promotions are stressful for all concerned. The success of the promotion becomes extraordinarily important, and everyone feels the tension. Actually, tension can be good — that energy creates a sense of urgency and importance. Certain concessions will be given to you. Be smart enough to take full advantage of them. A promotion that isn't a "fire sale" is much more fun. Everyone is relaxed and cheerful, and the sword of Damocles isn't hanging over everyone's head.

SELLING YOUR PROMOTIONAL IDEAS

How do you create a promotional idea and sell it to the buyer? As I have said, most buyers are desperate for promotional ideas. They are in a race with the competition, a contest for the consumer's dollar. Anything that will improve their chances in that contest is eagerly sought.

Every promotional situation is different from another. The type of merchandise, the kind of retail outlet, the price range, and the targeted consumers are just some of the factors to be considered. Let's take an example and devise a promotion.

Suppose you wanted to sell ice skates to preteens. Your customers are sporting goods stores, and the major customer is a chain with fifteen stores. You are competing with four other makers of ice skates, and your brand is not the best seller, not because of a lack of quality or salability, but because of the unenthusiastic marketing support by your customers.

Almost every product has a slush price — money that can be taken out of the price that is charged to the retailer. This may take the form of discounts or advertising and/or promotional allowances. Most retailers demand these allowances, and most vendors are happy to permit them, because the money is used to promote and sell their products. If, as may be the case with smaller customers, the slush monies are not used, the vendor has added to his or her bottom-line profit.

To sell your ice skates, you would first determine the amount of slush money available. Explain to your sales manager the promotion you have in mind and ask if additional funds might be made available (usually not, but it doesn't hurt to ask). Let's assume the skates cost $40 per pair wholesale, and there is $6 per pair in slush money. You have 300 pairs of skates in inventory that you must sell, which means that you have $1,800 in promotional money to spend. Work with that amount, but try to stretch it, if possible. You will see how this can be done.

Second, since you are targeting the preteen market, you must develop a promotion that will particularly appeal to them or to their parents (who buy for them). What do preteen kids universally like? Movies and music. Most music tapes cost around $7, and motion-picture theater tickets cost about the same. Kids are pretty smart nowadays, and the promotion must convey the impression that everyone has a reasonable chance at winning. Therefore, we will give away 150 prizes. Winners can choose either theater tickets or music tapes — the tickets to local movie houses and the tapes in the form of vouchers, redeemable at large, well-known music retailers (in the same mall, if possible). A visit to "participating" movie houses and to music store managers will very likely allow you a significant discount when you include their establishments in your promotional materials and advertising. It is even possible to get the promotional prizes for free! It is also possible to have the movie houses and music stores include your promotion in their normal advertising plans. Push for a team effort whenever you can.

Let's assume you can secure the tapes and tickets at half the normal cost. This means you spend only $525 for prizes and have $1,275 available for counter cards, flyers, mailers, and printed advertising.

Naturally, you have already met with and explained the promotion to your account, and you have asked if they have advertising money they can contribute. Let's assume they agree to the promotion, but can contribute no additional promotional money. Now you return to the buyer and work to design powerful selling spots in the stores: entry-way stack displays, for example, and additional stack displays throughout the store (the bigger, the better). If you were able to tie in another vendor, you should get additional spots. All checkout counters would, of course, have counter cards (and collection boxes) announcing the contest and inviting all to enter.

It is worth mentioning how we design a contest so that it is most effective. It must be easy to enter: Name, address, telephone number, and age must be submitted on every entry. This allows you to begin a database of customers in each store area, which may be very useful in future promotions. Since every jurisdiction forbids lotteries, you must allow entry into the contest without purchase. However, you want to sell skates. One way to discourage entrants who do not purchase is to make the contest open to all, but make entering difficult if the entrant doesn't buy. Having the nonpurchaser fill out and mail in a 3"x 5" card, for example. Few preteens will take the trouble to do this, so most of your entries will have purchased the skates.

Add to the strength of your promotion by displaying additional counter cards at locations that have at least peripheral interest, such as ice rinks, schools, gyms, and car washes.

Purchasers receive entry forms when they purchase the skates. These forms, along with all entries, are placed in a drum for a drawing. The drawing should be advertised as much as you can afford. This usually will draw a lot of kids, so hold the drawing on a weekend. A drawing should be held in every store of the fifteen-store chain, so that local kids will be the winners. Winners make great publicists, and having ten winners per store raving about their new skates will help build your entire territory.

The prizes are given out at the site of the drawing, and the winners must be present to win. This requirement will help to ensure a good-size crowd. Large crowds mean possible last-minute entries, additional sales of your skates, and additional sales of other merchandise in the stores. (You are gaining points by the minute with this buyer!)

As you can see, there is a fair amount of work involved in planning and holding a sales promotion. But the rewards are tremendous. Major companies have national campaigns that offer fabulous prizes. These campaigns are carefully planned, professionally managed, and run with military precision. Obviously, they work, or the companies wouldn't run them year after year. However, your little "homemade" promotion can actually outperform a national campaign in terms of people taking part and merchandise sold vs. money spent. Small, representative-planned promotions reflect your personal interest and energy. The consumers feel they have a better chance of winning, and the excitement level is generally much higher.

THE MYSTERY SHOPPER

Promotions can be used to accomplish any number of goals. One goal is getting the retail salesperson to offer your goods first to a shopper. If you could manage to get your merchandise offered first to every shopper who tells a retail salesperson: "I'd like to see a pair of binoculars," for example, your brand would quickly become the best seller in that store. The reason is simple. Clerks always offer the product they most prefer personally. That means they know that product best, can sell its features and benefits easily, and will recommend it to the consumer. That, of course, carries tremendous strength. How often have you asked a retail clerk, "What do you recommend?" and then ignored the recommendation? Not often, I would bet.

A number of years ago the marketing manager of a major brewery observed how often customers ordered a beer without specifying a particular brand. On a hot day in St. Louis, he sat at the end of a bar in a busy tavern and watched as more than fifty patrons ordered beer. Not one of them asked for a particular brand. "Gimme a beer," was the usual order. And, surprisingly, the bartender would reach for the same brand every time. After visiting a half dozen watering holes and noting the same pattern, he interviewed all the bartenders, asking them about their personal choice in beers. Not surprisingly, each bartender served his or her preferred brand when a generic order was placed.

The marketing manager struggled with the problem of how to get bartenders all across the country to reach for his brand when the order, "Gimme a beer," was made. Direct mail appeals to the bartenders didn't work, nor did advertising urging the customer to specify (that had been part of their and everyone else's advertising campaigns for years). "If," he thought, "I can only think of a way to *reward* the bartender who reaches for my brand first, my sales will increase at least 35 percent!" His company was third in the nation in sales at the time, and a 35 percent increase would catapult his company into first place. This was something worth working on, so he deepened his research.

Some interesting facts came to light. Getting beer drinkers to switch brands, he was told by his "experts," was nearly impossible. They were brand-loyal, and drinking one brand or another reflected on their neighborhood, nationality, ethnic origin, and even religion!

"Maybe," he thought, "but if that is true, why do consumers say 'gimme a beer' or just 'beer,' instead of 'gimme a Kidney Buster beer'?" It just didn't make sense to him. His marketing team ran survey after survey, they conducted on-the-spot interviews, offered discounts to bar owners, but nothing worked and no new information seemed useful. The problem seemed unsolvable, but he was determined.

Then, in the middle of the night, he awoke from a sound sleep with an inspiration! "That's it! I'll use a Mystery Shopper!" he fairly shouted — much to the anger of his sleeping spouse. "What the heck is a Mystery Shopper?" she asked. "I'll hire people to visit taverns, bars, and restaurants all across the country — first in test markets, and then, if it works like I think it will, nationally." "Mystery Shoppers" would order beer without specifying the brand at every stop they made. If the bartender served them the company's brand, he or she would be rewarded with a five-dollar bill along with a note which read: "I am the Kidney Buster Mystery Shopper.

This $5 bill is your reward for serving me a Kidney Buster beer when I ordered a beer. Keep it up. I or another Mystery Shopper may be back at any time with another reward."

If, on the other hand, the bartender served a competing brand, the Mystery Shopper would pay for the brew and hand the bartender a card that read: "I am the Kidney Buster Mystery Shopper. If you had served me a Kidney Buster when I ordered a beer, I would have rewarded you with a $5 tip. Sorry! But you will have another chance: A Mystery Shopper may stop at your bar at any time. Be sure to serve Kidney Buster when anyone says, 'I'll have a beer.' You never know, it could be the Mystery Shopper."

The marketing manager was so excited, he could hardly wait for morning. It was a brilliant marketing idea and, he was sure, the answer to his problem. The bartenders had nothing to lose and $5 to gain. It didn't matter to them or their employers which beer the customers drank, and once a bartender got his reward, he eagerly would spread the word throughout the bartending fraternity. Soon, every bartender would be serving the company's brand when a generic order was given, hoping that the customer was the Mystery Shopper.

Tested in a minor market and two major markets, the Mystery Shopper idea was an immediate success. The idea was implemented nationally, and in just a few weeks, sales skyrocketed. Before the end of the year the operation was running full speed, and sales were going crazy. The marketing manager was justly proud of his idea, but he was wrong about one thing: The sales didn't increase by 35 percent — they shot to more than 50 percent!

Needless to say, the Mystery Shopper idea can be utilized in almost any industry. There may be a few problems, however. Some retailers object to having one brand of merchandise favored over another. Their thinking is that if their people concentrate on selling one particular brand, inventories of other merchandise will back up and cause many problems. In addition, since some merchandise is more profitable than others, the retailer may want to feature the brands that are more profitable than yours. But, if you can have a meeting of the minds, most accounts will allow a Mystery Shopper for a specific, limited time period. It is an opportunity to reward the clerks, and it adds a little excitement to their day. For you, even a limited promotion can pay big dividends.

THE UNEXPECTED TARGET

A spin-off of the Mystery Shopper was conceived by the owner of an Italian restaurant in St. Louis. The restaurant was located in an Italian-American neighborhood populated by tradesmen and blue collar workers, most of whom were engaged in the building trades. Fair weather meant steady paychecks, but winter snow, rain, and bitter cold meant tight budgets that didn't include eating out. Of course, trade was not restricted to the neighborhood families only. On the contrary, most of St. Louis had known about this restaurant's excellent food and reasonable prices and traveled to the "hill," as the area was known, when business or pleasure led them in that direction. Nevertheless, the business was unpredictable and erratic.

Several serious problems existed. First, the neighborhood customers preferred to eat at home, and dining out was on special occasions only. Second, except for a handful of regulars, customers came only when a nearby sports stadium held an event. Third, the owner wanted to improve the service and price level of his menu, and that was impossible given the trade he now had. There was no escaping the fact that, without a drastic change, the restaurant's fortunes were tied to the economic and social conditions of the neighborhood.

Not far away, just across a park, was a cluster of quality hotels filled with prosperous business people, members of visiting professional sports teams, and tourists. Getting those guests into his establishment was the answer. All he had to do was figure out how.

Then one particularly miserable night, as he sat in his office that overlooked the main entrance, he watched as taxi after taxi pulled up to the door and unloaded groups of wealthy, expense-report-supported diners! "Taxis," he mused. "Most business travelers and others staying at those fancy hotels take a cab to dinner. Normally, they ask the cab driver for a restaurant recommendation." In that instant, he had his answer.

First, the owner renovated the basement of his restaurant and turned it into an attractive, comfortable dining room. The atmosphere was warm and friendly, and the food was exactly the same as that served in the dining room above. Next, he contacted every cab company in town and posted on the drivers' bulletin boards an offer of a free meal for every ten customers delivered to his door. When a cabbie delivered a diner, he received a chit for each passenger. Ten passengers delivered equaled one free meal.

Almost overnight the restaurant was packed, upstairs and down. Taxis lined up to unload their fares, and the bar did a brisk business from the patrons who were waiting for tables. The telephone rang constantly with requests for reservations, and as the restaurant's popularity grew, a banquet room was added, which also proved very successful. This restaurant became nationally famous and is a favorite hangout for sports figures, business people, politicians, and visiting celebrities.

The practice of rewarding taxi drivers continues to this day, even though the restaurant is one of the most popular in that city and probably doesn't need that help any longer. If you visit St. Louis, ask a cab driver to recommend a restaurant. Chances are you'll end up on the "hill."

Thinking up promotional ideas can be fun. It takes imagination, and it also takes cooperation and understanding. Promotions will disturb and disrupt the everyday operations. That is what they are supposed to do. But some retailers dislike the idea of noise, decorations, or any sort of activity outside the norm. You must sell the idea to the buyer and to the store manager. One of the most important things is to make sure your promotion doesn't violate laws — lottery laws, in particular. Everyone must be allowed to enter your promotional contest (if a contest is involved), without having to buy anything. However, under certain circumstances, you can have a contest where a contest prize is awarded to the purchaser of merchandise.

For instance, some soft-drink companies, fast-food chains, and others will award a prize if you should be lucky and buy their product with a winning "scratch-off." No one can win without first buying that particular drink or eating in that particular restaurant. Generally speaking, retailers are uncertain about the laws and resist any promotion that they think might cause problems. For those reasons, you may find it easier to take the prize money and use it in retail price reductions or in advertising instead.

TIE-IN PROMOTIONS

Generally speaking, I think tie-in promotions are the strongest. They give you additional promotional monies, spread the work, increase the number of stack displays, and sometimes double the amount of promotional advertising. On top of all that, if the tie-in product is strong in its own right, there is a residual benefit as consumers relate your product with the companion product.

Getting another vendor to join in your promotion is usually rather easy. Companies want to promote their goods, and if the tie-in makes sense, few vendors will have a reason to refuse. The trick is in getting the companion product to contribute monies to the promotion. But if you can show where the money is being spent and why it is needed, usually there is no problem.

PROMOTING TO THE "TROOPS"

Promotions can be very successful without giving prizes or even deep discounts to the consumers. As previously mentioned, spiffs, special commissions to retail salespeople, are extremely effective in making promotions worthwhile.

Most retail salespeople are not paid very well. They have a difficult job working eyeball-to-eyeball with the buying public, handling customers' complaints, and dealing with the many problems that arise daily. Once retail clerks (a term that most despise) were highly trained, respected, and well paid. It was not at all unusual for retail salespeople to work in the same store for their entire career, and with their earnings, they could comfortably support a family. But, with the changes in retailing (especially in the United States), the bulk of the retail sales staffs are often homemakers who work to earn enough for a specific purpose, college or high school students who work part-time, or someone who is working and waiting for something better to turn up.

Naturally, any additional income they have an opportunity to earn will be enthusiastically pursued. If, in addition to the spiffs, you can offer a retail prize, such as a color TV, a CD player, or other similar enticements, it will help ensure a solid effort from the clerks and almost guarantee a successful promotion. One key to that success is to hold a meeting with the staff, carefully explaining how the spiff program works (keep it simple to administer and understand), stressing how anyone can win and how everyone has an equal chance of winning (there are usually retail "stars" who outperform everyone else, which can reduce the zeal of the others), selling them on the merits of your products and the tie-in products, and winding up with everyone getting a reward.

That reward might be a one-dollar bill taped to the underside of every chair in the meeting room ("You're sitting on money, so get up and get going") or a similar "out of the starting blocks" tidbit.

PLAY IT AGAIN, SAM . . .

Naturally, your promotions are limited only by your imagination and the imagination of your customer. The breadth and scope of the promotion are limited by the funds available to you and the objective of the promotion. Objective? Yes, promotions all have certain goals, both short range and long range in nature.

A long-range goal that is frequently sought is gaining repeat customers. One promotion that will accomplish this is the "Punch Card Promo." This promotion is often used by car wash businesses, some restaurants, barber shops, and similar establishments. When customers buy a particular product or service, they are given a card with ten or more numbers printed on it. After each purchase, a number is either punched out or stamped, until all ten spots are used. At that point, customers are entitled to a free car wash, dinner, haircut, or whatever. All things being equal, consumers are more likely to come back to the establishment with the punch card in order to work their way toward the free item or service. Although this promotion is common with companies that sell a service, product-oriented businesses recently have adopted this method of gaining and holding customers.

Banks and similar institutions have tried premium promotions for many years. "Open an account and get a free toaster" is almost expected. The toaster promotion has expanded to include color TV sets, stereo systems, and even Hawaiian vacations. Lending institutions are very familiar with these promotional ideas. However, researchers report that the customers believe all such businesses are pretty much alike and that "banking" promotions have little impact on the average customer. People tend to return to businesses that know them personally. In other words, if your bank teller calls you by name, you are more likely to maintain your account there. Banks that are impersonal, cool, or snooty lose out regardless of promos.

Armed with that information, many banks are now aiming their promotions at their employees instead of their customers. This practice is somewhat similar to a spiff program, except in these promotions, depositors are asked to vote for "the friendliest" or the "most helpful" employee. At the end of three months, the "friendliest" employee is given a small bonus, a special parking space, a commemorative pin or scroll, or lunch with the boss (oh boy!).

We may sneer at these promotions, but you cannot question the results they bring, not just to the winner and runners-up, but to the employees and customers, too. Overall, morale is improved, along with service and the level of friendliness. This gain is not short-lived, and that is the biggest bonus of all!

Promotions do more than help to increase your territory sales. They inject an element of excitement in the retail outlets. The salespeople associate the fun and excitement with your promotion and in the future, will be more likely to recommend your products to the consumer.

The buyer, basking in the warmth of the promotional success, will look to you for future ideas and will add you to the "inner circle" of preferred vendors. Even the consumer's awareness of your product line will be heightened. So we have a win-win-win situation.

A closing word of caution: If you design a promotion, make sure you are more enthusiastic than the most enthusiastic sales clerk, department manager, or store manager. Get involved and stay involved. Be ready to get more stock instantly, handle questions from consumers or clerks, restack displays, arrange point-of-sale materials, or do whatever else needs to be done. Your example will be noted by the buyer, and what is even more important in this case, it will be noted by the sales clerks. Your enthusiasm will transfer to them, and the promotion's success or failure will be determined by your influence and example.

11

The Business Letter

In the previous chapter we discussed various ways to promote sales within a retail establishment. The business letter is another method of promoting sales that is effective and inexpensive. Moreover, the business letter can accomplish a number of other objectives that may be difficult or even impossible to accomplish in any other way.

The written word is an extremely powerful and dangerous method of communication. Dangerous? Yes, very dangerous, because it is an indelible record and can't be retracted easily. Unlike the spoken word, which can be claimed to have been misinterpreted, misunderstood, or misheard, the written record is there for all to see. Without proven statistics to support me, I would say that written communications have gotten people — especially salespeople — into more trouble than cheap liquor.

However, if used properly, the power of writing a business letter, a memo, an entreaty, or a solicitation can immeasurably strengthen you as a salesperson. There are many ways to develop this powerful skill. Countless volumes have been published about how to write a business or personal letter. Most community colleges offer courses that can give you a solid foundation as well. Tapes and correspondence courses are also available. One way to learn how to write is by reading. Read whatever you enjoy reading — newspapers, magazines, fiction, biographies, history, or anything! You will gain a feeling for words and phrases.

Once you develop the habit of reading, you will discover styles that appeal to you, and you will begin to write like the authors and writers you enjoy. Obviously, a mystery novel will not read like a business letter, so you may not see the connection at once, but as you increase the volume of your reading, you will expand the scope of what you read, and that will add to your writing ability. In this chapter, I hope to expose to you several types of business correspondence: the selling letter, the employment letter, and the letter of appreciation. Each can be forceful methods of accomplishing explicit purposes in a most personal way. Letters always reach their targets.

THE BUSINESS LETTER

A letter written to the president of a company will very likely be read by him or her. A secretary may open and read the mail, but you can be reasonably sure that the mail will be passed on to the addressee. You can also be sure you will receive a reply if the letter is addressed to a major decision maker. Lesser lights are often too busy or too important to be bothered, but the big brass will always find time, I guarantee it.

Some years ago, a friend of mine wanted to promote a new product, and his budget looked more like an area code than a zip code. Even so, he thought he had enough funds to run a national promotion if he could entice a major pizza company to join his promo. The idea was terrific, as was his product, but I warned him of the difficulties he was going to encounter. First, his product was unknown; and second, his competition was not only well entrenched, but also it was ranked among the largest companies in the United States. Companies with well-developed, large marketing departments and virtually unlimited funds usually join hands with similar companies.

Large companies are highly suspicious (and rightly so) of people who want to tie in to their name and image. Rarely will a major company gain anything of value from such a union. Major companies are not charitable organizations.

Nonetheless, my friend was determined. He engaged a commercial artist to draw up his contest promotion with his logo and the logo of the pizza company handsomely displayed. Along with that, he outlined his promotion in detail, complete with sales and profit projections by regions. The marketing plan was well done and after talking with the pizza company's sales promotion office, he mailed the entire bundle to them.

His hopes were high, and his outlook, positive. I admitted the promotion looked strong, but I was still very skeptical. In a few weeks, after numerous unreturned telephone calls to the vice president in charge of promotions, my friend received a poorly printed form letter advising him that the company had committed their promotional budget for the year to other projects. This is like saying the army has used up all its rifle ammo and will have to use bayonets until the new budget period. Ridiculous. My friend was furious. He had spent so much time, effort, and money on the project, and he was so sure his ideas would be favorably received that the letdown was devastating.

He couldn't let go of his anger, and he asked me what I felt he should do. I told him the best thing was to forget the whole matter and try something else. But that wasn't what he wanted to hear. Instead, he wrote a letter to the president of the company. It was a detailed, stinging letter about the shabby way he felt he had been treated and the unprofessional conduct of the vice president! A few days later the sales promotion vice president telephoned to discuss the promotion and to apologize. A letter from the president's office arrived in the mail instructing my friend to contact him again if he was unhappy with the vice president's behavior. Actually, nothing came of the entire episode, but it does illustrate how potent a letter can be: The president of a national enterprise and the vice president of sales promotion responded to a single letter of complaint!

Politicians are also sensitive to the written word. I have heard that just a half dozen letters have changed the vote of a senator or congressional representative! Advertising campaigns costing millions of dollars have been junked or altered because of a relatively few letters. All of these examples illustrate the power and vigor of written words in a positive way. There is a negative side as well. Letters written without a great deal of thought to how they may be interpreted have produced chilling results. People have been fired, reduced in rank, divorced, and even imprisoned! It pays to be careful and thoughtful when you write a letter. A good idea is to sleep on it overnight, and read it again the next day before mailing.

THE SELLING LETTER

In our rapidly changing business world, solicitation by mail has become more and more important. We all have found our mailboxes stuffed to overflowing with "junk mail." These unsolicited communications from companies that conduct their sales efforts in this way are an annoyance to some. But, it is obvious that this practice is very successful and less costly than "normal" sales programs. Some companies, especially in the publishing field, use mail as their exclusive method of selling. The Book of the Month Club, an early pioneer in direct-mail selling, and several magazine marketers are prime examples of selling by mail.

During the Christmas holidays, we soon realize we are on mailing lists when we receive handsomely printed offers to buy cheeses, smoked meats, fruits, cookies, wines, fruitcakes, and clothing. After the holidays, we can expect mail from credit card companies, mutual fund companies, stockbrokers, estate planners, health clubs, and who knows what else to invade our homes through our mailboxes.

Accompanying these flashy, attractive mailings will be cover letters. These letters try to develop a sense of obligation, to make recipients feel they must buy something. The companies even get tough in these mailings! I have seen letters that actually admonish the addressee for not having bought something within the recent past. That admonishment included a threat to stop mailing unless something was purchased immediately. This, when the addressee never asked for anything to be mailed in the first place!

This sort of mailing is the ultimate "numbers game." Tens of thousands of letters are mailed with the expectation of possibly receiving a 1 or 2 percent response. This should give you some idea of the profit margins these companies harvest. The cover letter is usually cleverly written and seductive in its appeal. In recent years, the trend is toward a dignified and logical approach, although the emotional appeal is still very strong. The goods offered are higher-priced merchandise. Expensive paintings, objects of art, prints, sculptures, and collectibles are all sold by mail these days.

Selling letters are not restricted to the mailings we receive daily in our mailboxes. Territory salespeople utilize selling letters to entice the buyer to accept a personal interview and to provide "teaser" information so that when the interview takes place, the buyer will have a healthy interest.

Like a personal interview, the selling letter should immediately grab the interest of the reader and tell just enough to whet his or her appetite for more information. Normally, letters loaded with statistics, charts, graphs, and testimonials are not effective; and the mention of sales success with the recipient's competitors is more annoying than provocative. Instead, a letter with a straightforward, candid approach should be written, with statistical information withheld until a personal meeting has been arranged. Statistics can be included, if necessary, but they should be separate from the cover letter.

Letters that request personal meetings are written only when distance, time, or cost prohibits using normal methods. The following letter was used to secure an appointment with an out-of-state prospect, which resulted in a sale. Study the structure of this letter and adapt its form to fit your sales circumstance. Names, addresses, and locations have been changed.

Great Expectations Appliance Company
August 18, 19–

Mr. Jacob Morley
Morley, Scrooge and Cratchit
2334 Florence Blvd., Suite 112
Hawthorne, CA 90617

Dear Mr. Morley:

Would you be surprised to learn that small appliances are the largest profit centers in convenience stores all across America? Well, it's true!

Why should this interest Morley, Scrooge and Cratchit? Because the rich rewards being harvested by hardware stores can be shared by you! In a pilot program here in Mississippi, small, hand-held appliances were introduced into such diverse outlets as supermarkets, drugstores, convenience stores, and even gasoline service stations! Each of these outlets has discovered that small appliances sell themselves when properly displayed and when adequate stock is available. Profit margins and stock turns are impressive. In fact, the profit margins exceed every profit center in these outlets by more than 17 percent!

Enclosed are more information and statistics that you will find of interest. I plan to be in California on the 12th through the 19th of September. Would it be convenient for us to meet and discuss this profitable opportunity during that time? I'll telephone to see if we can mesh our schedules.

Sincerely,

C. Dickens,
Vice President of New Markets

This letter tells the reader just enough to arouse interest, but it stops short of telling too much. The reader, it is hoped, will want to know more about this profitable idea and how it might be used in his stores. He will review the enclosed statistical information, and will be sufficiently interested to schedule an appointment. In this case, it is important that Dickens's secretary make the follow-up call, so that Morley can't get more information that might result in no appointment.

The letter's emphasis is on profit, ease of marketing, and rapid turnover. The letter makes it all sound simple. Had the seller used the telephone to make this first contact, he may well have been brushed off without even reaching Mr. Morley. A secretary, ever vigilant to protect the boss from those pesky salespeople, will screen the call and often will make the decision or be instructed to tell Dickens that "Mr. Morley isn't interested at this time." The following letter is another example of giving just enough information to pique the reader's interest.

July 10, 19–

Mr. Horace Greeley
Greeley, Thompkins and Edison
9921 Speedway Blvd.
Tucson, AZ 85732

Dear Mr. Greeley:

The John Reilly Company has increased its sales of air rifles by more than 150% in the last year by installing our portable Test-a-Range in their stores. These easy-to-install ranges are proven sales builders not only for air rifles, but also for slingshots, BB guns, small-caliber rifles, and hand guns.

The Test-a-Range encourages serious shoppers and almost eliminates the "Lookie-Loos."

The retail salesperson works within the Test-a-Range itself, so there is no need for special personnel or equipment. Tested and proven, the Test-a-Range can do for Greeley, Thompkins, and Edison's sales what it has done for John Reilly and so many others throughout the Southwest and Far West.

I would like to schedule a specific time to meet with you during the upcoming "Shooters and Hunters Show" at the Tucson Arena on September 15–19. That show is so busy that we must schedule our important clients well in advance. I'll telephone next week to firm up our appointment time and date.

Very truly yours,

Franklin Haweye,
Sales Manager/Western Region

THE BUSINESS LETTER

The John Reilly Company, we can be sure, is a well-known and respected retailer of similar merchandise. Its success is something the reader will surely wish to duplicate. What is this "Test-a-Range" thing, anyway? No special training or equipment is needed, and it has caused sales to increase dramatically! Certainly, Mr. Greeley will want to investigate, especially since he is "an important client." Notice that the letter has left many questions unanswered: Will special insurance be necessary? Will the noise level be too high? Will waivers need to be signed by consumers who use the Test-a-Range? But those and other questions are purposely left unanswered. They will be addressed during a face-to-face meeting. Finally, the letter leaves open the days and time when the appointment might be made, so that Mr. Greeley can't refuse on the grounds he has something scheduled at a particular time.

The next letter is meant not to arrange an appointment, but to sell a product or service. This is normally used in direct sales and is rarely used by wholesalers.

January 6, 19–

Mr. Bob Bentover
9865 Fastwater Lane
Provo, UT 86773

Dear Mr. Bentover:

May we offer our hearty congratulations on your candidacy for the United States Olympic Ski Team? Needless to say, we are proud of you and all the candidates, especially since our climbing skins have the team captain's endorsement.

As you know, climbing skins are invaluable to skiers operating in areas without lifts or T-bars, and since the U.S. team will be training on Snow Bear Mountain — a difficult and undeveloped area — I am sure you will have an interest in our newest product, the Quick Skin slipover climbing skin.

Tested in Canada and Alaska for four seasons under all conditions, the Quick Skin has outperformed every climbing skin on the market in terms of grip, ease of application, and durability. As a potential Olympic team member, you are entitled to a 30% discount. To claim your discount, you must order before February 15, 19–.

Sincerely,

Buzz Snowplough
Director of Sales

    The preceding letter is obviously aimed at a narrow target market. How many Olympic tryout candidates can there be? If Mr. Bentover is proud of being considered for the team, the chances are good he will buy the equipment that the "big boys" are using and endorsing. In this particular case the market is limited; therefore, a mailing campaign is the most practical. But suppose you need to reach a broader market? What kind of letter do you write then? Consider the following example.

THE BUSINESS LETTER

May 9, 19–

John Rigghouser
16223 Biscayne Road
Miami, FL 27339

Dear Mr. Rigghouser:

Hey — how stupid can you be? Are you really that dumb?

That's what I feel like saying to customers when I find they are buying term insurance.

What? You think term insurance is a good deal? Why? Because you have to die to collect? Or is it because you like having your hard-earned dollars flow into the pockets of the insurance fat cats?

Of course, I never say that to a customer — or to anyone else. I'm much too polite for that. Actually, it really is foolish to throw your money away on term insurance when so many better options are open to you, and I do feel like saying something to shock folks into at least investigating the new Income Builder by Grasp & Devour Insurance Company. In today's insurance market, you can actually get FREE life insurance! You don't believe it? OK, let me prove it.

Call 1 (800) 998-2435 right now and talk with a G & D representative. There is no cost, no obligation, and no sales pressure. Do it now, or would you rather have your cash go into someone else's pockets?

Grasp & Devour
Serving the public since 1995

This is called a shock letter because it is literally meant to shock the reader. Few people expect to receive a letter that starts by asking "How stupid can you be?" If you received such a letter, would you read it? The odds are ten to one you would, just to determine who was so brazen. Once the letter has the reader's attention, it quickly softens the attack with, "That's what I feel like saying" and then starts selling by attacking a term life insurance policy and the fat cats of the insurance industry — always a popular target. It also sets up an "Us against Them" relationship, although it is they who are writing the letter.

The letter also teases the reader with an offer for free insurance. If you are paying insurance premiums, wouldn't you like to know how to get free insurance? Of course. Is free insurance possible? The only way to find out is to call and see. After all, if you don't like what you hear, all you need do is hang up.

This is a terrific selling letter. It gets and holds your attention, it makes you do something (call), and it educates (to a point). The follow-up telephone contact will be critical in making the sale, but the letter will have set up the circumstances for a positive, selling atmosphere.

Note the hard-selling tone established in our next example.

THE BUSINESS LETTER

October 10, 19–

Ms. Nellie Osgood
731 Windy Way
Chippewa, MT 76953

Dear Ms. Osgood:

We were sorry to learn of your recent skiing accident, but were cheered to know you are on your way toward a complete recovery. Upon your release from the hospital, your doctor will put you on a home therapy program designed to strengthen your muscles and aid in regaining your coordination. Very likely, various mechanical devices will be suggested to aid in that recovery. I'm sure your doctor will vigorously endorse the use of the *Phys-aid* therapy machine. It is the one most often recommended by health professionals. *Phys-aid* was designed by a sports-medicine doctor and a physical therapist, both of whom have years of experience in getting trauma patients back on their feet and as good as new in record time — without pain. Warm, soothing, heat flows through the *Phys-aid* machine, bringing immediate and lasting relief to damaged bones and muscles.

Frank Webber, one of our therapy specialists, will be in the Chippewa area for ten days starting the 19th of next month, and would be pleased to spend some time with you explaining the *Phys-aid* therapy system in detail, adapting it to your specific needs, and showing you how to get the most from this amazing machine.

Phys-aid is covered under most insurance programs and is unconditionally guaranteed. Frank or his assistant will telephone within a few days to arrange a convenient appointment. Please have your insurance information available to facilitate billing.

With very best wishes for a speedy recovery, we remain,

Phys-aid Corporation

This is a strong, hard-selling letter. It creates a need, fills the need, hits the right emotional buttons, and assumes the sale. "Please have your insurance information available" really means you just bought a Phys-aid machine! Notice the letter tells you only a few things about the machine: You know that warm, soothing heat flows through the machine, but you have no idea how the unit works. You know that doctors will (probably) endorse the use of the Phys-aid, but there is no mention of cost. And, the letter implies, why should you worry about costs? Your insurance will pay for it (a dangerous, but all too frequent attitude today). Finally, the letter assumes you will want to see how this magic machine works, and the salesperson, calling himself a therapy specialist, will be in touch to confirm an appointment. Moreover, he will adjust the machine to fit the customer's particular needs! So there is no question; the Phys-aid is sold.

THE EMPLOYMENT LETTER

I'm sure you've heard people say, "You've got to sell yourself before you can sell a product." I don't agree. Some of the most successful salespeople I have known were not particularly well liked by their customers. They were recognized as knowledgeable, smart money-makers (for the client), but not necessarily likable as individuals. But, at some point in their careers, the need to sell themselves arose. Normally, that was when they first applied for a job, changed jobs, or were considered for a promotion.

Seeking work is a difficult and often degrading task. If you are in a tough economic climate, you may be refused and rejected time and again. This is an ego-deflating, physically exhausting experience. Trying to guess what is going to be asked of you, what information will boost your chances, and what kind of experience the interviewer is looking for is a mental strain. That is why a cover letter which accompanies the résumé is so important. It allows you to take control of the interview, which should be forthcoming.

The following letter was sent to a sales/marketing vice president friend of mine, who was so impressed by it that he hired the applicant and kept the letter for more than ten years! He particularly liked the "take-charge" tone and the maturity of the letter (considering the writer was only a college senior). Look for the power words and the way the letter sets up the selling sequence.

THE BUSINESS LETTER

April 4, 19–

Nationwide Merchandising Corporation
11965 Indiana Avenue
Seattle, Washington 90062

Attention: Howard Popejoy,
Marketing Manager

Dear Mr. Popejoy:

I'm sure it is no surprise for you to learn that *Popejoy's Guide to Marketing*, your current best seller, is a standard text at Gonzaga University. For the last two years, *Guide to Marketing* has been my constant companion, my guide, and my inspiration and a valued part of my personal library.

As you pointed out in Chapter 7: "The infusion of new blood, college-trained, eager, and ready to learn their craft, is vital to the ensured growth of any marketing organization." How true — and how descriptive of myself! [*He has set up the need and proposed a way to fill that need.*]

At Gonzaga, I prepared for a career in marketing and will graduate Summa Cum Laude. I'm proud of that, but I know I have just scratched the surface; there is so much more to learn. [*I've got smarts, but I'm humble, too!*] At the risk of sounding like a first-class, unabashed apple-polisher, it would be the fulfillment of a dream to work with and for a recognized leader in our field.

Only two companies, Nationwide and Continental, offer the direction, continued education, and the creativity that I seek. Although Continental's offer is enticing [*Better grab me before they do!*], the opportunity to work under your direction makes all other offers pale by comparison.

Allowing for normal mail delivery and your crowded schedule, I would think you will have had time to evaluate my potential worth to NMC by the end of next week. May I telephone you then to arrange a personal interview? [*Forcing a decision — namely, closing the sale.*] Thank you.

Sincerely yours,

Les Atkins
9975 Lost Hills Dr.
Los Angeles, CA 92336

   The compliments probably seem a bit too much to you and me, but they impressed my friend — and how! Please understand, the compliments were deserved and not without basis, so they were palatable. Popejoy had written a worthwhile marketing book and was considered a marketing whiz. The kid did his homework, had good credentials, was aggressive, and ended up with the job. The letter assumed that Mr. Popejoy would arrange a personal interview, which is the same as assuming the sale. I'd call that a pretty strong, wouldn't you?

   The letter to Popejoy was, in fact, an employment letter and a selling letter. The following employment letter would be accompanied by a résumé. In today's economy, applicants often send literally hundreds of letters and résumés and receive few replies for their efforts. You may be tempted to ask if anyone actually reads these letters. Someone does, and so it is important to take the time to prepare your letter carefully. You want it to have the maximum impact.

THE BUSINESS LETTER

Ms. Deanna Chance
Evers, Tinker, and Chance
10 Bank Tower Blvd.
Chicago, IL 60005

Dear Ms. Chance:

I must admit one of my least favorite things to do is to seek employment. Fortunately, due to an exemplary business history and excellent educational preparation, that loathsome task hasn't fallen on my shoulders very often in the past ten years. But business mergers and consolidations have at last caught up with me. When Downwind Aircraft and Flimsy Aeronautics joined hands this past May, I was released along with 3,000 coworkers.

I've spent the month of June carefully considering various opportunities in our industry and trying to decide where I would most benefit a company and advance my career as well. Only Evers, Tinker, and Chance seemed to offer that dual opportunity.

I am well aware of your company's reputation in the investigative field of digital computer analysis, and since my education and experience have been in that discipline, I'm sure you would agree that an early personal interview may benefit us both.

I am in and out most of the day, so to make sure we touch base with the least amount of frustration, I will telephone in a few days to arrange a mutually compatible time to meet. Until then, I remain,

Yours very truly,

Fido Betakappa

Do you see how the writer takes control of the situation? The letter starts by stating how much the writer hates to look for a job! I don't know anyone who might enjoy applying for work, but how many people express that to the potential employer? Very few, I would imagine. So this may grab the attention of Ms. Chance.

The letter immediately tells the reader why he is seeking work and explains what he has been doing since being dismissed. That time was well spent, considering and evaluating various business opportunities and companies. This leaves the impression that the writer isn't desperate for work (a very important impression to leave). It elevates the applicant above others who have a terrible sameness. In disclosing his qualifications, the writer is almost arrogant about his skills and at the same time compliments the company's reputation.

Finally, he takes the responsibility for future contact out of the reader's hands. He doesn't intend sitting by the phone all day; he is a busy guy, not about to accept a "We'll call you" response. Now, when he calls Ms. Chance and is asked the purpose of his call, he can honestly answer, "I promised Ms. Chance I'd call her this week." Can you see how he has improved his chances over the run-of-the-mill applicants?

The next two letters serve different purposes. The first is another cover letter seeking employment. The second is a follow-up letter when the job had been given to someone else. Bringing an opportunity back is difficult, but not at all impossible. Your persistence may indicate to the employer your tenacious character and your approach to getting a job done. Depending on the job, this could well be enough for the employer to take a second look or even create a job for you.

THE BUSINESS LETTER

October 11, 19–

Rowen Merchandise Company
321 River Front Drive
Downhome, OH 05771

Attention: Alexis Crabapple

Dear Ms. Crabapple:

How often does an ideal situation present itself? Rarely, I would say, but the job opportunity you advertised and my business background and educational training seem to present just such a situation.

If I were to write a perfect job description that would parallel my talents, skills, and experience, it would be an exact copy of your requirements.

The enclosed résumé will supply you with all the normal information you might require, but, of course, only a personal, in-depth interview can determine if we can help each other.

I am presently employed, and it would be awkward to receive a telephone call at my office. Therefore, I'll call you on Tuesday, the 26th, to arrange a meeting.

Sincerely yours,

Marigold Fields

Is this the perfect job applicant? Surely the reader of this letter will want to know more. It will encourage Ms. Crabapple at least to peruse the résumé and, I would guess, set up a personal interview. Once again, the writer has taken the response out of the recipient's hands and has assumed an interest.

August 2, 19–

Alicia Montoya
Harcourt and Wiseman
5353 Hope St.
New Orleans, LA 60711

Dear Ms. Montoya:

I was disappointed, of course, to learn you had decided on another applicant for the sales position in San Francisco. Nonetheless, I want to thank you for the time you spent with me and for the fairness and concern with which the interview was handled.

This setback will in no way diminish my interest in eventually working for Harcourt and Wiseman, a company I have long admired. With your permission, I will stay in touch from time to time, and I hope you will remember me for some future opportunity.

It was a pleasure meeting you and getting to know more about Harcourt and Wiseman. With sincere best wishes, I remain,

Yours truly,

Fred Wallace

(Address/telephone)

This thoughtful note was the only one of its kind ever received by Alicia Montoya, so you might imagine the impact it had. Not only does it show a determined job applicant, but it also suggests he would be a sales representative who follows through and ties up loose ends. A few weeks later, another job opened and Wallace was hired.

THE LETTER OF APPRECIATION

A letter of appreciation can be a powerful tool for reinforcing your relationship with a customer. It requires little effort, yet it reaps a bounty of goodwill. Favors bestowed, orders placed, invoices paid, or many other circumstances can be the motive for sending a brief, friendly, and appreciative letter.

May 15, 19–

Jim Rowlings
Rowlings Sporting Goods
888 Touchdown Lane
South Bend, IN 67554

Dear Jim,

There are times when the English language fails me. This is one of those times. How can a simple thank-you possibly express my appreciation for your generous contribution to the Special Olympics scholarship fund?

I deeply regret you were unable to be at the presentation ceremonies to see the love, the joy, and the growth these special people experienced. I'm not ashamed to admit that tears welled up in my eyes when the Special Olympics chorus sang our national anthem.

Your name will be inscribed on a plaque hung in our Hall of Fame, and I hope you will soon visit for a personal tour. Again, thank you for your contribution — you may never know how important and far-reaching it is.

Sincerely,

Bob Houseman,
Financial Director

    Mr. Rowlings will want to keep and frame this letter. It will certainly keep the door open when the next fund drive is launched. Notice that this letter is simple, sincere, and short.

Our last example expresses gratitude for business placed. We must be careful when sending this type of letter because we do not wish to project the image of a beggar giving thanks for alms. No, we are businesspeople, and we merely wish to express our thanks for a successful business completion.

April 19, 19–

Carl Lakeside
Lakeside and Moore
9099 Dimmer Drive
Cashmere, MN 77540

Dear Carl,

Thank you sincerely for your confidence in my company, as expressed by your recent order for 10,000 jackhammers. I am sure you will be as delighted with the performance of the Man Jack, as the more than 5,000 contractors in Minnesota and throughout the Midwest have been.

My job doesn't stop when an order is placed. We at Goliath Enterprises pride ourselves on follow-up after the sale. I will visit each job site to instruct your people on the use and maintenance of the Man Jack and will continue to be available to assist should the need arise.

Next month we are introducing our newest product: the Diamondback Auger. I've seen this amazing tool in operation, and I am sure you will quickly recognize its value to your company. I'll be in touch early the week of the 20th.

Sincerely,

Larry Winston,
Engineering Sales

THE BUSINESS LETTER

A letter like the above does three things. First, it thanks the customer for business placed; second, it lets the customer know that service after the sale is guaranteed; and third, it gets the foot in the door for the introduction of a new product. Expressing appreciation for business is acceptable and expected. But always remember that in any business transaction, both parties should — and usually do — benefit. Never lose your dignity or self-worth by groveling.

Letters are another valuable tool in your sales arsenal and should be utilized whenever their particular value can be maximized. Always remember that letters are a written record, so be careful what you write. Never make promises you are not certain you can keep. Once a letter is posted, it is out of your hands and is an indelible record that can cost you dearly or propel you to new heights.

12

ASKING QUESTIONS, BEING QUIET, AND GETTING ANSWERS

I have stressed the importance of initiating a dialogue between you and your buyers. In general, if you can get buyers to talk, you can get them involved; if they are involved, they become interested; if they become interested, they usually buy. Some salespeople interpret "initiating a dialogue" to mean that they must talk incessantly. They feel they must dominate a conversation, force-feeding buyers with facts and figures until, I suppose, they collapse under the weight of it. That is not what it means to start and maintain a dialogue.

When buyers start talking, asking questions, and raising doubts, they reveal an interest in what the seller has said. That information is what the salesperson needs to focus on in order to close. When a sales presentation is made, the salesperson must ask probing questions that demand more than a yes or no response.

When buyers answer questions, sellers must listen; and in order to listen, the sellers must stop talking and be quiet. There is an advantage to silence. As salespeople work toward closing the sale, they also close "doors" — escape hatches that buyers may try to use to avoid making a positive decision. Consider the following example:

SELLER: Mr. Prospect, I've demonstrated the need for a lightweight, water-resistant windbreaker, isn't that so?

(Door #1 is being closed. If the buyer answers "Yes," he can't say "We don't need this particular garment — we have too many of these windbreakers in stock already.")

BUYER: Oh, yes, there is definitely a market for your product.

ASKING QUESTIONS, BEING QUIET, AND GETTING ANSWERS

SELLER: And we agreed that the retail price is perfect for the Back-to-School sale?

(The seller has shut door #2.)

BUYER: Yes, the retail price is perfect, but I just want to get that inventory down. Give me a call in a few weeks. The inventory should be in shape by then, and I'll see what I can do.

SELLER: Mr. Prospect, isn't that like saying, "I have too much salami, so I'm not going to stock ham, until I sell more salami"? *(Said with a smile and a "get real" tone.)* We've already agreed that the windbreaker is perfect for the Back-to-School sale and that the retail price is right on the money. Do you really want to lose all those sales while hoping and praying for your inventory to right itself?

(The seller has made an emotional appeal to the buyer's desire for more sales and a logical appeal to his common sense. Now the seller should not talk until the buyer answers.)

BUYER: Well, I'd like to buy your deal, but I've got a budget problem just now.

(Now we are getting to the real cause for his reluctance to buy — he is worried about money, not inventory.)

SELLER: We'll work on quantities and a billing that I'm sure you'll find manageable.

(Now the salesperson has made a partnership and has assumed the sale. Actually, the final door has been closed, the sale has been made but has not yet been completed. At this point, the buyer may start talking about quantities or terms or other details of the sale.)

SELLER: *(maintaining control)* Considering the traffic in your stores and the age of your customers, this jacket will be a strong seller. What would you say to two dozen each in small, medium, and large sizes, and one dozen in extra large per store to begin with?

BUYER: Oh no, that is way too much. I'd say a dozen in the small, medium, and large sizes and half a dozen in extra large.

(The seller now has an order for at least that amount, and will now try to edge it up to his original suggested order.)

SELLER: *(after a few moments of silence)* Tell you what, let's make it eighteen of each size and a dozen in extra large per store, and I'll get you sixty days billing. With the way these jackets sell, you'll be out of stock in ten days.

(Now the seller clams up and waits for an answer. No matter how long it takes, he shouldn't say a word until the buyer responds.)

BUYER: Can you get me ninety days?

(The buyer has bought, but sixty days is all he is going to get unless he gives something up.)

SELLER: (laughingly) Give me a break! You're already taking money out of my pocket. I can't give you ninety days on this quantity. If you can make it two dozen each size and one dozen in extra large, I might be able to get you ninety days.

(The seller now shuts up, and the waiting game begins again.)

BUYER: OK, make it two dozen each size and a dozen extra large in assorted colors, but I must have ninety days billing.

SELLER: Don't worry, I'll get it through for you.

(The seller always had the extended billing on a creditworthy account in his back pocket, but he makes the buyer think he is "going to bat" for him.)

I hope this example illustrates how effective silence can be in making a sale and how a good salesperson will control the interview. By reinforcing and confirming the points of agreement, the salesperson ensures that the buyer will not be able to use those points as escape hatches at the close. For instance, when the salesperson suggested a quantity of jackets for each store in the buyer's chain of stores, the buyer could have said, "I don't think our customers will buy this kind of jacket," if he hadn't already agreed that there is a definite market for the jackets. The seller had closed that door. Suppose the seller had not reached an agreement on the retail price of the jackets. The buyer could have said, at the close, "Well, the retail price is too high (or low) and doesn't return the margins we want." That would have been the end of the subject and the end of the interview. The open door allowed the buyer to escape.

But you ask, what if the buyer never agrees to the need for the jackets or to the retail price of the windbreakers? What then? As I've said many times before, never fear a negative reply from the buyer. Suppose the buyer says, "I don't believe we need this lightweight, water-resistant windbreaker. We have ten different styles, all of which are selling well." The seller's job is now focused. He knows he hasn't done a good job of creating a need. Thus, he goes back to square one, creates the need, and *gets the buyer to agree to it!*

WHAT ARE THEY **REALLY** SAYING?

I hope it is clear that by asking questions and waiting for *the answers you want*, you establish a positive climate for the sale. This is another way of saying, never take no for an answer — at least for the first five times. When buyers say no, they are usually saying, "Tell me more. Convince me."

Naturally, I've known this for many years, but at a Christmas week party several years ago, I had the point brought home to me again in a very forceful and dramatic way. The party was a charity fund-raiser and was attended by a number of high-profile individuals — minor celebrities, news media people, and a well-known Catholic clergyman. I observed the priest and admired his deft way of turning potentially troublesome people or embarrassing situations away from him. The man was a splendid speaker and an extremely good salesperson. I had talked with him earlier, and he laughed as he admitted we were, after a fashion, in the same business. "But," he pointed out, "I have an edge on you, Bill — a superior 'product' that I know well and believe in without question." I had no comeback for that.

As the afternoon turned into early evening, several guests were beginning to exhibit the "spirit of the season," so to speak. The noise level went up several decibels, and the hostess started arranging for taxis for some of the "merrier" celebrants.

The priest was shrugging on his topcoat and saying his good-byes when an obnoxious and loud young man approached him. I didn't hear everything he said, but I got the idea he was challenging the priest. "I don't buy into your scam," he slurred, "you can't prove . . ." I lost the rest in the hubbub.

At first the priest tried to dissuade the man, asking him to call sometime or visit when the holidays were over. But there was no stopping this guy. He insisted on an answer and grew louder and more surly. The hostess tried to hush him up and apologized to the priest, but he simply smiled and assured her that he would handle the situation. He took the arm of the protester and walked him to a relatively quiet corner of the room, where they sat and talked for about thirty minutes. Finally, they stood and shook hands, and I was happy to see they were both smiling.

The man, who was now calm, sober, and even tranquil, thanked the priest profusely as he gathered his coat and left the party. What a turn-around! I congratulated the priest on a great "sale." "That was something to see," I said, "I would never have thought you could have turned that situation around. He seemed so vehement." The priest smiled at me with a questioning look. "I'm surprised at you, Bill. You of all people should have known that the young man wasn't saying he didn't believe in God. Rather he wanted someone — in this case, me — to give him a reason to believe. He wanted to believe, but he just needed a little push."

We all can learn a lot from that story. The priest remained calm when he was challenged. He was sure of his ground and confident he could turn aside any attack. He understood where the young man was coming from and what was really bothering him (why he wasn't "buying"). Most of all, he allowed — in fact, he encouraged — the young man to talk, to vent his anger or frustration. He asked questions which led the conversation where he wanted it to go. In essence, the priest directed the flow of the conversation, listened, and when the "prospect" was ready, he "closed."

I don't want to trivialize the important decision the young man made that day, but isn't that what buyers do when they question a statement, ask for more proof, or demand more evidence? Like that unhappy young man, they are saying, "I want to buy. I do believe some of what you've said, but now give me a bit more proof!"

STAYING ON COURSE

Buyers are only human, and occasionally they will go off on unrelated tangents during an interview. If buyers start to stray from the topic by telling you about their kid's Little League batting average or the price of pork bellies, you should appear interested and impressed, but gently lead them back to your product. Asking questions is, perhaps, the easiest and fastest way to accomplish this, because it forces buyers to refocus on your product if they want to give an intelligent answer.

Even if the answers are negative and not the ones you want to hear, you will gain a great deal by listening. Often when buyers rant and rave, they will, eventually, sell themselves. I recall the game that kids play called "Why?" Do you remember playing that? No matter what statement is made, you reply by asking "Why?" It was very popular and probably still is, because it drives parents absolutely nuts. Somewhat modified, the technique can be applied effectively in a commercial situation.

BUYER:	I don't think we need your roller skates in our chain of stores.
SELLER:	Why?
BUYER:	Because we have too many roller skates in stock as it is.
SELLER:	Why?
BUYER:	Because they aren't selling well.
SELLER:	Why?
BUYER:	I don't know.
SELLER:	I do. You need the Downhill In-Line Skate with the new braking system. This is the fastest-selling skate in the country, and you have the opportunity to sell it in your stores now. Not only does the Downhill Skate sell well, it stimulates the sale of all other brands as well. Don't take my word for it! Here's documented proof in *Roller Retailer*.

Simply playing a kid's game — asking why — can dig down to the root of the reasons for the buyer saying no. Asking questions and listening intelligently cause a number of good things to happen: You are forced to listen to the answers, and you may learn what the buyer really wants. You avoid being tiresome. Some salespeople fall in love with their own voices and think that everyone else has, too. They drone on and on and then are stunned when the buyer terminates the interview! When you are listening, the buyer can't do that. As buyers talk, they reveal more and more about what they want, what they need, and what they will buy. They will often tell you what they object to in your product line, allowing you to answer those objections. As I have seen it happen, time and again, they will sell themselves if you just give them the chance.

THE SILENT CLOSE

Normally, you must first create the need for your product, develop a dialogue, and direct and control the conversation before you can close the sale. After asking your closing questions, you should become still and wait for the answers. To some salespeople, that is the toughest thing to do. The silence is deafening. The clock on the wall sounds like Big Ben. The buyers may cough or squirm. Let them squirm. Inexperienced salespeople will panic and rush to fill the conversational void. They will pour out additional features, benefits, and statistics, and frequently make wild or silly claims.

Buyers may detect uncertainty or a touch of desperation. They may latch onto one of those desperate and silly claims and use it as an escape route. All because the salesperson talked when he or she should have remained quiet. When you stay silent and exhibit patience, one of three things will happen:

1. You will get an order.

2. The buyer will ask a positive question such as, "Can you give me extended billing?" or "Will you guarantee the sale?" or some other last-minute attempt to get something extra thrown in.

3. The buyer will say no.

If you get the order you want, write it up and leave. Hanging around after the sale can be annoying to the buyer and may give rise to thoughts of rescinding or reducing the order.

If the buyer asks for something extra to be thrown in, two things are possible: (1) you may have something you can give up, such as extra billing days, special discounts, or free goods; or (2) you may have nothing to give.

If you do have something you can throw into the deal, never give it up at that time. Tell the buyer you will "do your best" and will be in touch later that afternoon. After you've convinced the buyer that you battled for the extra whatever, call and deliver the good news. Better yet, get something in return for the extra. For example, "I can get you some extra billing, Jennifer, but not with this quantity. Can we up the order to three gross a store?"

If you have nothing to give, don't be afraid to say so. Never hold out false hope. It is much better to face the music then and there than it is to call back later and dash the buyer's hopes of extended billing, for example.

Once you give something away after the sale, *that the buyer asks for,* he or she will harbor the suspicion that you are *always* holding something back. This buyer will grind you into dust or even cut you off as a vendor, unless you regularly "sweeten the pot." You create a monster that may haunt you for a long time. Giving extras away is a dangerous practice and must be handled with great care.

One last thought on this subject: If you shift the responsibility to the buyer, you can usually come out on top. For example, if the buyer asks for a 2 percent discount, you will say you want something in return. After complaining that you are "down to bare metal" (that is, working on a short mar-

ASKING QUESTIONS, BEING QUIET, AND GETTING ANSWERS

gin), you make a bargain. "Tell you what, if you order a gross for each store instead of a hundred, I think I can get an extra 2 percent." Now if the buyer refuses to increase the order, and he or she won't get the discount, but it won't be your fault. The buyer will understand and will assume the responsibility for not getting the discount and hold the salesperson blameless.

If the buyer increases the order and gets that extra discount, he or she feels great about the entire transaction. In all circumstances, utilize silence as your partner. Try never to answer quickly, and always use thoughtful, careful replies.

The third possibility is that the buyer says no. This is the answer so many salespeople dread. They feel that a negative answer is the end of the selling opportunity, and that isn't at all true. Some sales trainers say that selling begins when the prospect says no. That is a little convoluted by my way of thinking. Selling should begin long before the close — long before the buyer makes a decision. However, I do agree that receiving a no answer isn't the end of the line and that sometimes the strongest selling begins after an initial refusal.

Suppose the buyer slowly shakes her head and says, "No, I don't think so. Maybe next time. If you have literature, leave it and I'll look it over."

What has the buyer said? Was it really a no, or was she asking you to convince her to give her a reason to buy? She must be interested, or why would she want you to leave literature [ask that question]. Dig, dig, dig. The skilled salesperson will remain positive. "Becky, I know you have an interest in Acme Sweeper. Why else would you want literature? *[Now, the salesperson re-establishes the need.]* We've agreed that the Acme Sweeper reduces dust in the plant by 37 percent. That is important for your employees and may reduce your Workers Comp Insurance, right?" *[Wait for the agreement. We are collecting positive responses.]*

Remind the buyer, by reviewing the content of the interview, that the need was agreed to and all the key points of the presentation were accepted. As you recollect those yes answers, you refresh the buyer's memory. This will bring to the surface the real reasons why the buyer did not place an order. The reason is probably something you haven't addressed or, more likely, something the buyer has kept hidden. As you review the presentation and the buyer's agreement with all the key points, it will soon become obvious that the buyer is withholding the real cause for not buying. It may be a reason of which he or she may not even be consciously aware. When that reason is exposed, you can deal with it and overcome it.

Remember: *Do not assume you know* what the prospect wants or needs. Get agreements.

"Having an exclusive on this product is important, wouldn't you agree?" "Doesn't it?" "Aren't you?" "Isn't it?" Those questions are all tie-down questions that involve the buyer. When you get an answer, make certain you understand it so you can answer objections intelligently.

SELLER: You say you must have the local high school's colors in the mix, is that right?
BUYER: Yeah, that's what we need.
SELLER: Is that the only thing keeping us from doing business?
BUYER: Well, er . . . yeah.
SELLER: We have no problem. I'll make certain that 35 percent of the shipment is in red and black, OK?

SELLING OR COSIGNING?

Today more than ever, buyers are looking for or demanding a "guaranteed sale." I've had buyers tell me flat out: "If it isn't a guaranteed sale, I don't want it." When that happens, I try to save the sale opportunity by impressing them with the need, and then shoring that up with benefits and features. Sometimes it works, but if it really is company policy, nothing but guaranteeing the sale will work. Buyers in this situation really aren't buyers.

Anyone can place orders and anyone can buy, if there is no responsibility or liability for the sale of the merchandise. Under a guaranteed sale, the goods are actually on consignment. Buyers — real buyers — must be able to determine which products the consumer will want. However, fewer and fewer companies allow their "buyers" to make that decision. Instead, a computer operator hands a printout to an executive, and the decision is made far from the selling floor.

Normally, buyers will tell you early in the interview that the company demands a guaranteed sale. So if buyers wait until you close to say they must have a guaranteed sale, you can be fairly certain it isn't company policy and that this is a ploy to sweeten the deal. That's fine. It's just part of the

ASKING QUESTIONS, BEING QUIET, AND GETTING ANSWERS

game. If you can't guarantee the sale or if you have nothing to give, nothing to surrender, what happens then? Don't fret. The order is probably yours anyway. An interesting story illustrates this point. We talked earlier about the unfair demands that many chains (especially grocery chains) make of their vendors. One unfair demand in particular is the demand for "shelf space payments," normally referred to as "slotting fees."

An acquaintance of mine owns a small, successful vitamin company. He is a shrewd businessman, but he's a terrible "people-person." He has a personality like a wet sock, and that has retarded his company's growth. Nonetheless, sometimes things just fall in your lap if you're lucky, and this fellow is very lucky. He "inherited" a major grocery chain account when he first bought his company. Then, because of an unusually gutsy and innovative buyer who bought a unique merchandising idea, his products were featured in areas other than the vitamin and health and beauty sections of the stores. It was a bold idea and one that proved highly popular with the consumers. His product line became an immediate success within the chain.

Several years went by with record sales being posted annually. Then a new buyer took over, and as the old saying goes, "a new broom sweeps clean." This "new broom" was going to earn his keep and make some headlines for himself. He called my friend in to a meeting, and laid it out for him: "Come up with slotting fees, or lose the account." This is like being robbed or mugged in a back alley. It is nothing short of larceny, but most of us would have rolled over and paid the fees just to keep the business.

Not so with "Mr. Personality." He flatly refused to play the buyer's game. He pointed out his excellent record with the company, the fat profit margins they enjoyed, and the excellent service his company had provided — a service, he assured the buyer, that was largely responsible for the annual sales increases. "If I'm forced to pay slotting fees, I will not be able to afford point-of-sale merchandising aid." To my (and everyone else's) astonishment, he kept the account. I was told that a vice president of merchandising interceded and instructed the buyer to back off. It was a courageous management decision on the part of the vendor, and he has my deep admiration. In most other instances, he would have lost the account. He was both tough and lucky.

This is an exceptional case. Generally, the buyer will insist on payment of slotting fees *or else*. There was an NBC news special on this very topic, which dramatized how harmful this practice is to small companies with fine products that are trying to break into the mainstream marketing system. Also, a few courageous small and medium-size companies are trying to get their congressional representatives to push for reform. I am hopeful that the FTC or some other agency will act to protect the integrity of doing business in the United States.

13

THE BATTLE OF THE BUDDY SYSTEM

As a rule, regular contact between people will eventually result in friendships. This is especially true when entertainment is part of that contact. In surroundings other than an office, both buyers and salespeople will let their hair down, relax, and talk about their interests: professional sports, current events, hobbies, family, and countless other possibilities. They may discover a common interest that deepens the relationship. For instance, if both parties are fishing "nuts," then very likely, they will arrange a fishing trip. Before long, a strong friendship has been formed. That can be very good or very bad.

Friendships carry with them unspoken responsibilities. Friends look out for each other and help each other whenever they can. Business friendships are no different. I'm sure you know people who are "in tight" with certain buyers. Whoever they are, their goods are featured in most of the ads the account runs and are prominently displayed in the stores. That's fine, but there is a price to pay. Some of these friendships last a lifetime; most are short-lived. Buyers change jobs, get fired, or retire, and sellers follow the same route. All too often, the friendship ends on a sour note.

FAMILIARITY BREEDS CONTEMPT

Once a friendship is formed, some salespeople will begin to take their buyers/friends for granted. Instead of servicing the account as before, they begin to rely more on the friendship than on the basis that started that friendship. Buyers will immediately notice this slackening, but instead of calling their new friends and expressing disappointment, they will allow it to continue and worsen because they want to protect the friendship. Both the sellers and the buyers are heading down a slippery slope that can only end in a catastrophe.

Suppose, on the other hand, that the salesperson continues to service the account as in the past. Imagine what course the buyer could take. Buyers in this situation will often expect special treatment from the seller — deeper discounts, first refusal on merchandise, relaxed return policies, and extended terms of sale. If salespeople give in on these and other "requests," someone else will have to pay. Other customers or prospects will not get a share of the extra services now being gobbled up by the friend.

If the salespeople refuse the "requests" of their friends, you can be sure that hard feelings will result. The refusal is no longer a business matter, but a betrayal of friendship. In selling to friends, as in selling to anyone else, salespeople must sometimes push for a larger order, or apply pressure for payment, or even refuse to ship for one reason or another. Suppose they have to push for a larger order. Buyers may treat this effort as if it were a joke. They don't take their friends seriously any longer, no matter how strong the entreaty. In return, the sellers become angry with their buyers. They expect their friends to come through when they (the sellers) need it, and sometimes that isn't possible.

Trying to collect money from a friend is very difficult. Once again, a buyer may expect special treatment. "Come on, George, can't you let this one rest until next month?" the buyer might say. The seller may stretch his own credibility to the limit, trying to accommodate his friend. When the credit department puts its foot down, and the salesperson has no choice, the buyer may very well feel his friend isn't doing as much for him as he could. He isn't only angry about the tight credit policy, but he's also upset that his friend did not come through in a clutch.

THE COST OF DOING BUSINESS

Usually, salespeople pick up all entertainment expenses and ensure that the entertainment is first-class and expensive. Buyers become accustomed to the best. Most sales managers will allocate a percentage of sales for entertainment; between .25 to .50 percent might be an average figure. Let's say an account is buying $50,000 per month on average. That means the salesperson could spend up to $250 monthly. In today's world, that means a dinner out for a party of four; or a few lunches, a golf game, and maybe a small business gift. But buyers don't seem to understand that. They will ride a salesperson's account into the cement if allowed. But how do you tell a friend that his or her account isn't worth more to your company than $250 a month?

A few years ago, a salesperson who worked for me made friends with a powerful general merchandise chain buyer. While cultivating the business, she stretched her expense account to the limit, entertaining the buyer and his wife. I didn't say anything about it. Before long we started to see some strong sales activity from this new customer, and everything seemed to be going along just fine. However, in approving the expense reports, I noticed that an inordinate amount of her expense allowance was being spent on this one account. I talked to her about it, but she assured me that everything was under control, and for a time, she was right.

The business increased monthly, and in no time we were the dominant line in that chain. The buyer and my salesperson, along with their spouses, spent virtually every weekend together. Golf weekends, fishing weekends, skiing weekends, and Las Vegas weekends were interspersed with weekday luncheons and sometimes cocktails after work. I continued to monitor her expense reports and was alarmed by what I saw. Virtually the entire expense allowance was being spent on this one account!

When I spoke to her about it, she made two points: (1) Her overall business wasn't hurting yet, from the lack of entertainment money; and (2) She, too, was aware of the lopsided spending. In addition, she was now spending a lot of her own money to continue these lavish rounds of entertainment. "John never reaches for a tab. He thinks my expense account has no bottom, and I don't know what to do about it. I think I will hold on to the business; in fact, I'm sure of it. But we are such good friends, I'm embarrassed to ask him to share in any expense."

I made a number of suggestions, none of which she liked. I even offered to talk with the customer myself — a prospect that didn't appeal to me. "I got myself into this mess," she said, "and I'll get myself out." The next afternoon she invited the buyer to lunch and had a "Dutch uncle" talk with him. Fortunately, he was an understanding fellow, and their friendship was based on much more than the entertainment she was paying for. Still, it was a difficult and delicate situation and could have had disastrous results.

THE BATTLE OF THE BUDDY SYSTEM

More than anything else, building a strong friendship with a buyer will prevent both you and the buyer from doing your jobs the way they should be done. It can build frustration and a feeling of helplessness in both parties. If you push for more business, which is your job, the buyer feels compromised. He or she feels obligated to give more orders, bigger orders, and more frequent orders. The buyer may not feel justified in doing this; he or she may not be able to explain to the boss why so much of the budget is going to a single vendor. The boss will probably be aware of the friendship, and the buyer may feel that he or she must defend every order, as well as the friendship itself. Any negative decision on either side of the buyer-seller relationship may be construed as one or the other taking advantage of the friendship.

There is nothing wrong with entertaining business acquaintances or developing friendships with your customers. The trouble comes when the relationship becomes too intense. It's the wisest course to maintain a certain distance between the customer and yourself. Build a business wall to maintain a slight formality, a respect, and a definition of each other's roles. I recall a nasty story that illustrates this situation well.

An important buyer of stamped parts had the reputation as a womanizer and a heavy drinker, and the salesperson was a clone. Trying to nail the account was difficult, and it seemed impossible. One evening when the salesman was at his favorite watering hole, the buyer walked in. Needless to say, they hooked up at the bar and ended up having a wild night together. This was the first of many wild nights. Both were bachelors and had so much in common that they became fast friends. The business was switched to the salesperson's company, and all was right with the world.

All was right until the buyer's birthday. The salesperson wanted to throw a birthday party, and he arranged for coworkers, vendors, and friends to attend the party and surprise the buyer. Well, the party was indeed a surprise, and the buyer soon was feeling no pain. As the night wore on, the party became increasingly bawdy and tawdry. The next day, the buyer was given a good talking to by his boss. His conduct was unacceptable, and corrections would be made, or he would lose his job. Now sober and feeling disgusted with himself, he began to blame his sales friend. After all, he had set up the party complete with witnesses and entertainment. On the salesperson's next call, the buyer refused to see him! He also refused his telephone calls, and the orders grew smaller and smaller, until they stopped completely. I admit this is an extreme case. However, it does demonstrate how friendships can actually damage or totally destroy a business relationship.

INSIDER DEALS

When you develop a strong friendship with a particular buyer, others in the industry become aware of it almost immediately. Many salespeople are terrible tattlers; they love gossip. Not everyone is guilty of this, of course, but enough are to make keeping a friendship or any other secret impossible. How do you think this friendship might affect other buyers? It is only natural to help your friend and to give the best at the lowest price to your buddy. Do your competitors notice that? You bet they do. If the friend gets a special deal, the competition hears about it. Even if the friend doesn't get a special deal, the competition will think that he or she has gotten one. Either way you lose. Keeping friendly buyers at arm's length is the wisest course to follow. That is the only way to defuse a dangerous situation.

Entertainment is a very big part of some sales efforts and can aid in developing a friendly climate and warm feelings in a normally cool and formal business setting. The trick is to keep your business wall up and at the same time make sure your guests are comfortable and enjoying themselves. Golf tournaments, company picnics, the annual Christmas party, a group night at the ballpark, and similar activities can bring customers closer to the company, give them a feeling of belonging, and let them meet the faceless voices they deal with daily. At the same time, that protective barrier is maintained, and the business relationship is kept distinct from a personal one.

I don't think that talking business at social functions makes good sense. The buyers know why they were invited; they aren't dumb. Let them enjoy themselves. Follow up the affair with a note thanking them for attending. During a normal week, you may find it useful to invite your customer to lunch. That is a totally different story. Business lunches should be just that — business extensions of the day. "Let's talk this out over lunch," is a way to express the invitation. Then, after ordering, it is perfectly acceptable to discuss business, ask for the order, or solve a problem. The business lunch should never be interrupted with telephone calls (cellular or otherwise), ingoing or outgoing, pagers beeping, or anything else. This is an opportunity to have the buyer all to yourself without telephones ringing, secretaries running in and out of the office, or other distractions. Make the most of the opportunity.

I've had sales applicants tell me they had this or that account "wrapped up." "Fred Forsythe and I are the best of friends. Hire me and I'll bring the XYZ account with me." Is that true? Can a salesperson control an account to the degree that he or she can change the product mix a buyer feels is the best for the company? I don't think so. Naturally, if the salesperson has a good relationship with a buyer, he or she will get an interview, the conversation will be relaxed with the customary give-and-take, and the buyer might try to throw some business that way. But I have never seen a quality line of merchandise replaced with another because the salesperson switched companies. There is just too much involved and too much at risk for the buyer to cause that kind of disruption in his or her company.

Consider the stress that is put on a friendship when a salesperson, who is starting a new job and must make a good impression, asks his or her friend for business. The friend may not be able to grant the request or in good conscience cannot replace existing products with what he or she may consider inferior goods. In this instance, doesn't the buyer have the right to feel used? How far can a friendship be stretched?

Another point must be considered from the buyers' perspective. Usually, all buying decisions are reviewed by the merchandise manager, unless it's a purchase of regular-line goods. Buyers may want to help their friends, but they also want to keep their jobs. A major switch of vendors will require sound business reasons. What justification can the buyers make unless the new line is obviously far superior, far cheaper, or both?

Having friends is, of course, always desirable in your business as well as your personal life. The point I want to make is simply: never allow the friendship to spill over into the business relationship. Understand the limitations and the conditions the buyers work under, and make sure they understand your limitations as well.

OVERCOMING THE BUDDY SYSTEM

Competing with a sales entity who is on the "inside" is a problem that you can be sure you will face at one time or another. The one thing you never want to do is compete by trying to develop a friendship of your own with the buyer. Instead, learn all you can about the needs of the customer and show how your products can relate to those needs. In other words, be a professional salesperson. Be fair and honest, and you will be rewarded and respected. The following eleven points can be used to compete with the salesperson who is the buyer's friend:

1. **Discover your customer's needs.** He or she may not know (probably doesn't know) what that need is, so study the customer's business and demonstrate how your products will fill that need.

2. **Remember the mechanics of selling** and never stray from the rules.

3. **Involve your buyer in the sale.** Develop a dialogue with every presentation you give.

4. **Ask questions.** First, ask questions to initiate the dialogue and gain information. Then, ask closing questions.

5. **Listen.** The buyer may be trying to tell you something. He or she may even be trying to buy!

6. **Always close early and often.** If necessary, review the steps involved in selling until they become second nature.

7. **Don't take no for an answer.** When the buyers say no they may only be saying, "Convince me."

8. **Don't overstay your welcome.** When buyers say yes, write the order and leave.

9. **Get the reputation as a follow-up person.** Follow through on all the promises you make.

10. **Be persistent, but be patient.** Solid selling techniques, coupled with hard work, will pay off. Persistence is a virtue if it's not overused. Persistence is the root of the word *pest*. Don't forget that.

11. **Maintain a courteous, professional relationship.** Count yourself lucky that you don't have to suffer from the strains of combining friendship and business.

THE BATTLE OF THE BUDDY SYSTEM

You may have noticed that the eleven points for overcoming the buddy system are basically the same formula I have recommended using with all buyers, regardless of the problem you're trying to overcome. When attempting to compete with a salesperson who is a friend of the buyer, many salespeople overreach. They feel extra pressure and struggle to overcome their disadvantage in such a way that they forget their professionalism. If, instead, they simply follow the intelligent mechanics of selling and if they isolate the need for their products and close as they would with any buyer, they will get their share of business most of the time. As we all know, nothing stays the same for very long. Buyers are switched to other categories, some die or get fired or resign. Contrary to what many sales trainers and managers teach, patience is a virtue in sales if it is used with moderation and mixed with common sense.

14

FINDING THE MARKET

Throughout this book, I have touched on the changing face of business in the United States, changes that now stretch worldwide. The changes that impact the market now began in the late 1970s, accelerated throughout the 1980s, and have continued to gain steam in the 1990s. These are what I call *contemporary changes*, but the fact is they are not really contemporary. Change represents growth, and growth is what business is all about. The only thing constant in the world is change. Nothing ever remains static and survives. A company grows, or it withers and falls, and it is replaced or taken over by another company that has changed and adapted to the newest technologies and the latest management theories. Management concepts change with the demands of the marketplace and, at least to some degree, with current political ideology. These political doctrines have swung like a pendulum from extreme liberal to rigid conservative.

THE AGE OF THE TITANS

At the present time we are experiencing a dramatic change in retailing. There are fewer and fewer retail outlets that can be classified as mass merchandisers. By mass merchandiser, I mean any national chain of retail stores that represents a major force in the marketplace. Kmart, Wal-Mart, Sears, JCPenney, Target, and Montgomery Ward dominate the markets within which they operate, and they are, in fact, without major competition (outside their select club of six).

These companies force prices down to such a point that smaller retailers collapse because they are unable to depend on mass volume to offset smaller profits. We have seen this same phenomenon in the grocery industry. Huge chains with almost unlimited resources have turned the neighborhood grocery store into a distant memory. These giant retail companies buy from large manufacturers and distributors both in the United States and abroad. Their buying power is so massive that they can and do make demands on their vendors, demands that smaller distributors and manufacturers can't possibly meet. In addition, the staples sold in supermarkets, super drugstores, department store chains, catalog houses, and mass merchandise stores are distributed by huge companies. Smaller companies simply do not have the capabilities to service these gigantic operations. At first glance we may consider this a frightening turn of events. But, like most changes, this trend has an upside, as well as a downside.

THE UPSIDE

Thanks to these massive retail operations, efficiency is excellent. The stores themselves are, in some ways, run robotically. The cash registers tell the operator what change is due, print out an itemized receipt, and in some stores, even give the customer a robotic "thank you"! Merchandise is pre-priced and carries a scanner-ready ticket marked with an inventory number. Thanks to this technology, reporting to headquarters the inventory levels has been facilitated, and placing new orders is automatic and simple. Department managers and store merchandise managers have a simple time placing orders and are rarely out of stock.

Consumers can depend on a wide selection of quality goods in a concentrated area and at low prices. Some "super stores" combine soft goods with hard goods, groceries with drugs, and they offer dry-cleaners, delicatessens, and bakeries to serve almost every need. The convenience factor is enormous, and the low prices are almost an extra.

THE DOWNSIDE

In spite of their virtues, these operations also have a downside. Service at point-of-purchase is almost nonexistent. I'm sure we all have wandered about a huge store looking for a particular item, unable to find anyone to ask where that item might be. If, for some reason the item is not priced, we usually have to wait until we pay before we can discover the actual cost. This lack of personalized attention has given birth to a submarket of smaller, service-oriented businesses that spring up and thrive alongside the giants. These service-minded stores carry very high-quality, expensive merchandise that the giants won't touch because the volume is low and the turnover is slow.

Of course, from the sales perspective, the downside is a reduction of sales jobs. With a smaller number of retailers, the giants' need for salespeople is also reduced. In one real sense, these gigantic suppliers don't need salespeople at all. For example, little selling is done by General Electric to the Wal-Mart stores. Both parties know that GE will be represented in Wal-Mart stores, and the only questions remaining relate to quantity, discounts, and allowances. Even these matters are mostly cut and dried. Computers talk to other computers, and the "salespeople" merely keep things in order. As the need for salespeople diminishes, the need for buyers also shrinks. Fewer buyers are needed because the computer age has simplified and quickened the placement of orders, and the list of acceptable vendors has grow smaller.

For small and medium-size vendors, the opportunities to sell to the giants have all but vanished, so they, too, need fewer salespeople to service those accounts. All this is referred to as *downsizing*, a term we have all come to know.

Downsizing is at its zenith right now, and it is reported as job losses in our morning newspapers. The cost of labor is a major expenditure in every company, and the downsizing experts are quick to attack that area whenever possible. As a nation, we have apparently come to accept the fact that we will not be a manufacturing country. The production-line jobs are quickly moving to Asia, Mexico, and many third-world countries. Many of the remaining manufacturers in the United States are modernizing and using industrial robots to eliminate errors, improve efficiency, and reduce costs. This trend results in fewer jobs.

I'll never forget a visit I made to an all-robotics factory in Texas. This plant supplied plastic-injected parts to the auto industry. It operated around the clock in order to meet the demand of the company's large, national market share. The thing that amazed me was the size of the plant in relation to the small number of people it employed. The plant stretched for blocks and, as I recall, the entire payroll consisted of only seven or eight people: Two computer programmers supervised the flawless performance of the robotic functions; a few people handled shipping and receiving; a "production supervisor" coordinated the changing of tools, which was also automatic, and other similar tasks; and two janitors kept the place clean.

That was it! Seven or eight people in a factory that is a major source for plastic parts in the country! It was a wonder to see. Raw materials were received and placed into hoppers by automated equipment; the computer programmed the injection-molding machines that formed the product and trimmed the parts. As the parts left the conveyors, they were automatically placed in shipping containers, sealed, labeled, and forwarded to the shipping department. I think they call this kind of plant a "lights-out plant." There is little need for lighting because there are so few employees. It was incredible — and it was scary.

THE UPSIDE OF THE DOWNSIDE

Production workers who lose their jobs because of downsizing may have difficulty finding other work, but salespeople should have no problem. Small and medium-size manufacturers and entrepreneurs are eager to get their products sold and to find new markets. The customers may have changed, but the opportunities abound for selling to the specialty-store market, representing higher-quality merchandise, and selling to new and very different venues.

These opportunities are exciting and fruitful. They offer the satisfaction of accomplishment and rich financial rewards. They require selling skills, hard work, innovative thought, and in some cases, an entrepreneurial spirit.

Currently, it is estimated that a person entering the job market now will change jobs an average of five times before retirement. I know that bothers some security-minded people. But we have all seen that security simply doesn't exist anymore, at least not the security we had come to expect in the past. Today the only security is the security we build for ourselves. And that is OK with me.

BRANDS VERSUS THE NO-NAMES

In the new specialized marketing arenas, virtually all products are new, low-profile, and unknown to the general public. The cost of advertising is so great that all but the largest companies are hard-pressed to mount an ad campaign. At the same time, the consumers are brand-conscious.

They have been programmed by heavy, repetitive advertising to believe that a particular brand is superior in all ways to any other similar product. Brands become indelibly stamped on the consumers' consciousness, and sales are almost automatic.

Consumers are suspicious of "off" brands, or products that are new to the market and have not been introduced by companies they have learned to trust. This is just one of the many challenges to the salesperson's selling skills in the new marketplaces.

Adaptation is another challenge faced in today's new breed of shifting markets.

Without the safety net of a large corporation and without the power of an organized marketing group, the salesperson engaged in the new sales arena must shed the methods used in the past. Consider what might happen when the small vendor ventures into the arena of the titans.

Suppose you have produced a new kind of window shade. Your shade never tears, wrinkles, or splits. Moreover, it blocks out sunlight, but it allows fresh air into the room. It is a great idea and, being ambitious, you present your product to Sears, Montgomery Ward, Target, Wal-Mart, Kmart and JCPenney. If you land just one "serious" order from any one of those companies, your entire inventory could be wiped out for the year. Your production facilities probably will not be sufficient to fill even the first segment of the first order. The demands of that customer can actually mean your complete collapse. Once your production is in the hands of that single customer (at the expense of all the smaller companies that supported you as you grew), the giant will probably *demand* a price reduction. Since you have put all your eggs in one basket, you will have to give the price cut, or the customer will cut you off as a vendor. With raw material invoices due and binding contracts for large future shipments signed, your small plant will be facing some difficult times. Fighting to meet the demands of the giant customer, your company will have to hire more people, rent more equipment, and incur more taxes and other costs. Suddenly, you find yourself working for the customer.

That scenario has been repeated time and again. Smaller companies have learned to be satisfied with selling their products in new and different ways and growing in a more orderly, less chaotic, and less traumatic fashion.

But many products are bought and sold that do not involve the retail consumer or retail store. Before we go on to discover the selling jobs and opportunities in the new marketplaces, let's look at other types of selling jobs.

INDUSTRIAL SALES

Industrial sales serve as an example of a field in which there have been monumental changes, modernization of plants, and widespread use of robotics. Nevertheless, industrial selling is relatively unchanged. The industrial salesperson is usually a technically trained person who can converse with engineers, production managers, and construction supervisors. As with all industries, certain suppliers have a controlling share of the business, but industrial buyers are normally open to any qualified vendor. If vendors have the capacity to supply, and if their quality is acceptable, industrial plants appear willing, indeed anxious, to add them as vendors. Many small, precision machine shops, parts distributors, and other suppliers act as subcontractors to many manufacturing giants. Hughes Aircraft, for example, utilizes more than twenty-five thousand independent suppliers in its far-flung operations. Hughes is only one of many similar operations that buy from small vendors/suppliers — all of whom need salespeople.

SMALL INDUSTRIAL OPERATIONS

In the construction business, many products are needed that can't be bought in large quantities or on contract, such as hand tools, specialty products, and products that will be used sparingly. All of these and hundreds of other items are stocked by supply companies that count on subcontractors, small general contractors, "do-it-yourselfers," and others for their sales.

Major contractors, on the other hand, will order shipments directly to the job site from building supply companies. Lumber, cement, pipes, wiring, wallboard, nails, rivets, and other major building components are contracted out. Yet, there are hundreds of products needed that cannot be bought in that way. Like their small and medium-size colleagues, the big contractors depend on the smaller vendors to fill those special needs.

SERVICE SALES

Service sales include products and services such as linen, uniforms, janitorial products, coffee, food, snacks, restroom supplies, security services, communication products, insurance, investments, and everything from diaper services to burial arrangements. These are "invisible" things we all take for granted, and we are shocked and angry when they occasionally aren't where we expect them to be.

Few companies in the service business could be classified as huge. There are a couple of big companies, but no monoliths. Opportunities for small companies to break into this market are good. Although some of the larger accounts have annual contracts in force, those contracts are reviewed annually and are changed frequently. Janitorial services for office buildings, plants, and warehouses are lucrative. I know of a fellow in the Midwest who had a fairly successful insurance agency going for him. One day, while trying to sell a policy to an account, he discovered the general manager was upset because the cleaning crew didn't show up the night before, and the place was a mess. He couldn't get another crew in right away, and in his fury had fired the tardy janitors. The insurance agent sensed an opportunity and told the manager that he had a cleaning service and would be delighted to take on the job. To make a long story short, he now owns the largest janitorial company in the Midwest.

There are many sales opportunities in the service industry. It is not a particularly glamorous industry, but it is steady and resistant to the kinds of changes we have seen in other industries. Also, the chances of starting one's own business are good in the service industry.

MULTILEVEL MARKETING

A relatively new concept in marketing is the multilevel operation. The idea of multilevel marketing was actually forced onto entrepreneurs, small businesses, and individuals who had unique products and no place or no way to sell them. Suppose you have a product that safely allows a dieter to lose weight without having to resort to exhausting exercises. To get that product to market would be difficult, extremely expensive, and beyond the reach of most people. The chain drugstores, supermarkets, and discount store operations would probably not give it a second look. They are "in bed" with the giants who make diet products. They are protected by guaranteed sales, massive advertising campaigns, celebrity endorsements, and national promotional efforts. Buyers at such operations are not risk-takers. No matter how good your product might be, unless the public knows about it and asks for it at the store level, these buyers will continue to sell the guaranteed-sale goods they have always stocked. Start-up operations have no chance of cracking the mainstream retail operations, even if they could afford the slotting fees and advertising allowances demanded. So here you are, with a great product and no way to get it to the general buying public. This is a problem that has faced and is continuing to face hundreds of new young companies that are short on money, but long on ideas.

As this problem continued to grow throughout the United States, someone thought to recruit a direct-to-the-consumer sales force. This untrained, unprofessional sales force sells to their neighbors, friends, coworkers, and relatives. Most of these people work with the multilevel marketing company on a part-time basis.

In order to become a salesperson/recruiter, interested self-starters would buy a beginning inventory to resell. This accomplished two things:

1. It provided start-up cash for the fledgling company and reduced its cash-flow problem.

2. It provided some assurances that the new "employees" would actually get out and contact people to get rid of the inventory they just bought. The recruits would receive a generous commission for each sale made. As they racked up sales, they would also recruit their customers to join the multilevel marketing operations, thus permitting it to grow in size and power.

The multilevel marketing organization is structured in levels. The first level is composed of individuals who first join and sell for the organization. All those who join later (thanks to the efforts of the first-level people) are also expected to recruit and sell. Commissions are usually paid down to seven levels (sometimes less and sometimes more). Receiving their own commissions plus partial commissions of all those they recruited and on down to seven levels or more translates into big paydays for the first-level people. The beauty of all this is that no matter when you join, if you recruit and sell, the income can be sensational.

Some multilevel marketing companies force their recruits to "top out" at some point in time. This simply means that the first-level person must re-enter and begin all over again. It is amazing how quickly a first-level person's income can grow. When I first was exposed to a multilevel marketing company, I must confess that I thought a con game was being perpetrated. I had a difficult time believing that much money could be made, until it was explained to me how the multilevel marketing company could afford to pay large sums.

If the first-level salesperson receives just one dollar per sale on commission, his or her earnings could be as much as $78,000 in the first year! Naturally, most commissions are substantially higher than one dollar, so the earnings are also much higher. Suffice it to say that if done correctly, it is an extremely lucrative operation for the active, productive salesperson, as well as for the multilevel marketing operator.

A critical factor in success is getting the right product to sell. The operator must first sell the sales force. Most of these people have never sold anything in their lives. They will only respond if they are personally convinced that their relatives, coworkers, friends, and neighbors will want the product or service. The product should not be available in retail stores, and it should have some unique advantages or benefits.

As in all sales, the salespeople must be encouraged to work. Since most recruits are not professional salespeople, they tend to slack off after selling a few special friends or relatives. So the first-level salespeople have to be highly motivated, and they must motivate others. They must burn up the telephone lines, encourage the "down-line" people, and push, push, push.

More important than the sales is the recruiting. A multilevel marketing operation must continue to grow. Many started in a community, overflowed that community, went statewide, then regional, and finally national. In theory, an entry-level person, getting into an operation at the outset, could have a network organization of 7,000 people — each contributing to his or her monthly income. The potential is staggering.

There are a number of national companies that began and continue to be operated like multilevel companies. Avon is a prime example. Of course, Avon has grown beyond what most multilevel marketing companies ever dream. Its people are well trained, the company is structured, and it has some of the trappings of any large corporation (big fancy buildings, national conventions, and a top-heavy executive staff). Still, Avon is a multilevel marketing company, and all people involved in it pull their own weight.

As gigantic companies continue to reduce their employee rolls, out-of-work people start their own businesses. They develop new products and ideas and search for the best way to market them. When they run into the brick walls of business, which they will, we will see an explosion of multi-level marketing operations. The overhead is minimal, the profits are huge, and almost anyone can start one.

PROBLEMS WITH MULTILEVEL MARKETING OPERATIONS

The income to be gained is more than most first-level salespeople have ever earned. Many of them grasp the opportunity; their early successes encourage them to forge ahead. The problem is that these people are few in number. Typically, the first-level salespeople sell to a few neighbors or friends, and then simply stop selling. Remember, these are not professional salespeople. They don't know how to find and approach new prospects. There are no training programs, and these people are left to sink or swim. I discussed this problem with a successful multilevel marketing operator in California, who told me there really was no problem. "In a more structured sales organization, isn't it true that 20 percent of the sales staff will sell 80 percent of the goods? Well, it's the same with us." He had me there.

Many products introduced by multilevel marketing operations eventually find their way (usually under different manufacturers) into the mainstream retail stores. When this happens, it normally kills the multilevel operation. The California operator told me, "It is too difficult to compete with retailers. When a product hits the mainstream, we find something else to sell."

Operators are constantly on the lookout for new, unique products or services that will "fit." *Fitting* means that the product must have an instant appeal, must be professionally packaged, must be perceived to be valued beyond the asking price, and must be able to sustain a seven-level commission bite. In multilevel marketing, consumer products that are simple to understand are the most favored. Vitamins, exercise equipment, cosmetics, weight-loss plans, collectibles, gold coins, and thousands of other products are being sold successfully through these operations.

Operations that have this kind of money potential quickly attract the "fast-buck" crowd. However, because of the nature and structure of the organization, it is difficult for a scam operation to hold up in multilevel marketing. I know of very few salespeople/recruiters who have been cheated out of their commissions. Some of the fast-buck operators are good motivators and can paint a very blue sky. If you are thinking of joining a multilevel marketing operation, do not base your decision on the motivational speaker alone. Examine the product carefully and ask questions (where is it made, what are the contents, what are the guarantees, what is the competition, is it in the mainstream stores). Ask yourself if you would really buy the products if someone offered it at the price asked. Gather the hand-out materials and price schedules, and if possible try a few test sales. Find out if a friend or family member would buy the product. You might even consider talking to a few strangers to test their reaction. Self-discipline is a key to success in an multilevel marketing operation. No one will spend much time with you if you don't show production. You are pretty much on your own.

DIRECT MAIL

Another method of selling, which has been especially strong in the 1980s and 1990s, is direct mail. Direct mail is just what the name says: an unsolicited mailing of advertising or promotional materials sent through the U.S. Postal Service. Many of us classify direct mail as "junk mail," an annoyance that has little or no value. We find our mailboxes jammed to overflowing every day with letters, flyers, and even telegrams that offer a bewildering array of products and services. We throw most of it away with barely a second glance. Nonetheless, *more than 50 percent of all adults in the United States order one or more products by mail each year.* Enough responses are made to make direct mail one of the fastest growing marketing methods in the world.

Some well-recognized companies sell directly through the mail and send hundreds of thousands, even millions, of mailing pieces per year to existing and prospective customers, and they use direct mail as an adjunct to other marketing and sales tactics. JCPenney, Sears, and Montgomery Ward are typical examples of this.

Smaller companies and independent agents (real estate, insurance, investment brokers, financial planners, accountants, lawyers, and even doctors and dentists), make much smaller mailings and depend heavily on this method of selling.

FINDING THE MARKET

Large orders are normally the rule when selling to direct mail companies. The buyers for these companies are throwbacks because they are innovative risk takers. They know their markets and are willing to take the chance that their decisions will result in successful product sales.

Huge corporations with massive marketing departments and national television campaigns are using direct mail. Of course, some of our retail giants began as simple (and very small) direct mail or mail-order operators. Sears, for example, was started when Richard Sears sold pocketwatches by mail order to train stationmasters. This grew to be one of the nation's leading mail-order catalog houses. In that instance, as in so many others, mail order changed into a direct mail operation. Direct mail is a response to a postal delivered offer, whereas mail order is a response to an advertising offer.

If you were to consider direct mail as a selling tool, your first questions might be (1) "Whom should I mail to?" and (2) "How do I obtain the addresses?" The answer lies in mailing lists. Instead of sending mail to every home in a city, a mailing list will isolate these people who are most likely to buy the product. Lists are broken down into hundreds of categories by gender, marital status, and other considerations. The more qualified or specialized the list, the higher the cost.

If the product or service has a general overall appeal, then a telephone book or any general directory can be utilized instead of buying a costly mailing list. A roofer, for instance, might offer his services to an entire suburban community by direct mail, even though a relatively small number of homes in the area may need new roofs or repairs. If the response is satisfactory — 2 percent is considered a healthy response — then the mailing can be extended to a larger market.

The keys to successful direct mail selling are developing the proper mailing piece, selecting the proper mailing lists or area, and having the product or service that is suited for the market. The following are the advantages of direct mail:

1. Low cost compared to other types of marketing/sales efforts
2. Quick response from the consumer
3. Ease of testing in a minor market before a more elaborate mass mailing

4. Market selectivity, as the piece goes to the people most likely to buy the product

5. Elimination of several marketing levels, thereby lowering costs.

Business is rapidly changing in the United States and throughout the world. New and different kinds of markets are gaining market share. I have covered only a few of the possible areas in which salespeople can flourish. As we look toward the twenty-first century, new arenas will open up and others will fold, but the new will definitely outnumber the old. Opportunities for salespeople have never been better.

15

CREATING MARKETS, CREATING NEEDS

Many salespeople make the common mistake of trying to sell merchandise or services that have no relevance to the buyer's business. The salespeople see what they consider an ideal outlet for their goods and try to force-feed the product. They carefully prepare a presentation, set an appointment with the buyer, and do a great job of selling. They can't understand why the buyer turns them down. "Heck, if she just had a little courage, my widgets would sell like hotcakes there," they lament, never considering the image that the buyer and the store may be trying to create or maintain. They try to force merchandise onto an account that has no history of selling that particular type of goods. They try to fill a need where no need exists.

This is not to say that new venues can't be created or that an innovative salesperson shouldn't explore new markets. On the contrary, I've seen whole new markets started by creative thinking. But making sales calls in untried markets can be frustrating and costly. They are frustrating because many buyers either lack imagination or are afraid of making bold decisions, and they are costly because your time is money.

Nowadays, if you are selling groceries, you might also approach super drugstores because drugstores carry a varied selection of groceries. Conversely, if you are selling over-the-counter drugs, you might approach grocery markets because they carry a large stock of nonprescription drugs. But, in selling either line of products, would you approach a shoemaker? A barber shop? A tailor? Of course not. Nonetheless, some salespeople make sales calls that are almost as ridiculous. At the same time, so that you don't always stick to the existing markets and fail to explore, remember that someone made that first sale of groceries to the drugstore and of drugs to the grocery store, and that must have seemed daring at the time.

Anxious to expand sales, some salespeople will fly in the face of common sense. But what makes good sense to me may make no sense whatever to you. On a recent visit to the local hardware store, I discovered they carried a good variety of candy bars, chewing gum, and snacks. I asked the manager how sales of those items were doing. He replied, "Can't keep them in stock!" Frankly, I would never have thought of selling confections to hardware stores, but some salesperson figured that the workers, hobbyists, and "do-it-yourselfers" get hungry on the job, and candy is a quick-energy snack. A new and growing market was born.

I remember one of my salespeople thought that travel agencies would be a perfect sales outlet for simple, point-and-shoot cameras. Why not? People who are planning a vacation or even a business trip might be inclined to make an impulse purchase. The travel agent didn't need any product knowledge because the cameras were idiot-proof, and the extra profits were good. I told her to forget it because the time and effort wouldn't be worthwhile. I envisioned her going from one small travel agent to another, struggling to make a presentation and making a few small, insignificant sales.

I was wrong! This salesperson sold to a few small agencies, and discovered that her idea made sense to the travel industry. The cameras sold well, and the travelers appreciated the reminder and the convenience. Some agencies even started stocking film, flash guns, and tripods in addition to the cameras! My salesperson had, she told me, taken her "show" on the road — off Broadway, so to speak. Now that it was tested and proven (at least to her satisfaction), she zoomed in on the big tour operators. She was ready for the big time.

Before you could say "frequent flyer," a major travel organization bought a boatload of 35mm point-and-shoot cameras that they gave away to every tour member. Their promotion was a huge hit with the travelers, and it resulted in a giant commission for my sales representative. Later, she sold the cameras in tote bags with the agency's logo. The tote bags contained an X-ray proof film bag (so that the film would be protected from airport X-rays), a camera, extra film, and a booklet with tips on how to take good pictures. Sales ran off the chart as more tour operators jumped on a good thing, copying the example of the first big customer. You just never know.

NEW OUTLETS = SALES

Not long ago, a distributor of small, hand-held garden tools found that its market was shrinking in the conventional outlets: hardware stores and garden shops. Those kinds of stores continued to stock and sell the garden tools, but the sales were slipping as the retailers concentrated on major products with bigger unit sales and faster turns. Super drugstores, the distributor decided, could be part of the solution to its marketing problem. The distributor knew that some drugstores already carried potted plants and a small inventory of garden supplies and that they did a brisk business, so the idea wasn't a stretch of any magnitude.

Soon, the drugstore outlets were outperforming the hardware and garden shops in sales. Encouraged by this, the distributor decided that other not-so-obvious outlets might also prove to be successful if given the proper marketing aid. The marketing manager designed a handsome dump bin topped by an attractive, eye-catching header to display the hand tools. The profit margins were considered excellent in nontraditional outlets, and the space required to display the tools was small. Both the distributor and the marketing manager believed that their chances for opening those other marketing outlets were good.

Convenience store chains, gasoline service stations (independent and chain operations), and supermarkets were approached. Even the marketing manager was surprised when every prospect ended up buying! Of even greater importance, most were very successful selling through. When asked how he accounted for this amazing situation, the distributor replied, "I had no competition in the stores I was trying to sell. The products, although not exactly the kind normally sold in those outlets, were used by most of the store's customers. As displayed, my hand tools became impulse items, especially in the springtime."

This distributor's success story can be attributed to several factors:

1. A careful market research study was conducted prior to launching the program. This study "proved" the efficacy of selling hand-held garden tools in those outlets.

2. The cash outlay necessary to stock an opening inventory was small, and the profit potential was large.

3. The dump-bin displays were attractive and took up little floor space.

4. The product did not lend itself to shrinkage, nor did it have a timed shelf life.

5. The distributor had a successful example to point to (the super drugstores).

While we can admire this bright and successful marketing effort, we must also be aware that many similar attempts, not as well planned, have failed miserably. This has been especially true when the salesperson or organization was careless in selecting the alternative outlet. Success boils down to identifying an existing need or creating a need — the foundations of every sale. In the above case, the need for profit without a large cash outlay existed. The distributor was selling into outlets where he had no competition with which to be compared. He was the first on the scene. The retailers recognized the profit potential and knew that many of the products that the super drugstores sold, they could probably sell too.

Retail organizations work hard to develop an image. That image may be based on low prices, high quality, excellent customer service, product service, or uniqueness. Anything that might damage their image will be immediately scorned by the organization's buyers. A ritzy department store, for instance, wouldn't be caught dead with clothing sold in a discount operation. No matter how low the price, the ritzy store's buyer would never deal with a vendor of that merchandise. The discounter, on the other hand, can't afford the ritzy store's quality of goods. As a result, the respective salespeople never approach each other's customers. Image keeps the two apart. A salesperson with a line of inexpensive costume jewelry might find a market in the discount-clothing operation, and a salesperson selling expensive luggage totes may find an add-on market in the expensive store.

Some catalog houses have made their product mix so different and unique that they carry goods no retail store would dream of carrying. The catalog houses are, therefore, free to charge whatever they think the traffic will bear. These are interesting operations because they operate like no other business. Some expensive, very high-line houses actually charge for their catalogs! The consumer pays to see what the catalog house is trying to sell! In addition, those very same catalog houses charge vendors outrageous prices for having their goods included in the book. The catalog houses don't buy an inventory, not even the goods of the vendor who has just paid through the nose for the privilege of being included. The houses only buy as orders are placed by the consumer. Thus, their inventory and overhead are tightly controlled. At the same time, the customer pays a king's ransom for these space-age, cutting-edge, or one-of-a-kind items.

DO THE LEGWORK FIRST

Never attempt to sell a retail chain operation until you have visited the stores, observed the competition's merchandise, and talked with or questioned the sales clerks and the store manager, if possible. Then, when meeting with the buyer, you will be armed with strong ammo: "Mr. Kilgore, your inner-city store manager, and Ms. Snerdly, the manager of your western store, have both expressed a belief that our boxed chocolates would sell very well in their stores. In fact, Kilgore was enthusiastic about the possibility of placing our product right next to the greeting cards you recently added." If your visits to the stores and your interviews with the store personnel suggest otherwise, you will have saved yourself some time and trouble. The buyer will, without doubt, check with and gain the support of the retail people before forging ahead with what he considers this dramatic new idea. Being armed with those endorsements will improve your chances of making a sale by at least 60 percent.

Merchandising trends change as the general economy changes. A few years ago, quality and service were the major important factors. Today, low prices seem to rule the day. But some outlets never change their image; it works for them, so they stick with it. Trying to sell something out of the norm to this kind of account is an exercise in futility. You must find the trailblazers, the cutting-edge stores, the innovators — these are the customers that will be willing to experiment. But be forewarned, these are the kinds of accounts that will pare your prices and margins to the bone.

KNOW WHAT YOU SELL

I know that I harp on creating a need before ever approaching an account, but the importance of doing this can't be overemphasized. Consider the following illustration.

A salesman was having problems introducing his product, children's chewable vitamin C, into a national chain. All competitive products had basically the same formula, strength, and retail price. Only the flavors and minor price differences separated them. The salesman had children of his own and asked them and their friends to taste various flavors. He discovered that flavors such as pineapple, raspberry, and apple were not particularly popular. In fact, only one flavor was popular with all — strawberry. Now, most salespeople would have been content with that information and would have used that as their foundation to establish a need. Not so with this excellent drummer.

Visiting a local college library, he discovered a study that drew an identical conclusion to his own. Strawberry-flavored products are universally preferred by children over all other flavors by a considerable margin! Although some other flavors were acceptable or even preferred by some children, the strawberry flavor was the overall favorite and was the flavor they all would accept!

"Ms. Bayer," he enthused, "our children's chewable vitamins taste just like fresh, sweet strawberries. Here, taste one." The buyer tasted the vitamin and agreed that it did, indeed, taste like fresh, sweet strawberries.

"So what? I like the tart apple that Nature's Finest sells," she said. "Strawberries make me break out in a rash. I guess that's why I don't care for the taste."

"Respectfully, Ms. Bayer," my friend said, "I don't want to sell you the children's vitamins; I want to sell them to the kids and to the parents who want their children to have fortified vitamin C in a tasty, fruit flavor. Children's vitamins are of no value unless the kids like the taste. Wouldn't you agree?"

"Obviously. But my kids like apple-flavored vitamins," she said.

"Well," my friend continued, "we just never know what kids will like, now do we? But parents know, just as you know what your children like. And most parents know their kids love the strawberry flavor over all other kinds."

"Who says so? My kids like tart apple," she insisted.

"I ran a test with my own children and their friends in the neighborhood; all of them preferred the strawberry flavor. However, I didn't stop there. Their preferences may have been an anomaly, just as your children's favorite flavor might be. To prove to myself that strawberry is indeed the flavor that children prefer, I visited the university library and discovered a study on children's preferences for various flavors. Strawberry won hands down all across the United States. Here is a copy of the paper. Read it for yourself."

You can imagine the power and force this paper had. A university research paper supported the closing point. This sales rep used an important and respected outside source, with no bone to pick, as collaboration! The sale was, of course, in the bag.

Did the salesperson create a need? Yes, he did create a need for his product. But his competitors also had strawberry-flavored vitamins for kids. Why didn't the buyer choose their products over my friend's? Because he had done his homework, he had prepared his presentation, he was first to present the information, and he was focused. He was the only salesperson who took the trouble to really discover which flavor children preferred. He didn't rely on a guess or speculation; he used solid proof.

Support materials, particularly from outside your company, have great power. A newspaper article — probably one of the poorest researched sources you could find — has more power than anything any salesperson can say.

Search the newspapers and other printed materials for information that can help you forward your sales effort. If you can supply outside support materials to your buyers who then carry your message to a committee, your chances of making a sales are vastly improved. Buyers, no matter how sharp they may be, can't possibly recall all the positive points of your presentation. They may have dozens of products to present to the committee and will usually have incomplete notes and their own fading impressions to pass along. All the power and energy you brought to the presentation has been lost. Strong support materials that aid your sale will endure over time, from the buyer's office to the committee's conference room.

Committee buying is a pain in the backside for all professional salespeople. As I've said earlier, the whole idea behind buying by committee is to defuse the strength and passion of a strong sales presentation. When you know you are selling to a buyer who must turn around and sell to a committee, you should arm yourself as best you can. Find out how many people are on the committee and prepare a folder for each member with all the pertinent written information. Write a cover introduction and make it as informative and emotional as you can. Along with charts, graphs, surveys, pictures, and samples, include your sales/profit projections whenever possible.

In short, follow the old axiom in sales: "Plan your work, and work your plan." That tired expression still makes a world of sense.

BE JUST A WHISKER BETTER

When salespeople fail to plan and prepare for every call, they doom themselves to mediocrity. It takes just a little extra "something" to push you ahead of the pack.

I like to illustrate this point with the example of Man o' War, the famous champion racehorse of the early 1920s. That great animal won all but one of his races. Just think of that, he raced against the finest and fastest horses in the world, and he only lost one race! He was, for many years, the top money winner in racing. Even today, with bloated purses and many top-dollar races, he still ranks among the all-time money winners. But he didn't win all of his races easily. Some races he won by a length or more; others he won by a nose; a few he won by a photo finish! A photo finish — just a whisker of difference!

That is really all you have to be — just a little better than the competition. Just a tiny bit better prepared, just a mite more energetic, just a wee bit better. Make that extra call on the way back to the office or to your home. Be a little late for the racquetball game and make that extra telephone call. Get organized over the weekend for the next week. Be just a whisker better.

Being better includes looking out for new markets and new ways to sell your products. Many medium-size companies and almost all small companies overlook the military market. Unlike large companies that have military sales representatives who concentrate only on military sales, the little guys believe that trying to sell into this specialized market is a waste of time. Like all bureaucracies, it is confusing and frustrating to wade through the paperwork necessary to sell to the military and naval forces. Their rules are sometimes difficult to understand but their business can be rewarding. Most military salespeople (at least the ones I've met) are not top-notch hard workers. They are "in the system" and know the buyers, but most have poor selling skills.

There is another market that is often overlooked, and that is the premium market. Premium sales can be regular and big. I remember shuffling the premium market off on our resident "clown." This fellow was a joke to the office staff and a question mark to the sales staff. We all wondered why he was hired in the first place and how he kept his job. But, he stayed with it and starting "selling," almost by accident, to the premium market. At the end of the year, he was among the top sales producers, and he was acting like the hottest salesman in town.

The guy couldn't sell, but selling in the premium market is different than selling in most other sales arenas. The premium market has many product shows. The buyers always attend these shows, make notes, collect samples and prices, and then leave. Rarely do they place orders at the show, except at year's end. When they need premiums, they call the vendor and place an order. Sometimes the vendor is out of stock, has had a price increase, or for some reason can't honor the order. The buyer then goes to his second choice, third choice, and so on down the line. It isn't what I consider selling, but it is sales dollars.

Naturally, if you are building a territory, you are busy and some of these opportunities will have to go wanting. However, if you get a few extra minutes in your day, use them constructively to check out the local military base, keep tabs on the various trade shows and fairs, or just think about the new and different markets in which your product might be sold.

16

THE COLD CALL

In many sales jobs, it becomes necessary to find new customers by cold calling. The very expression *cold calling* is intimidating, impersonal, and unfriendly. Most salespeople detest the idea of making cold calls. They find it somehow demeaning, humiliating, and all too often, unproductive. "I feel more like a push-cart peddler or a beggar than I do a salesman," my prize rookie once told me. "I talked with one fellow who denied he was the buyer, and I knew he was, but what could I say? The entire office staff was looking at me; some were snickering. I couldn't wait to get out of there! I was red in the face. It was so abasing. It was awful."

Naturally, I understood his reaction to a rude and probably stupid person. But I pointed out that he was trying to sell a legitimate product and that finding customers was part of the job. He had, I continued, no reason to be ashamed or embarrassed, and the kind of person who caused that embarrassment is not worthy of consideration. That buyer lacked a sense of self-worth. He was so insecure that he ducked meetings with salespeople, and by doing that he hoped to avoid having to make a decision.

Is that the kind of person you are allowing to control your future and your personal success? The secret to making a successful cold call is *attitude*. You must be quietly aggressive, friendly, prepared, and confident. When you hit the street to make cold calls, your armor is a thick skin and a sense of humor. You know that some people will abuse their positions of authority or responsibility. These people will treat all visitors in a rude, unbusinesslike way. You have probably encountered some customers who behave that way. Some accounts are open and friendly, and eager to learn about what is out there. These are the intelligent buyers, the ones who do their jobs properly. Others are reclusive, gruff, rude, and closed to new products and new ideas. Eventually, these buyers fail because they restrict themselves. They fall out of the loop and behind in the race and rarely command respect because down deep they don't respect themselves. When you are digging out new customers to buy your products, you are doing a service to your company, to yourself, and to the customer.

FACING THE FEAR OF COLD CALLING

Equestrians say that if you fall or are thrown off a horse, the best thing to do is immediately get back up on the horse. Let it know who is the boss and overcome any residual fear you may have. That is just common sense, isn't it? We overcome any fear by facing whatever it is that causes that fear. Children are afraid of the dark. More accurately, they fear what might be in the dark; they fear what they can't see. Suppose that some terrible apparition really did lurk in the darkness of your child's closet. Would the child be any less afraid if he or she could see that apparition clearly? Actually, yes. The movie E.T. illustrated that point very well. In the film a strange, scary, weird-looking alien was accepted by a young boy once they faced each other in the light. It was interesting to watch as the audience, initially repulsed by the alien's appearance, slowly accepted this repulsive-looking creature and even found it "cute." Cold calling becomes less frightening once we see what we face. So let's take a look.

Someone once said, "A stranger is a friend you haven't met yet," and that is very true. When we meet new people at a party, for example, we don't know anything about them — what they do, how mighty they may be in the social order, nothing. We enjoy their company, and they enjoy ours. At the end of the evening, we exchange telephone numbers and promise to stay in touch. Regrettably, we seldom do. But if we make that extra effort and call, we will, in all probability, gain a new friend.

Making a new business friend is somewhat like that. When you enter an office, shop, or store, or when you knock on the door of a residence, you may be about to make a new business friend. That is the attitude you must develop and carry with you. I have devised a ten-point list of attitude adjustments and ideas that every salesperson who is about to make a cold call should read and take to heart. As you look them over, perhaps other ideas will come to you.

THE TEN-POINT ATTITUDE ADJUSTMENT

1. Before every cold call, say, "I believe this call will result in my making a business friend." Repeat this several times to yourself.

2. Then say, "I am enthusiastic about my company and its products (or services). This contact needs my products and will want to know all about it."

3. "I know what I want to accomplish with this account. But on this visit, all I want to do is meet the buyer, learn his or her name, and gather all the information I can about the business."

4. "If I meet a rude person, I will try to consider the source and reasons for the rudeness. I will overcome that rudeness by kindness, understanding, and love. And I will have fun making a new friend."

5. "I will be sincere and honest in my approach. I will not exaggerate the value of my product; instead, I will stress the *need* for it. I will ask that show my interest in helping this prospect improve the operation of the business and that will tell me why this business needs our products."

6. "I will not take rejection as a personal affront; it never really is personal."

7. "If the buyer can't see me today, I will understand. After all, I was not expected, and I may be calling at an inconvenient time. I will try to arrange a solid appointment to return at a time convenient to us both."

8. "I will record the name and title of the person I saw or have arranged to see. If unable to see the decision maker at this time, I will gladly meet with the assistant, but I will set an appointment to see the decision maker next time."

9. "If I am unable to see the buyer today, I will make my next call within three days. I want the impression I made to remain fresh in the minds of those I met."

10. "I am a likable person. This buyer will like me and will want our products."

Always make post-call notes. Record the name of the person you want to see and indicate which products appear to fit into the account's operation. But don't make a firm judgment in that regard. Never prejudge what the accounts might be interested in or how much or how little they might buy. Make your initial presentation based on what you believe will be of most interest, but remain flexible and leave your options open.

The second time you call, the prospect is no longer a cold call. The receptionist will recognize you and know your name. If you have an appointment, the buyer will know you were aggressive enough to have made an effort to see him or her earlier. That will be appreciated. If you left a brochure along with your business card, you have the start for your presentation: "Mr. Prospect, when I last visited here, I left a brochure like this one. Did you have a chance to look it over?"

If your second call is without an appointment, the buyer will probably feel an obligation to see you. The receptionist or secretary will say, "Mr. Blogett was here Monday, and is here again waiting to see you." The buyer might then think, "I better see what this person wants. I'll get rid of him." Take the initiative. When you are led into the office, shake hands and immediately say, "Mr. Prospect, I appreciate your seeing me without an appointment. I wanted to introduce myself to you because I believe we should be doing business. When I last visited here, I gathered some information that led me to believe that. I know you use an imported widget that is expensive and rated AA. Our unit is rated AAA and costs much less. I would like to make an appointment to come back and make a full presentation next week."

I know that many would disagree with this oblique and mild first contact, but I have discovered that a little extra time invested at the outset will set the stage for a nonadversarial interview. The buyer expects an aggressive, perhaps overbearing salesperson, but instead, receives a professional, low-keyed representative who wishes to arrange a selling appointment. The buyer might ask, "Why can't we handle this now?" or something to that effect. I recommend you resist that invitation. "I have a full schedule today, Mr. Prospect. I took a few minutes to stop by because I am anxious to talk with you. I had no idea you would be able to see me today. Would next Monday at ten fit with your schedule?" This establishes you as a busy, well-organized salesperson, who is interested in building a customer list, but isn't desperate for business — he has other fish to fry.

The third point in the attitude adjustment list is often neglected or ignored by many salespeople. If you know what you want to accomplish and what you want to sell to each account you visit, your success ratio will greatly improve. This sounds a bit silly, I know, but the truth is that salespeople (especially those who allow themselves to become bored with the routine of working a territory) often look for "targets of opportunity." They "shotgun" the account; that is, they throw everything at the buyer with the faint hope that something will appeal to him or her. It doesn't work.

Instead, if the representative does some homework, knows which products will fit the account's operation, understands the competition and its products, and establishes a need (impossible with the shotgun approach), the chances of selling the new account are excellent.

DEVELOPING A POSITIVE ATTITUDE

I stated earlier that attitude will lead you to success when making cold calls. Let's change that to attitude and preparation. Your attitude can be positively affected if you view your effort as a positive contribution to building your territory. Without a transfusion of new prospects, your business will dry up. Cold calls are important to your growth as a salesperson and with the proper attitude and preparation, they can be enjoyable.

Follow these three simple steps, and I believe you will have a different and more positive attitude toward making cold calls. To begin, let's call them new calls instead of cold calls.

1. Carefully consider the area of the territory you intend to cover and draw up an itinerary for the day or days you will be making new calls. Knowing where the prospects are located will allow you to cover more ground, make your day go faster, and eliminate the frustration of searching for addresses.

2. Examine the list of prospects and eliminate those that you *know* have bad credit or whose buying offices are outside your territory. Eliminate accounts that are obviously too small to place even a minimum order or too big for your company to serve, and rule out accounts that are captive (subsidiary companies who are supplied by parent companies). Finally, although you may be tempted, do not make calls outside your assigned territory.

3. Develop an introduction that will grab the attention and arouse the interest of the buyer. Instead of saying, "Mr. Prospect, my name is Chris Greenberg, and I represent Mega Trends Industries," say, "Mr. Prospect, I have a product that could save your company thousands of dollars in production costs every year. It's proven, guaranteed, and — believe it or not — underpriced. May I have a

few minutes of your time next Tuesday to explain how it will work for you?" Using this suggestion, can you imagine a buyer saying, "No, I don't want to know how to save my company thousands of dollars each year"?

Following these three steps will help you develop a positive attitude toward making new calls. You will know where you are headed. Your days will be planned, not catch-as-catch-can, but organized and productive. You will be confident that the people you are trying to reach are, in all probability, good potential accounts. You will be motivated and energized. Finally, you will know what you are going to say. You will control the brief interview. You will whet the appetite of the prospect with your attention-getting opening remarks. The buyer will want to know more, and you will be in charge.

OVERCOMING RESISTANCE

Buyers are busy people, especially in today's business world when most are overloaded. Some are doing the work formerly done by two or three buyers. In order to do their job, many establish open buying days when anyone is welcome to visit. Others barricade themselves behind a phalanx of secretaries, assistants, receptionists, and others — all of whom are determined to protect the buyer from the likes of you.

When you make a new call, you don't yet know the buying decision maker. Until you meet the buyer, treat everyone you talk to as if he or she were the buyer. Most will quickly advise you they are not the buyer and will tell you with whom you should be talking.

Most of the people who stand between you and the buyer are following instructions; a few act on their own. The ones who follow instructions have been told, "Screen everyone who calls to see me. I don't have time to talk to every Tom, Dick, and Harry." If the screeners are lax in their duties, you can be sure they will hear about it in short order. So cooperate. Never try to disguise your purpose for calling. If you do get an interview, that subterfuge will only anger the buyer and enrage the screener, and future contacts will be made difficult for you. Honesty and courtesy are the best policy.

SCREENER: May I help you?

SELLER: Yes, I sincerely hope so. My name is Chris Greenberg, and I represent Mega Trends Industries. I'd like a few moments of the buyer's time. Could you tell me his name and how I can reach him?

SCREENER: This is in regards to . . . ?

SELLER: I sell a product that will reduce production costs by thousands of dollars every year. I'm sure your buyer would like to know more about it.

SCREENER: Ms. Carlton is our buyer. But she is very busy today and won't be able to see you.

(If you get this sort of reply, you can be fairly sure the screener is acting on direct orders from Ms. Carlton, so don't try to force your way past.)

SELLER: I understand. Is that Eve Carlton?

(Just another way of getting the first name.)

SCREENER: No, it's Teri Carlton.

Seller: Could you tell me how I can arrange an appointment to see Teri?

SCREENER: She makes her own appointments, but you can reach her at 877-9087, extension 1242.

SELLER: Would she accept a call this afternoon?

SCREENER: No, she's very busy today. Why don't you call tomorrow morning?

SELLER: Thank you, I will. And your name is . . . ?

SCREENER: Bob Rogers. I'm Teri's assistant.

SELLER: Nice to meet you, Bob. I'd like to leave this information for Teri, and perhaps you'd like to look it over as well. Would you kindly tell Ms. Carlton to expect my call tomorrow before ten o'clock?

You may be surprised to discover that most screeners really want to help. No underlings will take upon themselves the responsibility of turning you away. They are only doing what they are told to do, so don't be angry with them. However, if a screener says, "We wouldn't be interested," do not accept that answer. The screener doesn't have the power or authority to determine what the buyer might be interested in buying. If you get that sort of answer, stay cool and calm, but reply as follows:

THE COLD CALL

Seller: I misunderstood. You are the buyer or the assistant buyer?

Screener: No, but I know the buyer would have no interest in this. (*That alone is stupid; how could anyone know that?*)

Seller: I appreciate your opinion, but I have rarely met a buyer who is not interested in being able to save thousands of dollars in production costs. Could you tell me when Ms. Carlton will accept a telephone call?

Screener: Well, she can be reached in the mornings.

Seller: You've been very helpful and I appreciate it. Could I ask one last favor?

Screener: Of course, what it is?

Seller: Would you tell Ms. Carlton to expect my phone call tomorrow morning around nine o'clock?

By using this approach, you effectively defang the screener firmly and politely. Posing the question, "Could I ask one last favor?" has made the screener your ally. Subconsciously, he feels he has worked well with you and will carry your message to Ms. Carlton, probably with his good impressions: "Mr. Greenberg will be phoning you tomorrow morning. He's with Mega Trends Industries and has a product that looks like it has some potential. He seemed like a nice guy."

Honesty will save you time and gain cooperation. "Oh, you don't want Ms. Carlton, you want to see Hopkins in our production office. He buys all products connected with production. You'll find him in building 10-A just across the quadrangle. I'll call him and tell him you're coming over." This is the kind of cooperation and reward you get from being honest with a screener.

Use common sense in making new calls. Most businesspeople are busy setting up their day until around 9:30 in the mornings and are wrapping up things after 3:30 in the afternoons. This is not a hard and fast rule. Asking the screener when the buyer accepts telephone calls and makes appointments, record that information in your post-call notes.

Different industries have different business hours. Construction accounts like early appointments, as do companies and people engaged in agriculture. People who work at home are busy in the mornings getting the children off to school and in the afternoons preparing for their return. Professional people are usually difficult to schedule. Calling on doctors, dentists, and others is time-consuming and frustrating. I recommend an initial telephone contact.

With the possible exception of construction accounts, all of these accounts will have some screening procedure. Deal with nurses, secretaries, assistants, and all other screeners as you do with a commercial account — with honesty and openness.

Some salespeople place too much importance on screeners. Remember that these people are not buyers; they can't place an order and probably have little influence over the buyer. Be friendly, but remember their position and their responsibilities. Never take a "no" answer from them and don't try to sell them.

THE SCREENING BUYER

Some buyers may act as their own screeners. Some companies have a policy requiring the buyers to meet with everyone who calls. These buyers sometimes will try to get rid of you with a terse, prepackaged brush-off sentence or two. If that happens, cut them off at the pass. Stop them in mid-sentence, if necessary. "I know you're busy today, and I apologize for popping in like this, but we really do have something important to talk about. When can I arrange an appointment to demonstrate how this will serve your company?" You have now accomplished several objectives. You have brought them back to reality, arranged an appointment, and set the ground rules for the next meeting.

Another tactic that buyers may employ is seeing you, but continuing to do whatever they were doing before you came, such as shuffling papers, accepting telephone calls, or reading reports. If that happens, and it will, stop whatever you are saying and just sit there. Don't say a word until the activity stops and the buyer's attention is yours. The buyer might say, "Go ahead, I'm listening," but don't do it. He or she isn't listening and can't possibly absorb what you are saying while doing something else. Instead, say something like, "Mr. Prospect, I can see you are busy today, as I am. I appreciate your trying to squeeze me in, but this opportunity deserves your full attention. Please continue reading your report, and when you're finished, we'll have our visit." The buyer will do one of two things: Either set up an honest-to-goodness appointment or put the report aside and give you his or her full attention.

I had a salesman working for me who told me that when a buyer treated him like that, he would continue to talk, but would gradually lower his voice until he was almost whispering. He told me that buyers usually started asking, "What? What did you say?" and then would give him their full attention. I told my salesman that it may have worked for him, but I don't recommend it in a one-on-one situation. Most of the time the buyer will just tune you out and then give you some breezy answer, such as, "OK, if I have any interest, I'll call you." Whatever that means.

NETWORKING

Another method of cold calling (new calling) is by networking. We've all heard of the "old-boy network," but I'm talking about a network of your happy customers. Suppose Company X is a satisfied customer of yours and does business with Company Y, but you can't get Company Y started. Ask the Company X buyer to help out. Does she know the buyer of Company Y? She probably does and can set up a luncheon for the three of you. With the support and endorsement of Company X's buyer, Company Y will likely be open to your presentation.

Professional societies, social clubs, and some fraternal organizations can be good sources of new business. But remember that most of the members of these groups join in order to have fun and enjoy the camaraderie, while serving their community. When someone intrudes on that purpose, the results are usually not positive.

A few years ago, a friend of mine offered to arrange a golf game with the CEO of a major chain operation. This was an account I really wanted for some time, and the CEO turned out to be a warm and friendly fellow with a great sense of humor and a wicked slice. We got along very well until I started talking about how my products would benefit his stores. "Bill," he said in a friendly, but unmistakable way, "I never get in the way of my buyers. I'm sure you can understand why." That was it! He had said it all, and I felt embarrassed. I am sure the CEO felt cornered as though he had been set up. I really thought we could serve his stores, but I had rushed the entire process. If I had simply enjoyed the day and allowed things to take their natural course, most likely he would have asked me how he could help me. But I didn't, and he didn't.

Later, in the clubhouse after the game while we were enjoying a drink, he took me aside and promised to make sure I could present my program in the best possible way. I should have known better. I had regained my senses by then, and I thanked him, but asked that he not get involved. Unless the individual is a decision maker *at your level*, or if you are certain a major player will intercede (which is very rare), don't solicit help. His or her intervention only hurts your cause. Buyers will feel you have gone around them, over their head, and they will naturally resent it. Displaying their independence, the buyers will resist your efforts and probably will not buy from you.

If you meet someone at a fraternal gathering who says, "Call me next week, I think we could use your stuff," by all means call. But don't push yourself on these people. Don't try to make them feel obligated because you happen to belong to the same group. However, do use the group rosters to discover potential new customers. If, by chance, the buyers for those new customers belong to the same fraternal group, so much the better.

COLD CALL BRUSH OFFS

I actually enjoy cold calling (oops, I mean *new* calling). I like to meet new people and discover what their needs are. I like making new friends, but in our insular society, I find that more and more people are turning inward. We don't talk to our neighbors. Heck, some of us don't even talk to our own families! We watch TV or read a book, secure in our cocoons and protected from outside interference in our routine.

People have become abrupt with one another, so I suppose we shouldn't be surprised when a buyer is curt and compendious. Buyers who act in that manner are just trying to get back to their desks to reduce their pile of work. "Yeah, I've heard of your stuff. It's good quality, but the price is just too much for my customers. I've been in this business for years, and I know." Now that is a brush-off. Do they really know what their customers will buy? Is price ever a consideration?

If you accept the brush-off, you're out the door. But don't accept it. "My products are much more than price. Will you give me a few minutes of your time, to show you why people will pay for results? That's what we deliver — results!" What buyer is going to say, "No, I won't give you a few minutes. I don't want to learn"?

Another brush off is, "Never heard of your product. I only carry well-advertised merchandise." You can say, "OK, well, I'll get back to you when and if we begin an advertising campaign," or you can say, "I'm sure there are many customers who will seek out the highly advertised brands you carry, but I'm equally sure there are a greater number of customers who will want a product of high quality that will fit their budget. Are you willing to surrender that segment of the market?"

New calls give you an opportunity to sharpen your skills. You can make full presentations because the buyer doesn't know your goods. You can challenge the buyer's knowledge of your company's success and compare it to that of his competitors. New buyers may resist change simply because it is too much trouble: installing a new computer program, getting rid of existing stock, or training store personnel. "The in-stock merchandise is selling all right, why bother?" is often their attitude.

What are these buyers really saying? They are asking for affirmation. They want you to convince them that the trouble of switching vendors will be worthwhile. I witnessed just such an exchange once, and the salesperson was prepared. He pulled out a stack of letters from people who recommended our products. "These letters," he said, "are from people who use and highly recommend our products. I didn't pay them to write these letters, and I didn't control what they wrote. They simply wanted to share with you the wonderful success they've had with our line." Cleverly, he added, "Advertising is paid for; anyone can buy advertising and say anything — you can't buy wholehearted recommendations."

The new prospect said, "I like your stuff, but ABC gives me a bigger margin of profit."

"Are you more interested in margin or dollars?" my salesperson asked.

"Huh? What's the difference?"

"The difference is more money in your pocket. You can't spend margin; you can only spend dollars. Here, let me show you what I mean." With that, the salesperson showed how a larger margin could mean less money. It wasn't a trick, although the buyer thought it was, at least for a little while. Eventually, he came around and became an excellent customer.

I have covered only some of the objections you probably will get from first-time cold-call buyers. There are many others. Be prepared to overcome the most common objections: Your product costs too much (or too little), we only carry advertised goods, I get a bigger margin with XYZ, I've never heard of your company, I've heard bad things about your company, and the all-time favorite, I've never had any calls for your products; when I do, I'll give you a call. That last remark is worthy of more space and consideration, and we'll deal with it in the next chapter.

I've tried to emphasize how important making cold calls is to your growth and to the growth of your territory. You grow as a salesperson because you become more confident in your skills and more in control of any selling situation.

Obviously, your territory grows as you add new customers. Making new calls can be interesting and rewarding if you are well-prepared and if your attitude is strong and positive. Draw up a good itinerary and stick to it. Know what you want to accomplish with every call you make, and don't push for a sale on the first call unless the opportunity is obvious. Reread this chapter the evening before you make your new calls, review the pointers, and have fun.

17

SELLING SENSE, COMMON SENSE

Selling is a dynamic profession that offers new challenges and new opportunities every day. Like other professions, its members rely on a foundation of skills and techniques. The outstanding members, however, are never content to rest on the foundation. They build on it by learning new skills, exploring new techniques, taking risks, and venturing into the unknown. In this chapter, we'll explore situations, techniques, and ideas that are grounded in common sense, but that are too frequently overlooked by all but the outstanding salespeople.

DEALING WITH NEW BUYERS

As with almost everything else in our world, buying becomes routine and boring after a time. Buyers become jaded with the tiresome and repetitive duties they have to perform. This is just one reason why merchandise managers switch product categories for their buyers. The theory is that if a buyer can buy sports gear, he or she can buy kitchenware or (fill in the blank), and the new challenges will keep the buyer alert and stimulated. That is basically, but not completely or uniformly, true. The buying procedure is the same, but the "feel" for a particular category may not be as easy for a buyer to transfer. Some buyers just seem to have a penchant for one category over another, and it is regrettable when they switch product categories. But the thinking about stimulation is, on balance, true.

Calling on a new buyer is almost like making a cold call. The representative doesn't know anything about the new buyer except his or her name. The first, introductory call can be critical. New buyers usually have their own ideas about the decisions their predecessor made, and having pride in their own abilities, they plan to improve on the record of the old buyer. Amazingly, some look on the vendors as an extension of the departed buyer and seem to hold a grudge against them! Moreover, taking over a new product category is often one of the few times these buyers really can make a decision based on what they think is best.

A good friend of mine was having a drink at the New Otani Hotel in Tokyo with the buyer for a national chain. My friend's company had been supplying the chain with a photo case for several years, and sales were excellent. As the evening wore on, the two were discussing how they might improve on an already strong market position. Finally, the buyer asked if his company could get — just temporarily — a lower price. He explained that with the lower cost, he could eat up the competition and control the market for that particular product. The buyer promised the volume would be substantially increased, and both parties should do very well. It was, he assured my friend, "a win-win situation." Either the Suntory bourbon or the atmosphere persuaded my friend, and the deal was soon agreed upon.

For almost a year sales were strong, but not as strong as the buyer had promised. Still, the account was one of the best around, and the hope was that the program would finally develop as expected. Then, without warning, the buyer was switched to white goods, and a new buyer took over photo accessories. This newcomer was experienced in women's wear and had done well in that category, and this move was considered a promotion, a reward for a job well done. Because orders on "required" goods came automatically by fax, my friend didn't pay much attention to the change. He had planned to introduce himself after the dust had settled, and the new buyer had had a chance to establish herself.

However, when the orders didn't come in as expected, he decided he should make a quick visit to the buying offices. His old buyer-buddy assured him there was nothing to worry about, and the two of them went to the new buyer's office to discover the cause for the delay. Both men were stunned when the new buyer announced she was *dropping* the line! Dropping a line that was one of the top sellers in the department? Dropping a line that had proven itself for years? It didn't make sense, but despite all arguments from the old buyer and my friend, the line was dropped! No honeymoon, just a quick karate chop.

What had my friend done wrong? First, he should have immediately called and arranged an appointment as soon as he heard about the buyer change. At the meeting, he should have had the records of sales and profits compared to projections (sales and profits *exceeded* projections!). With that kind of approach, I am sure he could have convinced the new buyer at least to forestall any changes in the basic product mix. When a buyer change is made, as I stated before, your first contact is almost the same as making a cold call. The salesperson has to go through the selling mechanics, resell the product to the new buyer, *establish the need*, and answer all questions or possible objections. The new buyer has to be sold just as the previous buyer was. My friend didn't even attempt to do these things until it was too late. That's what can happen when you become overconfident and lazy.

Other things can happen when new buyers take over. Demands for lower prices, longer terms, and relaxed return policies are almost always advanced by the new buyers. They all try to make a bigger splash than the previous buyer, and they're not too choosy about how they do it. They have no ties to the salespeople or their companies. All "IOUs" are voided and the new buyers don't owe anybody. A buyer switch is sometimes an open-door opportunity to vendors who have been banging on the door and getting nowhere.

I look at a buyer change as starting from scratch. Well, that's not quite true. Sometimes — in fact, most times — no changes are made for awhile. Business may go along as before or may even improve. Nevertheless, you should be concerned about buyer changes and immediately offer your services to the new person.

As with a brand-new account, the *need* for the product should be proven to the new buyers. In this instance, you are taking on the role of educator, not salesperson. Teach the new buyers why their department needs your goods and why your line benefits the consumers. Support your case with positive sales figures and profit records. Prove that consumers like and will continue to buy the merchandise. Prove that your company has a profitable product to sell.

TRANSFER THE FEELING OF OWNERSHIP

Most sales trainers will tell you that the feeling of ownership is important in selling. The old "puppy dog" close is based on ownership. Let's briefly review this remarkably effective close. The vendor suggests that the buyer take the puppy home to his kids "just to see how they'll all get along." Needless to say, they get along just fine, and when Dad or Mom tries to take the puppy back to the kennel, the kids go bonkers, cry and scream, and won't allow it. The puppy dog close can be used with almost any product.

A Midwest appliance store in Iowa set national sales records for color television sets when those products were new to the marketplace. The stores would deliver the sets to the home for a ten-day trial period. After that time, with the family completely delighted with color as compared to black and white, the store would call and ask when they could pick up the set. Of course, very few allowed that to happen. When the marketing team from a major manufacturer's headquarters went to Iowa to find out how this small city dealer could outsell the big city dealers, the owner explained by asking, "Did you ever bring home a puppy dog, let your children play with it, and struggle through the first few nights of its whining because it missed its mother? Have you ever picked up a puppy and felt that fat little tummy resting in your lap as you read the newspaper? Well, if you have, you've got a dog at home now. That's the way I sell television sets."

The feeling of ownership is a powerful selling tool.

USES THE SENSES IN SELLING

Smart salespeople utilize the *senses* when selling. Not only will they give the product to the buyer to hold (thereby transferring ownership), but also they will use sensual words (words that evoke the senses). "Mr. Buyer, I'm going to *show* you an interesting product that is new to the market. But first, I'd like you to *feel* the difference between these two fabrics." This opening immediately gets the buyer involved in the presentation. The seller transfers ownership by handing the product to the buyer. Even if the buyer responds negatively, "I don't feel any difference," a dialogue is started and an opportunity to sell begins.

"You don't feel a difference? Most people do immediately. But let me *show* you why this is different from any fabric you have in your store." The seller then takes half of the fabric and draws the buyer's attention to it by using the sense of sight. "*See* the difference in the texture and *look* at the close, crossed weave." The buyer will examine the fabric carefully, perhaps trying to find a way to discredit the representative's presentation. The representative knows the buyer is just fishing, trying to determine if his or her objections have merit. The buyer knows that these are the questions the customers will ask, and so will the department managers. The buyer's challenges and questions are a way of getting the answers that are necessary to justify the purchase. The salesperson may continue to appeal to the senses by rustling the fabric and asking the buyer to *listen* to the silk-like sound, and so forth.

Involving the senses in your presentation requires buyers to become physically, actively involved. They have to *touch* in order to *feel* the difference in the fabric. They must *look* to *examine* the weave. They must *listen* to *hear* the rustle. In other words, they must get involved, no matter how reticent they may be. By accomplishing this, you prompt them to ask questions. Once the questions start, you are well on your way to a sale.

Bringing the senses into the presentation is possible in almost any situation. "Just *smell* the rich, dark chocolate baked into these cookies. Doesn't that remind you of your mother's kitchen? And *look* how soft they are. Now *taste* one." "Can you *hear* the engine? Can you *feel* the smooth shifting of gears?"

A friend of mine, selling an orange-flavored drink, was having a tough time getting it into grocery stores and chains. His product was tasty, rich in vitamins and minerals, priced right, and looked just like fresh-squeezed orange juice. But his competition was nationally known, brand-identified, and vigorously advertised. My friend was stuck on dead center until one evening he saw an ad on TV about the aroma of fresh coffee. In the television ad, a college kid was returning home from school early one morning for Christmas vacation. Greeted by his baby sister, the two tiptoed into the kitchen and brewed coffee. The rich aroma of fresh-brewed coffee awakened the parents, and a warm family scene was enacted.

"Why couldn't my orange-flavored breakfast drink do the same sort of thing?" he wondered. Naturally, the smell of orange-flavored drinks will not fill the air as will coffee, but a blindfold test would work. A few days later, armed with a blindfold, three competitors' products, paper cups, and his own product, he called on a leading grocery chain headquarters. "Bob," he said to the buyer, "you know my product by now. It looks and tastes like fresh orange juice, and it has even more vitamins than regular orange juice." "Yeah, I know all that, but . . ." the buyer started to say. My friend held up his hand. "Even more impressive, my product *smells* like fresh oranges." Then, pouring his competitors' products into three cups and his own into a specially marked cup, he asked the buyer to put on the blindfold. "I'd like you to judge for yourself which smells like fresh-squeezed orange juice."

The buyer objected at first; he thought it was a little silly. But it was fun, too, so he finally agreed to the test. Needless to say, he picked my friend's product — as did several other people in the office when the buyer invited them to take the test. Now, I don't know how many people buy an orange drink because it *smells* like fresh oranges, but the buyer was impressed enough to place an order. Today, you'll find that product in every grocery store in America. Using the senses makes sense.

Some people compare selling with show business, and this story did have a show business flair. In a way, I suppose, salespeople are performing. Drama is certainly a part of selling, and entertainment is an important extra ingredient when you sell. Our business is not and should not be as staid as the products or industries we represent. Little "touches" can add a dimension to your presentation that will stick in the minds of the buyers. For example, a sales representative I know carries an electronic flash sample in a royal purple, velvet jewelry bag. When he makes his presentation, the bag is set in front of the customer, unopened. This intrigues the buyer and raises interest. "You can almost hear them saying, 'What's in the bag? It must be beautiful and valuable,'" the representative told me. At the proper time he takes the flash unit out of the bag with a slight flourish. But the show isn't over yet. Holding the flash in a caress, as one would a precious jewel or fine watch, he offers it to the buyer to hold (transfer of ownership). This technique must work. The representative has sold more flash units than anyone else in his company for the past five years!

SELLING TO GROUPS

Selling to a group can be an awkward and difficult job. In many respects, the term *group selling* is inaccurate. We may be presenting our products or services to a group, but in reality we are *selling* to the one or two people in the group who are the leaders or decision makers, the ones who exercise the most influence over the group.

A sales presentation is normally given to a group when the company is trying to decide on a product or service that will affect a large number of people. This employer-appointed committee may be charged with the responsibility of evaluating a health insurance plan or of determining how quickly and easily employees can learn to operate new equipment. A buyer may want to know if employees will have difficulty learning how to operate more complicated machinery, or if the weight of a new unit will be too cumbersome for people to manipulate easily.

This sort of group selling and teaching is very old. In fact, group "seminars" may date back to the early cave dwellers. On the smoky walls of ancient caves in France can be seen carved illustrations that demonstrate how to hunt certain animals. Imagine the tribal chieftain or the best hunter in the community teaching the others the best techniques. No doubt, some among the tribe would disagree, and the chieftain would have to "sell" the methods on the ancient "chalkboards."

Recall our discussion of multilevel marketing operations — a form of marketing that is gaining adherents almost daily. The operators of these businesses must address large groups of potential participants. Most feel that they must add glamour and excitement to the presentation to motivate the audience members to come forward and sign on the dotted line. This is a first-close business; the operator has one chance and makes the most of it. Some overdo the theatrics, frighten off potential prospects, and cheapen the presentation. But enough people are sold by these methods that no real changes are taking place. If operators can get their base group signed on, they make small fortunes.

THE COMMON SENSE APPROACH

Perhaps the finest group presentation I have ever witnessed was given before an audience of about sixty people, all registered nurses, the majority of whom were women. As with all groups, the audience is interested or the people wouldn't have bothered to come, but most are skeptical and wary. The product was a wrinkle cream that was purported to make grandmothers look like teenagers. By way of introduction, a woman, who was dressed in a medical-type smock, explained the ingredients, what each was meant to do, and how natural and harmless the formula was. She then showed slides of people in the "before and after" mode, detailing each slide with information about the age of the person, health habits (heavy smokers, we were told, wrinkle early), type of work (outdoor or indoor), and even ethnic background. She gave an interesting, fast-paced talk, and everyone seemed enthralled. She then opened the floor to questions.

The question-and-answer period is a critical juncture in all group presentations. Speakers can quickly lose the audience unless a lively and interesting discussion takes place. In this case, a woman in the back of the room asked a daring question, "Can you demonstrate the cream on me, here and now?" If anyone had even a modicum of interest, it is unlikely that he or she would have left then. The speaker eyed the questioner with a slightly cocked eye (which brought the expected ripple of laughter). "I was hoping someone would ask for a treatment. Come on up here and one of our cosmeticians will show you all how to apply the cream."

The tricky part in any group presentation is getting a group member to finally make a decision all alone. You can't afford to lose the "herd mentality." In a group, most people will follow their neighbor's action. If the person sitting next to you signs up, the chances are good that you, too, will sign. Some operators use *shills*, people who pretend to be attendees, who stir the audience, and who lead the group to the sign-up tables. These people are, in fact, employed by the operators. This may seem devious and a tad shady, but I prefer it to the arm-twisting and hard-sell methods that so many use. A good example of the use of shills can be seen at the gaming tables in Las Vegas and Atlantic City. Operators never allow a craps table or 21 table to be unoccupied, so they hire shills to play to encourage "real" gamblers to approach the tables. Casino operators know that gamblers are timid about approaching an empty table.

Back to the wrinkle-cream presentation. At this point, another woman, also dressed in a medical-type smock, stepped onto the stage and draped the volunteer and prepared her for a treatment. As she did so, she invited anyone "who might be interested" to come up and watch. Immediately, everyone got up and crowded around the test subject as the cream was applied. During the application, the cosmetician talked about the benefits and features of the "Miracle Cream." "The problem with such a demonstration," she warned, "was that most people forget how the subject looked before the cream was applied."

I thought this was a cop-out, but as it turned out, it only intensified the crowd's interest. A warm towel was placed over the face of the volunteer, and we waited for fifteen minutes while the cream worked its magic. During that time, brochures were handed out, and the floor was open to more questions. Not one minute of dead air was allowed. Every minute was filled with questions and information. If a question was stupid or weak, it was quickly answered and dismissed. The interest level was sky high! I noticed that questions with more general interest or those that underscored a product benefit were given more time and attention.

Finally, the towel was removed, the volunteer's hair was rearranged (it had been under a shower cap), and she was shown to the audience. It was amazing! She actually did look years younger, and I felt right then that this product was going to be very successful.

At this point, the woman in charge asked the audience a question: "How old do you think I am? Don't spare me; be honest." Guesses ranged from forty to forty-seven years of age. She smiled and then said, "I'll have a surprise for you before you leave this evening." What could that mean? She was older? Younger? We were all going to get free samples? What was the surprise? We would just have to wait to find out (and that was, of course, the whole idea). She now introduced the main speaker, the multilevel marketing operator, in glowing terms.

Instead of the carnival-type pitchman we have come to expect from these operations, this fellow was suave, businesslike, and low-key. "Could I see a show of hands, please? I want to know how many professional salespeople are in the audience." Not one hand was raised. "Splendid," he almost shouted, "because we are not looking for salespeople! We don't want you to sell anything." This, of course, caused a buzz in the room, and many relieved sighs were heard. "Let me pose a question. What would you do if you had a big nose and nothing, no surgical process or any other medical procedure, could correct that problem? Everything else about you was attractive: beautiful eyes, glowing skin, even white teeth, radiant hair — and that big nose right in the middle."

There was a ripple of laughter which, I'm sure, was expected. "Now," he continued, "you meet a person who says, 'I have a cream here — it will you cost $75 for just six ounces, it's expensive, but I unconditionally guarantee that with just one application, your nose will be reduced to be in proper proportion to your face. If it doesn't work exactly as I promise, I'll refund your money.' Would you buy the cream?" Now he picked out a person in the second row. Pointing at her, he asked, "Would you?" There was a giggle here and there as we all waited for the answer.

Finally, she nodded in the affirmative, but he said, "I can't hear you." She replied, "Yes." But it wasn't loud enough for the speaker. He said over and over, "I can't hear you," until her stage fright was gone. Then laughing as heartily as the others in the audience, she almost screamed, "Yes!" Then, milking the situation for all it was worth, he asked, "Yes what?"

"Yes, I would buy it!"

Now he pointed to another and another and got "Yes" answers from all over the room. "Would you promise me you would buy that product?" he asked everyone in general. And the entire room erupted in a loud, "Yes, we'd buy it!" This entire exchange was done in a lighthearted way, but at the same time it was getting the message across in an extremely effective way.

"The cream you saw demonstrated a few minutes ago will eliminate wrinkles from your face and body — that is the guarantee and my promise to you. I guarantee it, and the company guarantees it, unconditionally, and *(he paused for dramatic effect)*, you saw the proof for yourself right here tonight. I want each of you to take a jar home and try it yourself. We will require a refundable deposit, but I'm confident no refunds will be asked because the stuff really works. I promised earlier that you would not have to sell anything — and you won't. Just a moment ago, the consensus was that all of you would have bought that nose-reducing cream, right?" When there was no response, he asked his question again. Once more, the room rocked with a loud, "Yes!"

"What else would you do if you had a big nose, and the cream worked its magic for you?" He didn't wait for an answer, "You would tell your friends, your relatives, and your coworkers — everyone with a big nose — all about it. People would ask what miracle had reduced your big nose, and you would share with them the good news. Isn't that right?" Again, he pointed to the woman in the second row and repeated his question. Naturally, she responded with a loud "Yes."

"Of course, you would. We all want to share good things with the people we care about. That is what this is all about: sharing the good news. Take the cream home tonight, try it on yourself and on anyone else, get a good night's sleep, and tomorrow you'll see a remarkable difference. Then, when you've seen it work for you, when you see what a fantastic product it is, when you are convinced it works just as I say it will, then get your starter kit. Share the good news. There's no selling. Just tell your friends, relatives, and others what wonderful things, what miracles, this little jar can perform. Probably you won't have to tell anyone, because people will ask, 'What has happened to you?' 'You look wonderful!' 'Did you have a facelift?' If there were ever a product that sells itself, I hold it in my hand." He stepped a few paces back and repeated, "I hold it in my hand."

Then, the woman who had asked everyone to guess her age came back on stage. She flashed a slide onto the screen: it was her picture, but she was wrinkled and tired-looking. "That was me, just last week, before I used XYZ cream. Earlier, when I asked how old you thought I might be, the oldest guess was forty-seven. Now how old do you think I am?"

"Fifty," shouted one woman. "Fifty-five," said another.

"Most people think I'm in my early forties. Actually, I'm fifty-nine years old; here is my driver's license if you'd care to see for yourself. This cream really is a miracle in a jar, and I want everyone to share in that miracle."

It was a powerful presentation. Everyone in the audience was involved, entertained, occupied, and, most important, convinced. Of the sixty attendees, I think only four or five failed to sign up that night.

ANALYZING THE PRESENTATION

Why was that group presentation so strong? *Involvement*! Everyone was listening; some were asked to give replies, and they led the others to get involved; they were enjoying themselves and having fun; they belonged. The speakers had taken away the feeling of fear. Members of the group had lost the feeling of captivity that is so common in these situations. They lost the fear of being strong-armed into buying something. This was no longer a room of strangers, but a group with a common interest and purpose. The presentation was logical, yet very emotional. I was struck by the fact that the need was cleverly established by using an example of a *different* beauty problem (the big nose). That eliminated the need to embarrass anyone, by singling out someone in the audience with a wrinkled appearance. Before it was over, we all knew he was really saying, "You have wrinkles and I will guarantee they will be gone tomorrow."

Were the members of the group being asked to sell? Of course, but in a real sense, selling is sharing information with others. The key speaker was saying, "If you are convinced, you can convince others — and you will want to do that." Isn't that what selling is all about? Being convinced and wanting to convince others?

COMMITTEE SELLING

Some group selling is done before a small, select number of people who are considered experts in a particular field. These experts will be difficult and even hostile at times, because they are individually and collectively trying to establish their worth. Their questions will be thoughtful and tough, and your answers had better be just as thoughtful. The leader or chairperson of the group is the one to whom you should direct most of your presentation, without totally ignoring the other members. He or she will have the most power in the group, and probably the other members will adhere to his or her judgment.

When you sell to a committee, illustrations, charts, graphs, and similar audiovisual aids are highly recommended. Involvement is vital in all presentations, and even more vital (if that is possible) in group sales. Like the multilevel marketing operator, single out an apparently friendly member and direct your first questions there. Then, point to another member and ask a question. Don't be afraid to tell people to speak up. The more resounding "Yes!" responses you get, the closer you will be to your sale.

Prior to all group presentations, except those in which the group members will sign up or buy right then and there, ask the group organizer, the chairperson, or the person in charge if you can expect an answer immediately. If too much time elapses between the presentation and the decision, individual group members begin to dissect the presentation and question everything. Without your presence, without your being able to answer questions and defend your position, your chances of making a sale greatly diminish.

Some members of committees (usually newly appointed members) try to establish themselves as brainy, wise, and valuable. These people are the most likely to question the tiniest, least important points you've made and challenge every statement. They do this not to reach an informed decision, but to inflate their own importance to the group. If you allow these people to sucker you into their pointless discussions, they will destroy or at least obscure the main points you've worked so hard to establish. Their nonsense will kill the sale or, at the least, delay the decision. For this reason alone, it makes sense to poll each group member after every point is made. "Are there any questions? Does everyone agree to this?" These kinds of questions — the same ones that a salesperson uses in a one-on-one situation — close the escape hatches and set up the close.

Weaker members of the group will go along with the majority (the "herd mentality") or the dominant members. Usually a few members of the group will control the questioning and make themselves known by their demeanor. It is to these people you will direct your most telling arguments.

The longer you must wait between your presentation and the decision, the less are your chances for success. If you are allowed to close and get a firm decision immediately after your presentation, your chances are good.

"I believe I have established a need for my product, and I've demonstrated how you (your company, your organization) will benefit. Are there any gray areas I haven't completely touched on? Some question I haven't answered to your satisfaction — or, perhaps, an area we haven't touched on?" Wait for an answer or watch for a frown or a look that might mean that some group member has a comment or concern. You will probably get a question or two, which you will answer and expand upon. Once there are no additional questions, be candid: "Your chairperson has promised me I would have an answer tonight, so I'd like to poll the group." Go from person to person until you get a majority. If the vote is negative, ask each negative voter for a reason. Usually, you'll find the negative vote is unfounded and based on a simple objection that can easily be overcome. If you find the objection is major, go back and establish the need — always go back to the need. Then, if necessary, review the entire presentation.

USING VISUALS

We all agree with the well-known saying attributed to the Chinese, "One picture is worth a thousand words." We are told from our earliest years that "seeing is believing." Why is it, then, that so many intelligent salespeople fail to use visual selling tools and methods? In the wrinkle-cream anecdote, the entire audience was involved in a *visual* experience. They saw for themselves how effective the cream was, and that visual evidence stimulated them to buy.

Several years ago, during one of the many diet crazes that have swept the nation, a new product was reaching the market almost daily. A colleague of mine was introducing a weight-loss formula and was complaining about getting lost in the blizzard of products. He was, he assured me, happy to have a small piece of the market, and had set his sights on Southern California. Even with this limited market, he still felt the competitive pressure of every giant company that had millions of dollars in advertising backing it up.

My colleague had a weight problem of his own. Standing 5'7" tall, he weighed almost 225 pounds! These are dangerous dimensions and an absolute killer to someone who is trying to sell diet products; so my friend decided to take his own product and lose weight.

Busy with my own accounts, I didn't see him again for some time. When I did, I barely recognized him! He weighed about 165 pounds and looked great, except for one thing. His clothes hung on him like a tarpaulin; he looked comical. He could turn his head without moving his tie at all, because his neck was now fifteen inches and the shirt collar was seventeen and one-half! His trousers were so baggy that he reminded me of a circus clown. "Bobby, you look great, but . . ." I never got to finish my sentence.

"I know, Bill," he smiled, "I look and feel like a nitwit, but I have a call to make on chain headquarters today. The buyer hasn't seen me since last summer when I first tried to sell him the formula, and he turned me down flat. This is my way of visually demonstrating how well the formula works." I pointed out that wearing a smartly tailored suit might illustrate the point just as well, or even better, but he waved me off. "This is much more dramatic. Buyers are always so impressed they call others in to show me off. I haven't missed a sale since I started using this prop," he said. Who was I to argue with success?

Although I thought (and still believe) that my friend was extreme, there is no denying that he was using visual methods to demonstrate his product. I recall seeing a well-known and formerly rotund actor demonstrating how effective his diet aid worked by modeling his old trousers. I've often wondered if, somehow, my friend's idea didn't get back to Madison Avenue.

Whatever product you sell, use visuals to help. It may take a little thought and preparation, but it can be done. Recently, a salesperson called at my home to sell me a fire alarm system. He was awkward and unsure of himself, and the presentation wasn't going well. I was anxious to have a good system installed and knew nothing about how a good system works. I was already sold. I recognized the need, and now it was just a matter of finding the best system for my family and learning how it worked. No matter how many questions I asked, I could never seem to get the answers I wanted. The poor fellow stumbled and mumbled through meaningless statistics and boring facts concerning the cost of fires.

I was about to terminate the interview when he took a small model home from his sample case. Suddenly, he became animated and excited as he pointed out the tiny replicas of heat detectors in every high point in the model house. Then, after asking my permission, he set a small fire in the basement of the model house. Almost instantly, the tiny detectors activated and a shrill sound filled the air. The salesperson then explained that something called "superheated air" rises rapidly to the ceilings, which is why the heat detectors are installed there. I was impressed and asked a few additional questions about battery life, standby battery systems, and cost. These he answered easily, and today I have his company's system installed in my home. Without the visual aid that this salesperson utilized, almost as an afterthought, I would never have considered buying his product.

Was this salesperson's presentation effective? From the standpoint of making the sale, it was. In actuality, it wasn't. Although the need was recognized by me (the buyer), it is never wise to assume that the need is known. The salesperson didn't even attempt to establish need. His manner showed an uncertainty about his company and its products. This fellow needed a crutch to help him through the presentation. That crutch was a visual aid. Without it, he would have been on the street in a very short time. Over my wife's protests, I took a few minutes to advise him on how he might improve his presentations. I hope it "took."

COMBINING COMMON SENSE AND TAG-ON SALES

A wise person once said, "The interesting thing about common sense is, it's not common." Anyone who has ever engaged in any kind of business activity knows that to be true. It isn't that folks are stupid; it's just that we all have so much on our plates that we overlook the obvious.

Take, for example, the obvious add-on sale (sometimes called the *tag-on*). In the grocery business, certain foods are packaged or displayed together to encourage a higher per-unit sale. Chinese food lends itself to this marketing technique. For instance, a package of fried noodles is shrink-wrapped to a can of chop suey. The two products are served together, so why not sell them together? Why not, indeed?

Offhand I could give you at least a dozen reasons why that doesn't make marketing sense, but from a certain standpoint it makes perfectly good sense. If the chop suey and noodles were sold as individual products, the per unit sale would be smaller but the profit margin would be greater. However, the seller risks losing a sale by marketing in that way. A consumer might buy Great Wall chop suey, but switch to Dynasty noodles. To assure selling both products, the manufacturer packages them together — an add-on sale.

When I was actively engaged in the photo sales business, I saw this idea pirated by a prominent manufacturer of photo lenses, cameras, and electronic flashes. Battling to establish itself in the lens adapter business, this company packaged its new telephoto lens with a 2X adapter. It was a remarkably clever idea, and the consumers went wild! I had never seen anything like it. Customers, waiting to buy this package, were backed up into the street at some stores. Why? What was so great about it? A dozen or more manufacturers sold the same or similar products, except they sold those products separately. This really simple packaging/marketing idea grabbed the imagination of the consumer. I was intrigued. One day, while waiting to see the buyer for a local chain, I interviewed a consumer who was waiting in line for this lens package. "What makes this combination package so special to you?" I asked. "Well," he finally answered, "I figure the manufacturer has 'married' two perfectly balanced units: the lens and the 2X adapter." This was, of course, a completely naive and foolish answer, but not in the mind of that consumer nor, it appears, in the minds of many other consumers. People were lining up to buy the lens and adapter package because of the phenomenon of *perceived value*, which is a powerful motivator.

ASKING WHAT IF . . . ?

My insurance agent is an innovative guy. He sells all kinds of insurance to companies and individuals. Selling fleet automobile insurance to rental agencies and truck companies is a big part of his business. One day he told me he was thinking how nice it would be if he could sell these big operations a product separate from his insurance business. What did they need that would save them money? Naturally, because insurance was his primary business, his thoughts ran in that direction.

That evening while driving home, he witnessed a fairly minor accident between a truck and an automobile. Pulling to the side of the road, he walked over to where the two drivers were discussing how the accident happened. Neither could agree on exactly who was at fault, but both were sure the other was the guilty party. Finally, the truck driver, who was frustrated and angry, said, "The heck with it! Let the insurance guys worry about it." That was agreeable to the other driver, so they exchanged information and continued on their way.

As my insurance agent resumed his drive home, he asked himself, "What if the truck driver had an accident-reporting kit? Wouldn't that present a terrific advantage to the trucking line? It would help establish blame, reduce claims, save the trucking company money, and make the adjuster's job easier. More than that, the accident-reporting kit I have in mind," he continued to think, "would contain a small point-and-shoot camera with built-in flash so that the driver could take photos of the accident scene; a small tape measure to measure skid marks and distance from traffic signals, stop signs, and other traffic control systems; and finally, a simple guide telling the driver what information to gather from the other driver, the police, and any eyewitnesses!" With my help, the agent assembled the kit and presented it to one of his clients. This client had bought cameras for some trucks, but this idea would ensure that every truck had a complete accident-reporting kit. The buy also thought that freight damage could be photographed to help in adjusting those types of claims as well. It is a great idea, and although still in the start-up stage, should do very well.

That idea, which might become a very profitable business, came about because an innovative mind asked, "What if . . . ?" I recommend that everyone ask "what if": What if my product was lighter, heavier, stronger, better looking, faster, bigger, smaller, tougher, cheaper, more expensive, made from a different material, sold in a different way, sold to other outlets, sold overseas, or sold with another product? As you can see, this powerful little question can spark an explosion of possibilities.

I'm sure you've talked with salespeople who, when you mentioned a new invention or sales notion, have told you, "I had that idea ten years ago." Did they? I'm sure many did, but some people see something that could improve their products or services and do nothing about it. When someone else makes a move, takes the risks, and succeeds, they curse their "luck." These are members of the "coulda, woulda, shoulda corps," people who lack that aggressive, entrepreneurial courage to launch a new product or suggest a new idea. They may also lack the instincts necessary to envision an acorn as an oak tree. If you don't want to become a corps member, or if you wish to resign from the corps, just as yourself "What if . . .?"

18

Staying Motivated and Saving the Sales

There are many things I like about selling, not the least of which is the freedom and opportunities it offers. There are other occupations that offer freedom and opportunities, too, I suppose, but selling does more. There is a constantly changing mosaic of challenges that confronts us daily. New buyers with different ideas and different approaches are always coming on the scene. New companies are forcing their way into the market, and new products are always being presented. Yesterday's leaders may become today's also-rans. It's tough to get bored in sales. I have salespeople ask me, "I can't get excited about my job. How do you manage to stay motivated?"

STAYING MOTIVATED BY HELPING OTHERS

Having kids in college helps me stay motivated, but even without that wolf constantly nipping at my heels, I would still be turned on by selling. But selling is not for everyone. You should like people, and of equal importance, you should want to *help them succeed*. Their success will become your success. Like many in our business, I have won awards and accolades over the years. Some salespeople pretend (and I'm sure it's pretense) that awards, plaques, and other forms of recognition mean nothing to them. Not I. I'm not ashamed to admit that I am proud of those awards, and as I look at them on my office wall, I remember the fun I had selling, the great people involved, the intense rivalry, and the thrill of getting the sale and winning the admiration of my peers. Those awards represent many customers and many situations. I don't look at them as my personal accomplishments alone; I also remember that my efforts helped others reach their goals. Helping others is my motivation, and I'd like it to be yours, too.

STAYING MOTIVATED AND SAVING THE SALES

I realize, of course, not everyone in sales can be motivated every day. There are days when we all would rather play golf, go fishing, or just take it easy. I've done my share of that from time to time, and I always feel guilty afterwards. Like a kid stealing a pie from the cooling rack, I wish I could put it back. I haven't "stolen any pies" for a long time now. Whenever I'm tempted to play hooky, I read the following motivational reminders, and they usually work (especially when the weather is bad).

Motivational Reminders

1. I am the best-prepared salesperson in the country. I know everything there is to know about my product. I know my competitors and have matched my strengths against theirs, and I am stronger. I have considered all the possible objections I might hear, and no objection can stand up to my solid facts.

2. I have prepared a presentation that *identifies* and *creates* a need, and I can show how my product will fill that need.

3. I am the best there is. No buyer can resist my powerful presentation. I will follow the basic mechanics of selling. I will use props and power words whenever possible.

4. Buyers have a difficult job, and I will respect that job by not wasting their time nor by making my presentation unnecessarily long.

5. I have all the support materials I need to make my presentation entertaining and informative. This material will help me involve the buyers and convince them to place an order today.

6. The buyer will recognize the value of my products and will be happy to see me.

I gave this list to one of my veteran salespeople, who told me it was a silly idea. "That's kid stuff, boss. I don't need it."

Perhaps it seems silly to you as well — pumping yourself up, trying to make yourself do something you may not want to do at a particular time. But it works for me, and it makes me focus on the job at hand. You see, I never consider an account 100 percent sold on my product. I constantly seek ways to sell more and to make the account stronger and happier. What my mother told me when I was just a boy is still very true: "The only thing that comes easy in life is failure." That is a true and scary statement. It's been my motivator for a long time.

ANALYZING THE MOTIVATIONAL REMINDERS

Let's take the time to analyze each of the six motivational reminders. Perhaps you will discover, as I have, that they don't seem so "silly" when we don't pay attention to them and our sales suffer as a result.

REMINDER 1

I am the best-prepared salesperson in the country. I know everything there is to know about my product. I know my competitors and have matched my strengths against theirs, and I am stronger. I have considered all the possible objections I might hear, and no objection can stand up to my solid facts.

Consider this reminder and ask yourself, "Am I really totally prepared? Do I really know all there is to know about my product and my competition? What if the buyer asks me a complex, technical question? Have I done my homework? Do I have the answers?" When you grill yourself in this manner, you'll sometimes discover that you've been getting sloppy and need to trim your sails. You'll force yourself to do a more thorough job. As you review your post-call notes and find out that you promised something when you last called on the account, you'll ask yourself, "Am I now prepared to fulfill that promise? Did I take care of that credit? Did I get a bigger credit line? Did I reship those new parts?"

We must constantly remind ourselves to stay on the right path and to stay motivated, excited, and involved with every account. Granted, we're only human. We all slip and grow lax from time to time.

I remember a story that illustrates that point quite well. A young girl was just graduated from high school and had applied for a job as a cigarette girl in a very posh and snooty restaurant. The ambiance was French and magnificent, and she was duly impressed. Hired, she felt a duty to maintain the elegance and style of the café so she affected a French accent. "Ziggeretts," she would announce in a husky voice. "All-monds," she would say, dragging out the word. The patrons were delighted, and her sales skyrocketed. But, after a period of time, the job became boring. The same routine, over and over, began to dim her enthusiasm. Soon she reverted to her everyday, American accent. "Cigarettes, almonds," she would announce, and her sales reflected the change. Finally, the ambiance no longer held any charm for her. The kitchen smells made her slightly nauseous, and she began to notice chipped paint and other flaws in the club's decor. She was, she decided, at a dead-end job, selling overpriced tobacco products in an overpriced café. Now, instead of her charmingly accented "Ziggeretts. All-monds," she walked about saying, "Butts and nuts."

We all are in danger of becoming lax and sloppy about selling. We develop a great presentation, and it works just fine. We follow the mechanics of selling, and we determine if the buyer is introverted or extroverted. We are enthused and motivated and organized. People buy, commissions grow, and the world is our oyster.

After a period of time, we start to lose the zest we once had. We become tired of hearing the same words come out of our mouths day after day. We start cutting corners and taking shortcuts. We assume all sorts of things about the customers and what they will and won't buy. We decide that the prospect knows all about our product or service, so we delete that from the presentation. Or we assume the prospect will not want to hear this or that, and we cut that, too. The next thing we know, our presentation isn't anything like it once was. Our sales plummet, and our commissions match our shoe size! We can't understand it. What happened?

Some of us will blame our manager. "I'm not getting a fair deal. My territory is too small or *(fill in the blank)*." Others will blame the product. "Our stuff is outdated, too expensive, and the packaging isn't snazzy enough." A few of us will look in the mirror and ask: "What am I doing now, when I am failing, that I didn't do two months ago, when I was a winner?" Those few are the ones who will turn things around. I hope you will be able to state the first reminder with conviction and enthusiasm, so that you'll only have to look in the mirror to shave or apply makeup.

REMINDER 2

I have prepared a presentation that identifies *and* creates *a need, and I can show how my product will fill that need.*

Whenever I am in danger of taking shortcuts, this reminder forces me to review my presentation. Does it really identify the need? Does it create the need? It is too easy to fall into the trap of presenting benefits and features and deluding yourself into believing that you are identifying a need. I take this reminder seriously because it makes me analyze every account and every product. "What is the need here?" I ask myself. I write the need at the top of a legal pad; then below it, I write the benefits and features.

Doing this helps to isolate the need and make every presentation stronger.

REMINDER 3

I am the best there is. No buyer can resist my powerful presentation. I will follow the basic mechanics of selling. I will use props and power words whenever possible.

Like the "Ziggerett girl," we all have a tendency to stray from our original game plan and become sloppy and lax. I like to review my presentation and know that I am sticking to the mechanics of selling, not with just the new accounts and prospects, but with every account and every prospect. Just as athletes practice the basics, I, too, review the tools and techniques of my trade. You can't win the game if you fumble the routine pass.

REMINDER 4

Buyers have a difficult job, and I will respect that job by not wasting their time nor by making my presentation unnecessarily long.

This reminder packs a one-two punch. First, it jolts me out of my own world and forces me to remember that I am not the only person involved in the selling equation. Buyers have their own set of problems and pressures. Although I may neither like nor respect some individual buyers, I still respect the fact that their decision will affect my performance. Also, at the most fundamental level as human beings, if we don't treat one another with a degree of civility and courtesy, then what have we become?

Second, it reminds me of the old saying: "Talk is cheap because supply far exceeds demand." Words are our only way to convey an idea, and we must use them. But the verbose among us are also the most boring. (Could *verbal* and *boring* be the root of *verbose*?) I will make my presentations as efficient and concise as possible without sacrificing any of the power and strength needed to make the sale.

REMINDER 5

I have all the support materials I need to make my presentation entertaining and informative. This material will help me involve the buyers and convince them to place an order today.

When I consider this reminder, I also consider the expense and effort my company has spent to supply support materials. So much cost, thought and planning went into providing those materials that I can benefit by incorporating them into my presentation. I also recall the times I have successfully involved the buyers in my presentation by transferring ownership and appealing to the senses. Excitement is contagious, but I can't give it to the buyer unless I have it myself.

REMINDER 6

The buyer will recognize the value of my products and will be happy to see me.

Finally, in spite of the success we may have had in the past or the esteem we may enjoy, everyone can use a confidence booster. It is hard to come by sometimes; we may have a problem at home, the boss may be hounding us because our sales production slipped, or an unpleasant encounter may have left our confidence dragging. The last reminder reinforces that you're a wonder in the universe. There is no one else like you. Drop your baggage of failure and doubt. Every day is a fresh page, a new start, and you will succeed because you are the best there is, and the buyer will like you and what you are selling. It doesn't matter if you're tall or short, blond or bald, handsome or homely, black, yellow, red, or white; all that matters is who you are and how hard you work. Everyone likes and respects a hard worker. Think about that. Think of the hardest worker you know. You like that person, don't you? Do you know of anyone who doesn't?

PUT THE REMINDERS TO WORK

"Silly," my veteran salesperson said. "Kid stuff!" he scoffed. I should have fired that guy or perhaps taken the time to show him the error of his ways. Is it silly to tape a message on your bathroom mirror and remind yourself in writing of what it is you are working so hard to achieve? You would think that by working hard, your goal would be burned into your brain. Yet, too many of us lose sight of our goals. Motivational experts advise us to keep our goal in front of us, constantly reminding us of what we want from all our hard work.

Do me and yourself a *big* favor. Try this small motivational-focusing exercise for just thirty days — thirty working days. No backsliding. Read the list of motivational reminders before every call. Think about what each point means and is trying to say to you. I have no doubt that at the end of thirty days, your improvement will be so marked that you will continue the regimen without my urging. Now do one more favor. Pass the concept and the idea along to someone who needs help, too. That used to be a common occurrence in sales. It's rather rare today.

A PEP TALK FOR WHEN REMINDERS AREN'T ENOUGH

The week between Christmas and the New Year is normally slow in many businesses. It is during that time we analyze each territory, determine year-end bonus figures, set quotas for the next quarter, and ask the territory salespeople to make their projections for the new year. Also, during that time, people unload on the boss, complaining about God knows what. In the relaxed atmosphere of the holidays, one sales representative told me, "You're always pushing me to stay on an itinerary, but that's boring. I want to attack targets of opportunity. I want to spread my wings!" Poetic, I admit, but foolish, too.

"Sally," I explained, "I know that working a territory and calling on the same accounts can seem mundane, but that should only be as tiresome as you allow it to become."

"Huh?"

"How do you view the accounts in your territory? If you see them as a glob of businesses and not as individuals who have different personalities, then working a territory becomes routine, and the job gets boring. You see, Sally, every account has different goals. We tend to lump them all together and imagine that they all want the same things — more sales and higher profits. I don't question that those are important to all your accounts, but each one wants something else, too. Brown and Carter, for example, is trying to upgrade its merchandise mix and attract the 'carriage trade,' as it used to be called. Hobart's is trying to corner the teen and subteen market, while International House is aiming for the college crowd. All want more sales and higher profits, but they all have other agendas as well. Most salespeople never try to appeal to those 'hidden' agendas, if they even know they exist. It's fun to see your accounts grow, to watch their strategies, to mark their progress and see the changes, and to know that you had a part in their success.

"You already know my feelings about getting too familiar with the buyers. Nevertheless, I think of them all as friends. I want them to succeed, and I want to help them succeed. I was thrilled to see Lambert's open a second store. When I met with Frank Lambert, he was so delighted there were tears in his eyes. It's not all about money and profits; it's about years of hard work, of planning and sacrifice. To see those years of effort finally paying off is almost like being present at the birth of your own child. Did you know that Lambert wants to open a third store by late summer? I get a chill just thinking about it.

"Sally, we are servants. Yes, indeed, we serve the people we sell. If that is boring to you, then you might be in the wrong business. But I know that you're in the right place at the right time. You just need to look more closely. There is a lot more going on than you know, and it's exciting."

Sally looked at me with wide eyes. "Gee," she said.

SAVING THE SALE

CREATING PROMOTIONS

One of the easiest and most pleasurable ways to motivate yourself and inject interest and excitement into your sales territory is to devise promotions. By creating promotions, you become a closer, more important business friend to the buyer, and you increase your sales, as well. Promotions mean a lot of extra work and many overtime hours for the retailer and for you. However, the benefits far outweigh the costs. Planning promotions forces you to think, to concentrate on the business of the account, and to learn more about the needs and goals of that business. When you first suggest a promotion, the buyer may reject the idea. Buyers have been through this before. They know that promotions mean extra work and, unless you have an extremely appealing, extra-hot idea, some will be inclined to turn the idea down. Don't give up. Demonstrate how the promotion will be administrated and explain how the buyer's participation will be minor. Reluctant buyers will eventually come around.

REMEMBERING YOUR OBJECTIVES

You'll recall that many or even most salespeople don't know what they want to accomplish when they make a sales call. That sounds ridiculous and astounding, but it is totally true. The reasons for this is that they allow routine to become boring. Boredom transforms into less interest and a lack of complete preparation. Basically, these salespeople become uninterested in the job. Their sales turn downward, and only when the manager starts taking a firm stand, do things change. If you use the motivational points I've outlined earlier, you will remain motivated most of the time, and that terrible feeling of sales spiraling downward will never happen to you.

TURNING COMPLAINTS INTO SALES

I couldn't wait to get back to Columbus, Ohio. I liked the area. It was fall and the nip of winter was in the air, the leaves were changing, and it was beautiful. On top of all that, I had helped my sales representative open a major account on my last visit a few months before. The buyer was a wonderful, cooperative person, and I was sure that this was the "start of something big."

My representative was gloomy when we met for breakfast. I didn't have to ask what was wrong. I was immediately informed that the account was "very unhappy" with our goods. "I've only talked to the buyer by phone since we sold her. You know I was on a late vacation, and she was on buying trips. Anyway, the goods aren't selling, and I think she will want a return authorization." Suddenly, the air felt cold and bitter instead of nippy, the sky seemed gray, and the trees were stark. What did that buyer know, anyway?

"Does she expect me in town?" I asked. He nodded.

"Good. I want you to call and arrange an appointment today."

"No problem." When we entered her office that afternoon, I shook her hand and good-naturedly said, "I have a bone to pick with you." Obviously, this was unexpected, and she wore a puzzled expression as we got settled. I learned long ago that to ignore an obvious problem only compounds it. It's like a blemish on the end of your nose; everyone can see it, you can't hide it, so you may as well deal with it.

"What's the bone you have to pick?" she asked.

"Earlier today we visited three of your stores, and everyone had the same problem. Our goods are backing up. They aren't selling, and there is no reason for that. What seems to be the problem?"

This tactic shifts the burden of explanation for the product not selling from the seller to the buyer. Subconsciously, buyers feel responsible for the

STAYING MOTIVATED AND SAVING THE SALES

merchandise they made the decision to buy. By bringing the problem out in the open, a problem most salespeople would try to avoid, they feel they owe you an explanation. If you don't take the bull by the horns, they will dump the whole mess on you. Why should you take responsibility? After all, they decided the product would make their company money, they own the goods now, and they have a responsibility to sell them. (Note: There are times when you just have to take the goods back, but it is much healthier to work with the account. The "revolving door" of guaranteed sales is nonsense.)

"I just don't know what the problem is," she replied, shaking her head.

"Lori," I began, "please give me a few minutes to remind you what a fine line of merchandise this is, and to impress upon you why there is no excuse for merchandise to be backing up in your beautiful stores." I then resold her on the need and the utility of the goods. I carefully reminded her why she bought our products to begin with, and then I said, "Together we are going to turn this ship around. Together we are going to promote this line so that your customers understand the quality and value we offer."

Naturally, she was somewhat taken aback. She explained that she had "done everything possible," without results. "The product is apparently just not right for this market," she said.

"Lori, if you and I start to argue that point, we will end up angry with each other and we won't solve anything. I know for sure, and I think you suspect, that isn't true. If it were true, an outstanding buyer like yourself would never have bought it in the first place — isn't that so?" Could she say, "I'm stupid. You conned me into buying your trash and now I can't sell it"? Of course not.

"I thought it was perfect for us, but — well, you've seen for yourself, it just isn't . . ."

I never let her finish her sentence. "It sells in markets all over the country, and it sells right here in Columbus. You were right; it is ideal for your stores, and all we need to do is push to get it started." I had been thinking about a promotion to get us going, and I outlined the main features for her. "I want your help on this, Lori. I got her involved and obliquely assigned her a responsibility. By doing this, we gained her cooperation. Her motivation was no longer to dump the goods back on us, but to see that they sold through. "Before I leave town this week," I continued, "I want to see every department manager and, if possible, every store manager. Can you arrange that?"

"Sure, I'll start on it today."

"Good, I want to sell *them* these products while I tell them about our promotion. I want special displays and the hottest selling spots in every store. Then I want to meet with the retail people of the department in each store. This is the critical point. I need these people to believe, as you and I believe, that we have a sleeping tiger here. I'm going to 'spiff' them to keep them excited and focused, but I will sell them so that when the promotion is over, they will continue to sell our product because they believe in it."

It was a difficult week for all of us. Long days turned into late evenings. At morning meetings with the department managers, we outlined a special spiff program and explained how the promotion worked. Quite a few store managers attended and added their support. We then scheduled meetings with their retail salespeople. These meetings were the most important of all because without the hard work and cooperation of the retail salespeople, no promotion can succeed. These meetings were in the morning, and we had full breakfasts catered *after* the meetings. (That is important. If people are drinking and eating, they don't concentrate.)

The promotion was scheduled to begin on Friday morning, when I would be on a plane headed home. Naturally, I was anxious to hear the results, and when the telephone rang Sunday evening, the excited voice of my rep told me all I needed to know. The promotion was very successful, and the line was now solidly in the product mix. In fact, the representative placed an order for an express shipment because some stores were out or almost out of goods. What a rush! As I said, I like Columbus, Ohio, in the fall of the year.

I don't mean to suggest that every promotion is going to work miracles or small wonders. Some promotions flop. But isn't it better to do *something* — to take the offensive position — instead of simply saying, "Gee, I thought it would sell here. I'll get you a return authorization number"? Even if the promotion fails, you will have accomplished something. You will have eaten into the inventory, and you will have educated and stimulated the retail salespeople. The buyer will appreciate the effort, and all this means is that you are doing your job well.

I told this story because I want to illustrate how you can take the power out of the hands of the buyers and transfer it to yourself. You retain confidence in your products. You are saying, "If this merchandise isn't selling, it's not because of the goods, it's because of something else: poor merchandising, poorly informed sales clerks, or simply a poor retailing effort."

MOTIVATING THE CUSTOMERS

I remember trying to capture an account by selling a new, small, snapshot camera display. This popular store, located in one of the many suburbs of Los Angeles, was the most active in that community, and the weekend traffic was tremendous. The camera had a unique feature (for that time) — a built-in electronic flash. The store manager and department manager went crazy over it. The store manager, in particular, loved the camera and couldn't put it down. It was late on a Friday afternoon, so I invited him to take the camera home and shoot some pictures over the weekend, promising to pick up the camera on Monday.

On Monday, over his protests, I insisted on taking the exposed film to a one-hour developing lab. The pictures turned out great. When I showed them to the store manager, he was simply overwhelmed. From that little encounter, he and the department manager cooked up a promotion for the coming weekend. I tried to get involved, to add my two cents' worth, but they had their own ideas. It was an incredible sale and one of the best selling weekends that store had ever had.

I really didn't do much, did I? Or did I? Well, first and foremost, I identified a need. Up to that point, only 35mm cameras had flashes, and those weren't built-in flashes. Flash cubes were expensive, "razor-blade" items that people always seemed to run out of on rainy nights when all the stores were closed or closing. Now, here was a camera that really filled a need.

I was selling to qualified buyers — namely, the department manager and the store manager. I demonstrated a great little camera that was almost budget-priced; with very few words, the demonstration was my presentation. I transferred ownership by loaning the camera to the store manager. I closed by having the film developed, thereby proving that the need was truly filled.

So, in truth, I did a commissionable selling job. It is true that they merchandised and promoted my product, and, contrary to my rules, I never got involved in the promotion itself. But their enthusiasm was too high for me to get involved. I wasn't needed so I took the weekend off. I tell this story because it teaches us two important lessons:

1. **The customer can be as motivated as the seller.** This particular product actually motivated the store manager to promote it to his customers. I did a few things to assist in priming his motivation (allowing him to take the camera home, and later having the film developed), but basically the store manager and department manager were so intrigued and delighted by the product that they took over the promotion.

2. **Always establish and define the need** — even if the need appears obvious. By doing that in this example, the store manager was excited to have this newest boon to photography in his store. That was his and my motivation.

MOTIVATING THE SALES FORCE

Staying motivated isn't just a personal thing, it is also a company concern. Trips, special bonuses, plaques, and other forms of recognition are used to motivate salespeople. I know of at least one company that goes around the salesperson and sends motivational materials to the spouse. The company's rewards and prizes for reaching specific goals always include spouses. The managers believe the spouse will encourage hard work and an early start each day, and their success record is excellent.

As strange as it may seem, money is not considered the prime motivator by many leading managers and trainers. Of course, it is always important, but other motivational factors seem to work better in many cases.

I'm sure we've all heard sports announcers say, "They (the members of the winning team) wanted it more." What they are saying, of course, is that one team is more motivated than the other. I can easily understand this when we are talking about amateur athletics, but it is difficult to understand when discussing professionals. How can money motivate a running back who is making $5,000,000 a year? Can the lure of earning an additional $200K or more drive him to greater heights? It just seems to me the motivational factor is lost in that instance. "What *does* motivate these guys?" I asked a baseball scout friend.

"Most people can't understand the tremendous egos that these professional athletes have. These people have been praised and pampered all their lives because they can play baseball or some other sport better than anyone else. Along with that praise and pampering, they take on a heavy load of pressure to perform — and to win. In a play-off game, the World Series, or an All-Star game, they are competing with the best of the best. They are showcased to their peers, the people they really care about. First, they must have a driving desire to win, or they would never have reached such a high level. They know they're special, and now they are competing with other great talents. They want to prove something, to test themselves, and this is the way they do it. This is a high you and I may never know, and no amount of money can buy it. No, it isn't about the money; that's just a way of keeping score."

As I mulled over his ideas, I realized how right he was and how often I had seen similar situations in sales. Salespeople are strongly motivated by money, but plaques, trophies, and other such ways to acknowledge achievement will sometimes do more to gain sales than any bonus arrangement.

People want their coworkers, family, and friends to know how good they are and how well they do their jobs. It isn't likely they will pass around their paychecks for all to see, but they will proudly display a plaque, a trophy, or some other tangible form of recognition. Remember Napoleon's observation, "Men will die for a piece of ribbon."

AVOIDING A MOTIVATIONAL TABOO:
NEGATIVE REINFORCEMENT

I remember being the top salesperson in my company. I was young and loaded with enthusiasm, and I worked very hard. Because I was stationed in a city far from our headquarters, I hardly ever saw or spoke with any sales management people other than my regional manager. I would occasionally receive a letter of congratulations and, very rarely, a telephone call. For the most part, however, I was on my own. I was doing great, but the company's sales were sharply down company-wide. A national sales meeting was called. It was my first national sales meeting and I was excited. I wasn't sure what to expect, but negativity wasn't in the mix.

I realize now, looking back, the national sales manager must have been under a great deal of pressure. He had a large staff, but a rookie (me) was leading the pack. This was inexcusable. Rookie salespeople are never given the best accounts or assigned the finest territories!

The very first day of meetings — in fact, the very first minute — the national sales manager walked to the chalkboard and wrote *KYJ* in large, bold letters. "That," he announced, "is the promotion I have designed for the coming quarter. It stands for 'Keep Your Job.'" A nervous titter of laughter ran through the audience. It sounded hollow and forced, and it was short-lived. I looked around the room and tried to read the faces of my colleagues. The message I saw was disgust, anger, disappointment, and fear. The balance of the meeting that day was subdued, unenthusiastic, and waning.

After dinner that night, the talk was mostly negative. I remember hearing a lot of conversations about changing jobs. A few salespeople actually checked out of the hotel and returned to their homes, leaving their resignations at the check-out desk. Everyone was upset about the national sales manager's attitude, and almost everyone had suggestions for how he could have better approached a problem we all knew existed. Amazingly, the next morning was a duplicate of the first day. I couldn't believe the disrespect this manager showed to his sales staff. Even the compliments he threw my way were negative. ("There's a kid that's fresh out of college — and you clowns can't even equal him! Nice job, Bill!" Some compliment.) The entire meeting consisted of shouting, cursing, and berating. It was so negative that we all returned to our respective cities feeling useless and uninspired.

The negative tirade was a foolish way to try to motivate the sales force, if that was the manager's intent. To threaten, berate, or (as I've actually witnessed) fire someone in full view of others is the worst management gaff possible. Does anyone actually believe that fear and abuse will make a salesperson or any other employee work harder, smarter, or more efficiently? Apparently some do, but wise managers and inspired salespeople know that motivation — either self-motivation or group motivation — must be based on positive thought.

Like managers, salespeople must find solutions to problems. Virtually no problem is unsolvable if hard work, intelligent thought, and sales effort are applied. The individual must tackle most problems alone. A buyer is a problem? The salesperson must figure out a way to overcome that. Sure, the manager can help in most cases, but day-to-day problems are the salesperson's responsibility. Naturally, the big problem of staying motivated is the salesperson's alone.

If you will recall, earlier in this chapter I mentioned the need to keep your goals in front of you at all times, and I repeated the often-heard suggestion of posting a reminder of those goals on your bathroom mirror. Keeping your goals in sight and reviewing the reminders every morning will reinforce your reasons for working so hard.

That note on the bathroom mirror should also include a reminder of how important it is to be positive and to eliminate the negatives from your life. Once you have accomplished that, I believe you will be well motivated now and tomorrow.

19

DIRECT SALES

Direct sales is the selling of a product or service to the person or entity who will personally use or consume that product or service. Insurance companies, investment houses, legal services, landscaping firms, home improvement companies, real estate agents, automobile dealers, book companies, home study courses, cleaning services, magazine and newspaper publishers, plus many other purveyors of products and services all use direct-selling methods to build their companies and boost their sales. Direct selling is not to be confused with over-the-counter sales that is, (retail sales). Selling directly to the user usually means going to the prospect, rather than having the prospect come to you (as in retail sales).

DISCOVERING LEADS

In almost every instance, the biggest ongoing problem direct salespeople have is finding sales leads. Many direct salespeople spend hundreds of dollars every month for sales prospects. Others will "prospect" for leads. Prospecting (as in gold mining) is an advanced realization of something to come. Prospecting is the lifeblood of most direct sales businesses. As prospects decline, so do sales; therefore, the direct salesperson is on a never-ending treadmill of chasing after leads and prospects.

Similar to a cold call, prospecting is as detested by the direct salesperson as cold calling is by the territory representative. But, there is no escaping the need for new, fresh prospects. Some managers maintain that prospecting is 80 percent or more of any direct salesperson's success. This "monster" (the need for more and more prospects) is explained by the following insurance company statement:

> If it takes fifty names to make twenty-four contacts to get thirteen sales interviews, of which ten are closing interviews, which result in three sales with an average $2400 annual premium per policy and

an average $328 first-year commission, then each contact is worth $41.00 (3 x $328 equals $984 ÷ 24 equals $41).

Taking that a step further, if the salesperson makes ten new contacts each day, those contacts are worth $105,780 annually! In between the ten daily contacts and the $105,780 in annual commissions are a lot of sweat, much frustration, and hard work.

In other words, direct selling is a numbers game. The more calls you make, the more contacts you make. The more contacts you make, the more interviews you will have. The more interviews you have, the more sales you'll make, and the more sales you make, the more commissions you earn.

I once knew a sales manager who told me that if you walked into enough stores and simply asked: "Do you want to buy anything today?" without explaining what you were selling or making any other sales effort, eventually, someone would say "Yes, I do." I have no doubt that is true, although I do question this "broadcast" method, which is wasteful and expensive in terms of both money and effort.

Prospecting is selling the interview. Salespeople rarely try to sell the product, service, or company while they are prospecting. The purpose is strictly aimed at trying to set up qualified appointments. Very rarely will it include any selling. For example, the salesperson will canvass an area, visiting every store or office. He will ask to see the owner or manager, conduct a short interview to determine if there is any interest in his product or service, and qualify anyone who shows interest. He will then leave a card and promise to get back to the prospect at a specific time. A brochure or other printed material may or may not be left with the prospect. By way of qualifying, the brief interview will answer the following questions:

1. Does the prospect *need* the product or service?

2. Can the prospect *afford* the product or service?

3. Is the prospect *qualified* for the product or service?

4. Is the prospect *prepared* to do business immediately?

The answer to the third question is especially important in insurance sales. The prospect must *qualify* with regard to health and age. In other businesses, specific qualifications must be met. For instance, is the prospect a citizen of this country?

MINING FOR REFERRALS

In one way, prospecting is self-perpetuating. Once a sale is made, and before the salesperson folds up her tent, she asks the prospect for referrals. According to LIMRA (Life Insurance Marketing Research Association):

1. Referrals are the strongest leads — the most likely to buy.

2. The best source is gathered from someone you've already sold. (However, referrals may also come from people you haven't sold.)

3. Two-thirds of the people surveyed by LIMRA answered that they had never been asked for referrals!

4. Of those who said they had been asked for referrals, most reported that they did comply with the request.

One way of harvesting referrals is by placing an obligatory request on the table. "Mr. Johnson, in order to continue to offer this outstanding product to the public, we must have your cooperation. By that I mean the names and addresses of friends, relatives, neighbors, or coworkers who might have an interest in our product." The recently sold prospect may hem and haw or promise to "think about it," but that isn't good enough. The salesperson will ask the prospect to get out his address book so that, together, they can review it and see if "someone comes to mind." Should the prospect not have an address book (that is, refuses to retrieve it), the salesperson will ask for the prospect's best friend, closest neighbor, or best-liked coworker. In short, he or she will do anything that will jar the prospect's memory. I don't deny that this is a hard-sell situation, but the need for referrals is really the lifeblood of the direct salesperson. It *must* be done.

The savvy salesperson will ask for a specific *number* of referrals. "Can you refer me to *five* of your friends or relatives?" This actually forces the prospect to think in terms of a quota, a quota that he or she unconsciously feels obliged to fill. The prospect may not come up with five names and may struggle to find even three. But persistence and friendly persuasion will finally result in at least a few referrals.

Some salespeople would rather wait a day or two after the sale before calling the prospect and asking for referrals.

SELLER: Mr. Smith, I have good news! (*the close after the close*). Your application is approved and everything is in order. Now I want to ask a favor.

PROSPECT: Yes? What is it?

SELLER: As you know, we don't do a great deal of advertising, which is how we keep our price so reasonable. So, I need your help. I would like you to give me the names of five friends or neighbors who might also profit from (*fill the blank*).

PROSPECT: Well, I can't think of anyone right offhand.

SELLER: I know. It was unfair of me to ask, but I'll be calling back the day after tomorrow. Will you have those names for me by then?

PROSPECT: Yeah, I can do that.

And you can be reasonably sure that when they call back, the names will be waiting. But not always. The prospect may claim that his or her busy schedule forced a delay, "but I'll get it done." If that or any other excuse is used, the best thing salespeople can do is advise they will drop by: "I'll be in your area on Thursday, and I'll drop by then. I'd like to see you again, and I can pick up the leads at that time." This holds the prospect's feet to the fire and will probably result in some solid leads.

But you can see that by delaying the request for leads, the salesperson only makes things more complicated than they need to be. The chances of getting leads diminish with the passage of time. "Strike while the iron is hot" is a good motto to follow when mining for referrals.

REWARDING THE PROSPECT

Some states forbid, by law, giving any reward to the buyer in exchange for referrals. But many do allow this practice. If allowed, it is a nice gesture to send a thank-you note, together with a small, tasteful gift. It can even be a gift with your company's logo or your personal imprint. A pen, paperweight, money clip, or similar gifts are appreciated and sometimes result in additional referrals.

OTHER METHODS OF PROSPECTING

Canvassing, which means going "door-to-door," and asking for referrals are just two methods of prospecting. Many salespeople use *telemarketing* as their way to contact hundreds of people every day. These telephone specialists have a short script aimed at getting just one thing: an eye-to-eye interview for the salesperson they represent. Telemarketing is so popular and so widely used that it is losing its effectiveness. Knowing that the decision maker usually is at home around 6:30 P.M. (just about the time when most people are eating dinner), the telemarketer will call. Having been besieged by such calls and not pleased at frequently having dinner interrupted, the prospect may not be in the mood to be cooperative.

The telephone company reports an enormous increase in the number of customers who switch to unlisted numbers. Still, there are ways around that, and the onslaught goes on night after night. Calling lists — like their forerunner, mailing lists — are available for purchase. In addition, there are literally hundreds of other sources that telemarketers use to uncover personal telephone numbers.

So many "junk" calls are tunneled into our homes and businesses that the cost of each telephone lead has skyrocketed. With increased calls, the closing rate must increase (but doesn't necessarily) to justify the cost increase.

Direct mailings are another method of contacting and finding prospects. Thousands of pieces of mail are sent each year, aimed at discovering if the addressee is interested in whatever the addresser is selling. It is estimated that if just half of one percent of the people reply positively, the mailing cost is absorbed, and a profit is made. Nonetheless, direct mailings are generally considered an effective method of gathering sales leads, especially if the mailing is done from a qualified list. Like the telemarketing effort, the recent escalating cost of mailing is causing some to adjust their thinking and is sending them scurrying for other ways to find customers. Newer, more effective, and perhaps less expensive ways, such as e-mail and other electronic "mining" methods are being employed.

THE INTERNET

The latest and hottest method of selling, finding leads, and marketing goods is the "information highway." This electronic marvel is in its infancy, but it has already given rise to many new businesses. Travel agencies and travel-related businesses were the first to recognize the *worldwide* marketing potential of the Internet. With millions of computers on-line internationally, the seller can be in direct contact with the consumer instantly, twenty-four hours a day, 365 days a year! In some cases (at least initially), there is no cost or only a minimal cost.

This exciting new method opens tremendous opportunities for both sellers and buyers. It is just another indication of the changes taking place in the markets of America. Traditional retail distribution systems are starting to be challenged by the Internet, multilevel marketing, direct sales, mail-order sales, Blue Board selling, and networking systems. The Internet challenge, in particular, is very powerful and its potential is so great that some major retailers are quickly adapting and are presently utilizing this method to draw customers into their retail outlets.

For independent entrepreneurs, commissioned salespeople, and small business owners, the Internet can be a continuing source of business at an extremely low cost (or, in some cases, no cost). In addition, their products or services can be offered far beyond their normal selling territory, even worldwide, if the product or service is adaptable to such markets.

For example, a new service on the Internet feeds information into millions of computers throughout the world about hotels, motels, car rental agencies, bed and breakfast establishments, theme parks, points of interest, and other tourist data. This information bulletin board includes rates, space availability, year-round weather conditions, and fax and telephone numbers. It also tells the interested potential visitor if pets are allowed, what child-care facilities are available, and even if special diets can be accommodated. The service can also make reservations for the inquirer and will accept credit-card information if deposits are necessary. Can you imagine how lucrative and helpful this service can be to an owner of a hotel, restaurant, or other tourist facility?

I gave the example of tourist-related businesses only because of the dramatic impact the Internet is having on that industry. But literally all businesses can benefit from this electronic marvel as well.

Suppose you are selling insurance and you wish to reach people who enjoy a particular sport, such as skiing. The Internet puts the vendor right into the skier's home, informing him or her about skiing insurance, the approximate cost, the coverage, and other critical information. Obviously, I could give many other examples, but I am sure you get the point.

FISHBOWLS AND TEAR-OFF TAGS

You may have noticed the fishbowl method of gaining leads at the register or checkout counter of your local market, coffee shop, car wash, or drug store. These "fishbowls" are containers (made of glass, hence the name, *fishbowl*), inviting one and all to deposit their business cards or fill out a slip with their name, address, and telephone number. In return, they will receive information. This method is inexpensive and the leads gathered are usually excellent. All the people who ask for information are qualified leads in terms of interest.

Still another method of garnering leads is by using tear-off tags. You will find this gathering method on supermarket bulletin boards, in public telephone booths, and in other, similar places. A headlined master sheet with tear-off tags containing the salesperson's telephone number is posted. Anyone with an interest in the product or service simply removes the tag and calls the salesperson. Both of these sources of leads are inexpensive ways to gain access to prequalified potential buyers with very little effort expended by the vendor.

DIRECTORIES AND LISTS

Local telephone directories, the Yellow Pages, and reverse directories are all sources of names. Using these sources requires the salesperson to make a telephone call or personal visit in order to turn those names into leads.

Membership lists and directories are a rich source of leads. These directories list the names of members and often other valuable information. Churches, social organizations, temples, housing developments, alumni associations, and community fraternal organizations are only some of the groups that issue membership directories. Follow-up methods tailored to these specific groups must be created. Some of these organizations will allow (even encourage) a mailing to all their members, or they will include (usually for a fee) a sales message in their monthly statement mailings or in their information bulletins and newsletters. Usually, a discount or some other incentive will be offered to the members ("Special Discount for Craft Society Members Only!").

Professional associations, such as Women in Management, all have directories of their members and often produce many qualified leads. A mailing to this kind of prospect is recommended before any telephone or direct contact is made. That mailing may or may not include a notice that a representative will shortly be in touch.

FORMAL NOTICES

Newspapers print important information for the lead-seeker. Legal notices tell you what new businesses are starting and who the principals are. Divorce notices (often printed under the heading "Responsible for Own Debts"), notices of estates in probate, and new corporations will contain the names of those who placed the notice and other information that can be extremely useful and valuable.

The social section of the newspaper will yield information such as new arrivals to the area, birth announcements, graduations, and a list of marriages and engagements.

The business section prints announcements of all major and some minor employee promotions, retirement notices, reports of illnesses that strike key people, and announcements of new business openings, as well as business closings. It also provides news about buyouts, mergers, and new hirings of executive-level people, along with transfers of management people. I once knew a real estate agent whose brother worked for a major interstate moving company. The brother could and did supply a list of executives and middle-management people who transferred into the area. That was a bonanza for the agent.

The obituaries may be still another rich source of leads. The survivors may need financial consultation, accounting services, child-care services, insurance policies, boarding school information (if some of the survivors are children), job opportunities, and any number of other products and services.

MAKING PROSPECTING PAY

Why does one person prospect successfully, but another is so unsuccessful? There may be any number of reasons, but as with so many other endeavors, the answer is *planning* and *effort*. John Ruskin, the noted English critic and author, said, "Quality is never an accident; it is always the result of intelligent effort." Few of us can argue with that. Many sales managers seem to think that quantity will eventually produce quality. Their mistake is that they equate quality with making a sale. They really have little concern for the number of leads used to make those sales. I feel this is a great mistake and one that the insurance industry, in particular, makes consistently. It always seemed to me that a different approach to harvesting leads would assure the companies a more efficient operation, a happier sales staff, and more business. The cost of the leads could easily be transferred to the agents, who would be happy to take a lower commission for an assured bigger volume. Both the company and the agent would benefit. I just can't understand why these companies haven't seen the errors of their ways and taken steps to correct them.

PLANNING

Planning for fruitful prospecting involves answering the five *who, what, where, how,* and *when* questions.

1. **Who** are the most likely candidates for my product or service?

2. **What** method will best put me in touch with those candidates?

3. **Where** are these candidates most likely to be found?

4. **How** should these candidates be contacted?

5. **When** should the prospecting be scheduled into my daily routine?

It is too easy and all too common to waste time by burying yourself in piles of unqualified leads. These leads waste time, build frustration, increase costs, and produce almost no sales. To plan and improve your prospecting, I suggest the following:

1. **Always take the time to qualify the prospect carefully.** Don't be afraid to ask the questions you must have answers to before marking the prospect as qualified. Many salespeople and especially telemarketers delude themselves into believing that prospects are qualified simply because they *might* accept further contact from a representative. If prospects are seriously or even mildly interested in what you are selling, they will not be averse to taking a few minutes to answer questions. The concern over the interviewee terminating the interview is what causes salespeople and telemarketers to make the interview too brief (thereby not getting enough information) or too shallow (not getting qualified information).

2. **Never try to sell the product or service when prospecting.** Instead, remember the purpose of your efforts — obtaining the interview. That is what you are trying to accomplish. This leaves the prospect fresh and unfettered with preconceived notions about your product or service.

3. **Strive for efficiency.** If your product or service lends itself to a "broadcast" approach in gathering leads, determine the most efficient way to get those leads. In other words, plan your prospecting days carefully. In the chapter on cold calling, I stressed the impor-

tance of *attitude* and *planning* when making cold calls. Basically, there are no differences between making a cold call and prospecting. Hence, the same general principles apply to both.

APPEARANCE AND DEMEANOR

When you prospect, you are showcasing yourself, your company, and the way you conduct yourself in a business situation. People carry a subconscious image of how an authority figure looks and acts. Outside the family, our first contact with authority probably took place at school. The male teachers wore suits or, at least, ties. The female teachers wore dresses. Both male and female teachers were neat, clean, and well-groomed. The times have changed. Today's teacher and businessperson may well wear more relaxed, casual clothing. Still, someone dressed in "business attire" projects an image of authority, and people are more likely to pay attention to him or her.

When you maintain a businesslike demeanor and dress accordingly, you level the playing field or possibly even tilt it in your favor. The following suggestions have proven effective when cold calling and prospecting.

1. **Dress appropriately.** No jogging suits, golf togs, or jeans. According to a research source, when 2,000 people were asked what detriments they would likely notice in a salesperson's appearance, most people answered soiled or wrinkled clothing, poorly tied neckties, unshined and scuffed shoes, an unshaven appearance, poorly applied makeup, rundown heels, and dirty or chewed fingernails.

2. **Use your eyes.** Good eye contact is a must. It displays confidence and honesty. But don't stare or rivet the prospect with your eyes; just show an interest in what is being said. In other words, don't allow your eyes to wander.

3. **Be sincere, honest, and relaxed.**

4. **Start with a "grabber."** The opening in your window of opportunity is small. Know what you will say and practice how you will say it. Be friendly, businesslike, and clear.

5. **Choose your words with care.** Be friendly and open, but be professional and careful with your language. Do not use slang, and never use profanity.

6. **Respect the prospect's property.** Stay on sidewalks and paths; don't park in an area where you might be blocking the entrance or exit or in areas that are marked for specific employees, handicapped people, or special purposes (loading zones or fire lanes).

7. **Properly dispose of chewing gum and cigarettes** before you reach the door.

8. **Be confident, but not brassy.** Be polite and courteous, but not servile.

Some managers believe a good opening will relieve any anxiety the prospecting lead may have. For example, "Mr. Smith, I have no way of knowing if I can be of service to you, but I handle the needs of many of your neighbors, and the chances are I can help you, too. If you can give me a minute to answer a few questions, I might save you a lot of money (time, frustration, effort)." Opening this kind of dialogue with a feature or benefit may be more effective than trying to establish a need, which can surface during the interview. Therefore, stating that you can save money, time, trouble, or whatever, may grab the attention of the prospect immediately and more effectively than saying, "Mr. Smith, we all must realize the need for health insurance . . ."

QUESTIONS

As in all selling situations, you must ask questions. What kinds of questions? Prospecting questions must be designed to generate interest. "Mr. Johnson, do you have any retirement funds that currently earn less than 7 percent?" is a much stronger and more provocative question than, "Mr. Johnson, do you have a retirement plan?" The first question will pique the interest of the prospect. Johnson may think: "Seven percent! Wow. What does this person have up his sleeve? I want to know more." The second question offers the prospect an easy way out: "Yes, I have that all taken care of. Good-bye." If the representative tries to reopen the conversation with a "Fine, but what interest does it produce?" he or she appears intrusive and nosy and perhaps a tad desperate.

"Would you be opposed to comparing your present insurance policy with our policy?" presents an escape once again. It is what I call a "heavy opening." "Yes, but I just don't have any time today." That would be a good or acceptable answer because it opens the door for the salesperson to come back when the prospect has time. But, supposing the answer is, "Been there, done that. Just had that comparison made last week. I'm happy with the present policy." You're dead meat. It is better to get the answer you want by asking, "Would you be opposed to comparing your current coverage?" It's the same question, but it is less threatening because it doesn't say "I'm going to sell you something, twist your arm, and take your time." If the answer is "No," the prospect is allowing you to make the comparison and opens the door for the sale. If the answer is "Yes," meaning the prospect would be opposed to a comparison, a dialogue is opened, and you still have a shot.

When making prospecting calls, maintain a positive, friendly, and aggressive attitude. Even if prospects turn you down and their reasons are unassailable, you can still ask if the company or person across the street might be a prospect. If the answer to that is positive or uncertain, ask if you might use the prospect's name when you approach the other company or the neighbor.

FRIENDS AND NEIGHBORS

Direct salespeople often are embarrassed to approach friends with their products or services. For years they've heard, "Never do business with friends." I could never understand that. If the product is really useful, what does it matter if the customer is a friend or a stranger? Shouldn't a friend be given the opportunity to benefit, too? When you sort it out, there can be only one reason a salesperson is reluctant to approach a friend: a lack of faith in the product. If you really believe in the product, you'll want to share it with your friends, right?

Having said that, I do recognize to some degree, why the direct salesperson may not wish to approach their friends. It could imply an imposition; friends may feel that they must buy in order to retain good feelings. That is why planning is important when selling to friends. Employing the following rules may make approaching your friends more comfortable and relaxed.

1. **Be candid about the purpose of your visit.** "Fran, I just joined ABC company, and they have a product I know you will benefit from using. Don't feel obligated. Don't hesitate to ask questions, and most important, if after you've seen what this product delivers, you don't believe as I do — that you will feel stronger and have more energy — don't hesitate to say no."

2. **Remember, you are selling.** Make the same presentation to a friend as you would to anyone else. Exercise the mechanics of selling, define the need, and close. Get the prospect involved and ask questions, even if you know the answers.

3. **Lean on the friendship in an nonadversarial way.** "John, I've known your kids since the day they were born. I know you want to provide for their college education, but you haven't done it yet. This plan can send them to Stanford, Yale, or any top university in the United States. Would you like to see how this can provide the tuition without putting you and Alice in the poorhouse?" Because you know the prospect, you are in a better position to serve his or her needs. It makes sense, it's logical, and it's silly not to sell to friends.

4. **Be sensitive to the need for privacy.** Remember, depending on what you are selling, friends may not want to buy from you because it means releasing certain information. Some people are age-sensitive; others guard their financial situation from all save their accountant, attorney, and the IRS. Whatever those hidden causes might be, take the rejection gracefully, assure your friend that you're not angry or upset, and confirm that your friendship is still firm and lasting. You may indicate that all information gathered would be confidential, but even that assurance probably will not turn the decision in your favor.

5. **If your friends don't or can't buy, ask them for a referral.** "Jeni, I understand. I can see why this cream wouldn't serve your needs. But can you see how great it works for people with a lighter complexion? Whom do you know who would benefit from this kind of cream? Perhaps someone at your office? How about your sister?"

Whenever you are given referrals, make certain to follow up with the person who gave you the lead. He or she will expect that from you and will be annoyed if the referral reports no contact. Always report back. "Mary, thanks again for sending me to George. I was able to help him as I did you, and he is delighted." Never discuss what you sold to the referred, what he or she spent, or any other information that the person might not wish to share.

SETTING UP A DIRECT SALE

As I've said earlier, selling is selling, but direct selling is different because the user is the customer. Since the product or service will benefit the user, there is, of course, a more personal interest. Often, direct sales involve selling to a husband and wife or to two or more business partners.

Small details figure greatly in the psychology of making the sale. Seating, for example, is an important detail when you make your sales presentation. When selling to two people, for instance, you would be better served if you can see both at the same time (remember the importance of eye contact). Sitting between the two makes that impossible, so have them sit side by side. This is easily done by making a simple statement, "It will be easier if you sit here [*indicating where you wish each to sit*], so I can show you both just how this works."

Try to get the perceived decision maker seated closer to you. This gives you the advantage of eye contact and visual control with both people. That, in turn, helps you control the interview. It also allows you to use support point-of-sale materials more easily and prevents the prospects from sending signals to one another.

In virtually every direct sales situation involving two people, one will be more easily convinced than the other. One will like your product or service; the other will be reticent. That is why it is especially important to ask questions during the presentation *and* make certain that both parties answer. Do not proceed until both agree to every pivotal point during the presentation. "Mr. Sanders, do you see how this product will protect your home from the winter rains without adding weight to your roof?" "Yes, I can see that," he replies. "Mrs. Sanders, do you see?" "No, I don't see how that is possible," she says. If you would allow the presentation to go forward after only Mr. Sanders gave his answer, Mrs. Sanders would be a problem when you closed (a problem you would not be aware of and would probably have a difficult time uncovering).

When using point-of-sale materials, never point with your finger. Instead, use a pen or pencil sparingly. Once again this harkens back to schooldays. A pointer was used by the teacher, and people subconsciously pay more attention.

SALES, LIES, AND VIDEOTAPE

Most people are suspicious of direct salespeople. Many have heard frightening stories about cheats and charlatans, about overpriced goods and dishonest contracts. The governments of many states have recognized that some direct sales operations have been fraudulent and that others have abused the trust that should exist between seller and buyer. Because of this, many states have passed laws to protect consumers. These laws allow any contract to be canceled for any reason or no reason, within a certain period of time after signing (usually twenty to thirty days). The laws also guarantee the return of any down payment made. It is important to note, however, with some purchases (such as a new automobile), the buyer is only guaranteed the right to have the purchase made satisfactory. In other words, if an automobile doesn't function as it is supposed to, the seller must make the necessary repairs. Provable misrepresentation of the product or an improper contract protects the buyer regardless of the product involved.

Some salespeople, fearing the loss of the sale, may be tempted to withhold telling prospects about their rights. Some managers teach their sales staff to avoid mentioning consumer rights or to mention them only in passing (thus downplaying them). On the contrary, the protection of the law can be used as a sales tool: "Mr. and Mrs. Walters, I am obliged to tell you that our state has a law which allows you twenty days to cancel any agreement that we may make tonight. This gives you time to compare our plan with any other offer. Frankly, I know you won't find an equal to my offer, but please do compare us to anyone else in the business. I want you to be as convinced as I am."

A straightforward statement of the consumer's rights given early in your interview (immediately after the warm-up) will eliminate a lot of doubt and fear. The prospect feels protected, relaxed, and free to make a positive decision. Some managers disagree and feel that making this declaration only encourages cancellations. In a small and informal survey I made, my decision to disclose up-front seems to work best.

Some companies, unhappy with their sales staffs or uncertain that their message is getting to consumers in the best, unadulterated way, provide videotapes to the salespeople. These tapes are professionally produced, cover all the salient points, are glamorous and attractive and . . . totally worthless in my opinion. Sitting in someone's office or living room watching a videotape is awkward and seems to take forever.

Videotapes may cover the important points, but they don't and can't involve the prospects. The prospects may be paying attention, or maybe not. They may understand what is being screened, or they may not. Conversation is difficult if not impossible while the videotape is being screened. How can the seller harvest "yes" responses? How can questions be asked? How can you keep prospects in the presentation? The answers to these questions are that you can't.

I've known some salespeople to leave the tape with a prospect and arrange to pick it up in a day or two. Invariably, when these representatives return to gather the tape, they discover the following possible results:

1. The tape was never viewed.
2. The prospect has deeply formed (usually negative) opinions that the seller can't change.
3. The tape has been lost.

I don't oppose new ways of selling, and if videotapes are produced with the expressed purpose of heightening interest, then I would be all for them. But that isn't what the ones I've seen try to accomplish. Instead, tapes become surrogate salespeople, and that just doesn't work. Instructions that accompany some of these tapes tell the salesperson where to stop the tape, and interject comments or underline various points. In theory that is just fine; in practice, it simply shows that videotapes are not the answer.

This chapter, along with Chapter 16, "The Cold Call," is extremely important to every salesperson because it teaches the importance of gathering new business contacts, and instructs how those contacts can best be approached. I have seen the fear or concern and the distaste that many salespeople have when asked to make cold calls, or must discover new prospects. These calls are a challenge to anyone in sales, but there is no reason why this particular task should be so distasteful.

Planning, attitude, and organization, coupled with proper motivation, will turn aside this fear and distaste. I urge you to read this chapter and Chapter 16 several times, and refer to them frequently. Make margin notes, and carry the book with you — especially on those days when cold calls have to be made, or when prospecting is necessary.

20

Tips for Success in Direct Sales

When I was a boy we listened to the radio for entertainment. We didn't have television in those days. Radio was good for our young minds, in particular, because it forced us to "see" with our imagination. *I Love a Mystery, Gang Busters, The Green Hornet*, and some of the comedy shows were my favorites. I would listen intently and imagine the Green Hornet speeding through the dark streets on his way to capture a criminal. I "spent" many a day in prison with the Gang Busters. It was a great way to develop a youngster's imagination. Anyhow, one comedy program had a sad character who played the part of a door-to-door salesman. He would mumble to himself as he approached a door (the doors were always answered by funny characters), and his radio signature was "There may not be anyone home, I hope, I hope, I hope." That silly radio program of yesteryear unintentionally made light of a problem that's common to many salespeople.

It is hard to understand why some salespeople actually try to avoid meeting with the decision maker. That kind of direct salespeople will "burn" lead after lead until he or she finds a "rollover" (an easy sale). As the preceding chapter showed, leads are expensive and difficult to obtain, so direct salespeople must make the most of every lead they get. Organizations will not waste good leads on bad salespeople, and anyone with that attitude will disappear faster than beer at a boilermaker's convention.

Direct salespeople work on a straight commission; therefore, they must produce sales, or they don't get paid. The companies they represent depend on their sales staffs, and these companies are among the hardest-driving sales organizations that demand production. Although some companies provide leads, others do not. The salespeople must find their own customers in any way they can.

As stated at the beginning of the preceding chapter, direct salespeople sell a product or service to the entity or person who will use (consume) that product or service personally. This contrasts with territory salespeople who sell in the marketing chain — from manufacturers to wholesalers to retailers to consumers.

Direct salespeople may work for a company and enjoy some company benefits (health insurance, for example), but more commonly they are independent without any benefits. Nonetheless, whatever the product or service they represent, a company's reputation and future are at stake. So, although independent, these direct salespeople still have an obligation to the company and operate, at least to some extent, under its rules and guidelines.

ONE TIME SALES

Unlike their territory sales colleagues, direct salespeople usually have only one opportunity to sell the prospect. The direct salespeople drive for a decision here and now because there is no tomorrow. This forces them to become stronger closers. Some become so strong that they become overbearing and end up blowing sales opportunities due to their own impatience.

The arm-twisters of the sales business are, without question, the direct salespeople. If they are pushy, persistent, and sometimes a bit obnoxious, we must remember that the nature of their jobs leaves them little choice to be otherwise. In recent years I have noticed a sophistication in direct salespeople. Many now appear willing to make a second or third call in order to make the sale. That sophistication is by no widespread; most are still hard-hitting, one-time closers.

DIRECT QUALIFYING

An important part of any direct salespeople's life is obtaining qualified leads. So many seem content with shuffling through stacks of "B" leads (leads that have been worked before, sometimes many times before) in the hopes of breathing life back into them. This is usually an exercise in futility and almost a complete waste of time; their time would be much better spent making new contacts (prospecting) or getting referrals from old customers.

We can agree on the value and cost of obtaining qualified leads, and therefore we can agree on the importance of turning those leads into commissionable sales.

The first step in that direction is qualifying the lead. This is a step that so many direct sellers seem to fear. They believe that asking too many probing questions will scare off the prospects. That is nonsense, of course. If the prospects have even a mild interest in your product or service, answering a few questions isn't going to frighten them away. On the other hand, if you are just being fooled, it is better to know immediately instead of wasting precious time.

What is the best way to qualify a lead? There are many methods, I suppose, but the easiest way is to compose a short list of pertinent questions aimed at determining the depth of interest. A health insurance representative shared the following with me:

1. Do you pay for your own health insurance? (If the answer is "no," the salesperson ends the interview. Employer-supplied insurance eliminates the prospect. However, he told me, he always asks for referrals in that instance.)

2. What do you like most about your present coverage? (This question helps determine if the coverage being offered can at least meet the existing policy features).

3. What do you dislike about your present coverage? (Likewise, this question helps determine if the coverage being offered can eliminate or offset the negative aspects of the prospect's present coverage.)

4. When can we spend a few minutes together to determine if I can improve on your health insurance situation? (This is the close for an interview.)

This insurance salesman told me that most people know what they dislike about their existing policies, but few can articulate what they like about them. This gave him a terrific advantage over competitors. By asking these questions, he was able to post an impressive one-call closing rate.

It is difficult to draw up a list of questions that fit all situations, all products, and all companies, but drawing from the health insurance agent's ideas, anyone can formulate the best questions related to his or her own business. The following is an easy formula for making your own list:

1. Grab the attention of the prospect with a strong opening.
2. Define the need.
3. Qualify the prospect.
4. Close (that is, set the appointment).

Direct sales is a numbers game. The more calls you make, the more appointments you set, which result in more sales. Once again, the downside is wasting time and effort with prospects who are not qualified (can't buy or have no interest). It is a fine line and a difficult decision to determine which prospects have interest and which ones may have interest but are fearful of salespeople.

This is why subtlety in your approach is so important. The following tips will help you improve:

1. Never enter a business or approach any prospect while carrying a briefcase or an attaché case. That, to the prospect, indicates the presence of a determined, persistent salesperson. Instead, if you carry anything, just carry a brochure or something you might leave with an interested party and your business card.

2. Usually it isn't a good idea to stick out your hand by way of greeting. Instead, introduce yourself and wait for the prospect to offer his or her hand to shake. "Hi, my name is Bob Smith, and I represent Clear Lake Water Company." That is usually enough for the prospect to offer to shake hands. I'm not sure why so many people dislike shaking the hand of a stranger, but I suppose it has something to do with intrusion or possibly because so many people have cold, sweaty hands or bone-crushing grips.

3. Zap the prospect with your winning opening: "I suppose you've heard about the high bacteria levels found in our local drinking water, and the possible health hazards they present, particularly to children?"

4. Define the need by asking a question or making a power statement. "It isn't widely publicized, but it is thought that because of the high bacteria levels, many children are victims of internal parasites. Do you have kids?" This makes a statement and asks a question. Most

people would recognize a need for their families or for themselves. If they have children, they would no doubt be interested in learning more.

5. Ask a qualifying question: "What kind of water system do you have in your home?"

6. Close for the appointment: "I've got a very crowded schedule today, but I could visit with you either Wednesday or Friday. Which is better for you?" Or, "Because your family is very much involved, I'd like to meet with you and your (husband or wife) some evening this week. Is Thursday or Saturday suitable?"

TARGETS OF OPPORTUNITY

Sometimes we get lucky and discover that our golfing partner is looking for insurance, investments, or whatever else we are selling. Usually, that isn't the case, so we should always keep our eyes open for any indication of interest. Suppose you were selling annuities and you noticed a copy of *Forbes* magazine on the desk of your prospect. Chances are the prospect is an investor, so find out.

SELLER: I see you're an investor. Are you active in the market?

(*This approach is assumptive, but reasonable.*)

PROSPECT: Sometimes. I'm mostly into mutual funds and a few munis.

SELLER: Have you heard about the Wide-World investor's trust? It's paying over 8 percent, tax-deferred.

This is a good opening. We've discovered that the prospect is an investor and what investment venues are favored (conservative). The grabber is the 8 percent return, tax-deferred, which is something any serious investor would want to know more about.

Let's consider another example. While walking around a neighborhood, a local roofer stops to visit with a homeowner who is trimming his lawn.

SELLER: Hi, I couldn't help noticing your shake roof. Looks like it's tight.

PROSPECT: Well, I'm not so sure. Had some minor leaks during that last storm.

SELLER: Would you object to a free inspection? It'll take about eighteen minutes, and there is no cost. It could save you a lot of trouble and money."

When giving a time estimate for any interview, *never* give a rounded time — half an hour for example. Instead, always give an odd figure — 17 minutes, 22 minutes, or other reasonable amount. For some reason people are more receptive to an odd figure rather than a half hour, 45 minutes, or an hour.

In this example, we once again get information; in this case, it was freely offered. The prospect's roof has leaks, and he needs repairs or perhaps a whole new roof. Asking "Would you object" really disarms the prospect. After admitting to leaks in the roof, he would be rather foolish to say he didn't want to know the overall condition. By putting a time limit on the inspection (a limit the salespeople can adjust as needed), the homeowner is more likely to agree. Otherwise, if the time element is omitted, the owner may say, "Well, not today. I'm just about to leave" or use some other reason to procrastinate.

The successful opening should be accompanied with a friendly smile and good eye contact. Good eye contact, once again, doesn't mean staring or penetrating looks. I once attended a very high-profile "Master Salesman" and trainer's seminar and volunteered to act as the customer in a mock sales demonstration. This chubby-cheeked trainer has dark, penetrating eyes to begin with, and he fixed them on me as a cobra would on a mouse. I felt very uncomfortable, even though I wasn't in an actual sales situation. If I had been approached by this fellow in an actual sales situation, I wouldn't have bought twenty dollar bills for a dime.

The thing you must remember is that fear — consumer fear — is a real obstacle that all salespeople must overcome. The warm-up (see Chapter 7) is a very important step in the selling process, and it's especially important in direct sales. The idea is to relax the prospects and calm any anxiety they may have (and they all have some, whether they are conscious of it or not). There is a danger in being overly friendly, too. All too many people have seen the friendly, down-home character selling cars on television ads and recognize the charade. Overdoing friendliness might be considered insincere or false. Honesty, sincerity, and genuine friendliness are the keys.

Let's suppose you are selling real estate — raw, undeveloped land — and your prospects are a couple in their early fifties. They live in a nice, modest neighborhood, and the breadwinner has a steady job. These are bona fide prospects. After a short warm-up, the salespeople begins the presentation.

SELLER: Folks, did you know that every single great fortune in America is based on real estate? Every single one!

(The seller is using an emotional appeal to financial gain.)

PROSPECT: Well, yeah, I guess so. My cousin Freddy Watkins has done pretty well in real estate.

SELLER: *(Not getting sidetracked into talking about cousin Freddy's wonderful record.)*

It is the one commodity that cannot be replenished. Only God makes real estate.

PROSPECT: Yeah, but I've seen the real estate market plunge and fortunes lost. I really think you're wasting your time with us, Mr. Rankin. We never make an investment without carefully considering every aspect of the offering.

SELLER: Of course, and I applaud you for that. You would be foolish if you didn't. But it doesn't cost to listen, now does it? And, I'm going to make you a promise: The short time we spend together will be interesting, and you'll enjoy yourself. Fair enough?

(Don't be upset with the negativity; the buyer is just trying to build a little protective fortress.)

PROSPECT: Fair enough.

(The prospect is starting to relax. He's made his statement, and now he feels safe, and you have your first agreement.)

SELLER: Good. By the way, I haven't been in this part of town in some time. Is that a new condo development overlooking the golf course?

PROSPECT: Brand-new and sold out in ten days!

SELLER: Really! How long have you lived here, Mr. and Mrs. Brown?

PROSPECT: It'll be twenty years this April.

SELLER: Oh, so you folks lived here before the condo complex was built?

PROSPECT: Long before. Heck, when we first moved here, there was nothing but farms and orchards. Ours was the first house on this block.

SELLER: You don't say. Well, then you . . . that is, you did have a piece of that complex, right? You must have bought it for peanuts when you first moved here.

(This is said in a "Well, surely you saw the opportunity" tone of voice.)

PROSPECT: No, I missed out. I could have bought in as late as five years ago. Freddy offered me a piece, but I didn't have the money, what with kids in school, you know.

The sales agent has set up the prospect nicely. The prospect will recall missing out on an excellent opportunity, one from which his cousin made a fortune. He is contrite, perhaps even a bit angry with himself, and now is more interested in finding out what this offer is all about.

SELLER: Well, don't fret, Mr. Brown, there are still great opportunities in this town — and all they take are vision and courage — not a lot of money.

(The prospect now must be thinking, "Is it possible I can still make money, even with a minimal investment? But, maybe this fellow is talking big bucks.")

PROSPECT: I don't know. All the big money has tied up the worthwhile real estate around here. There's no room for the little guy anymore.

(He's just asking to be convinced. He wants to believe.)

SELLER: *(Setting the trap)*

Interesting you should say that. Let me ask you, what makes real estate valuable — in your opinion?

PROSPECT: Supply and demand?

SELLER: Bingo! And the supply is short, but the demand is great, right here in our town. Your cousin Freddy, he had vision. I'll bet when he started out he didn't have a lot of money. Am I right?

(Building to the close)

PROSPECT: Yeah, you're right. Old Freddy was working at the foundry with me.

SELLER: Like I said, vision, not money, is needed to make a fortune.

PROSPECT:	Yes, but it takes some money, doesn't it?
	(*Perfect! He is asking, "How much is this going to cost me?"*)
SELLER:	(*Qualifying the close*)
	Not much. Could you afford $125 a month — about the cost of a Big Mac and coffee a day?
PROSPECT:	I never thought of it that way. Sure, I can afford that.

Forgive me for dragging out this example, but it illustrates how a good salespeople will obtain information without seeming to pry, and how he or she will use the information the prospect gives to set up the sale. Notice how the example follows the mechanics of the sale, how the need is identified, and how the salespeople collects positive responses as the interview moves along.

Once the prospect agrees that he could afford the monthly payment, the sale is made. What possible objection could he raise at that stage of the sale? If the prospect still stalls or balks, the seller need only point out the other opportunities that have been passed over. Cousin Freddy will come in handy. I feel confident in using this kind of example, since everyone has met people who have passed up investment opportunities and have lived to regret it.

A good presentation overlooks the objections and capitalizes on the information that is given. Notice how the need was identified and how the seller followed the mechanics of the sale. Especially notice the subtle and nonconfrontational closing.

GUARANTEES

Direct salespeople often imply a guarantee without ever actually stating it. "Miss Bevins, if I could show you, *beyond a shadow of a doubt*, that your home will increase in value by 35 percent with a new Wear-ever roof, could you afford just $75 per month?" How is that going to be proven? It isn't. The onrush of verbiage obscures the need to explain how the statement can be proven (guaranteed). Instead, the beautifying of the home, the protection it affords, and similar features are stressed. By the time the salesperson finishes, the client will convince herself that the new roof will increase the home's value by 35 percent. No one can prove whether the home will increase in value by 35 percent or 3.5 percent. Such proof depends on many things beyond the salespeople's control: economic conditions, interest rates, building activity in the immediate area, and many other things. Suppose the prospect asks, "What is the value of my home now?" Chances are the seller would be stuck for an answer. These are guarantees that are not guarantees and are used only to make a point and dramatize a perceived benefit. (The homeowner may have no intention of selling her home, so the increased value is a moot point.)

OBLIQUE CLOSES

Often qualified and interested buyers are stricken with buyer's remorse even before they actually buy. They reach for some last branch, no matter how small or insignificant, to keep from tumbling into the sale. "Do you have that in a dark blue? No? Well, that's what I want. I only want dark blue." This is the kind of last ditch-stand a prospect might use.

"I like the area, but I wanted a corner lot." This is another objection and sales-killer that qualifying could eliminate or that reasoning might still overcome.

The first automobile I ever bought was actually a side mirror. I had saved every dime from a small allowance, every penny from every miserable job I could find, and every dollar from every Christmas and birthday since I was twelve years old. Now, I had enough — a grand total of almost $500 — which I carried around, secured with a rubber band. It was an innocent age.

I searched the newspapers and various used-car lots and discovered that my roll of bills wouldn't get me as much as I had first thought. Still, I was beside myself with excitement; I was going to have a car!

One Saturday morning, on an already typical hot and humid summer day in St. Louis, I saw it. A dark blue (slightly faded) four-door Roadmaster Buick. I stood in that blazing heat for a good five minutes staring at it, until I heard a voice say, "She's a beauty, isn't she?" Standing next to me was a tall, middle-aged man who was smoking a short cigar. I nodded weakly — yes, it was a beauty, indeed. He quickly qualified my ability to pay and then, taking my arm, led me over to "Old Blue." "Get in," he invited, "I'll get the keys, and you can take her for a spin." I slid behind the wheel and placed my hands on the scorching-hot steering wheel. I noticed the headliner was loose and dipped so that it touched the top of my head, but heck, I could fix that. The odometer read over 100,000 miles, the rear window was cracked, and there were holes in the floormats. I could see a dent in the hood, and the trunk wouldn't lock. The cigarette lighter was missing; the seats had a dank, musty odor; and the window crank on the passenger side was gone. It was the most beautiful car I had ever seen.

Handed the keys, I stomped on the starter (on the floor in that year), and after a desperate grinding struggle, the engine roared to life. A blue-gray cloud could be seen in the rearview mirror, as I carefully drove off the lot. What a joy! I honked the horn, played the radio, tested the brakes, and explored all the wonders of this marvelous contraption. I couldn't stop smiling.

However, as I reapproached the lot, a curious thing happened. An icy hand clutched my heart, I started to worry and think. After all, this was the first car I had looked at. There was no hurry. I had a list of ten other cars that I had promised myself I'd look at. Yet, this huge blue devil had a grip on me. I loved that car. Torn with indecision, I finally decided it wouldn't hurt to wait a little longer. You know, shop around.

"It's a beautiful car, isn't it?" the salesman beamed. I nodded. "It's a great road car. Do you ever take your girl to Creve Coeur Lake? Tonight should be a great night out there — out of the heat of the city, just you and ... what's your girl's name?" I can't remember answering. I had a picture in my head of us dancing at the pavilion, the lake shimmering in the colored lights, and my Buick parked nearby, ready for whatever the night held.

I was led to the closing office and sat sipping water as the salesman wrote out the contract. Once again, that icy hand grabbed my heart. I started thinking about gasoline, oil changes, repairs, insurance, and licenses. Why hadn't I thought of these things before?

The salesman was finished now. Without a word, he slipped the contract over to my side of the desk, pointing to where I should sign.

"The mirror," I blurted, "I hate that mirror." The salesman looked tired, I thought.

"What is it about the mirror you hate so much, Bill?"

"It's round. I hate round mirrors." He nodded. Did I detect a bemused smile?

"You prefer rectangular mirrors, do you?" he asked. I nodded vigorously. "Sign there, Bill, then go have a soft drink out of this heat. By the time you finish your drink, I'll have had your car washed and a new rectangular mirror installed. It'll take ten or fifteen minutes. OK?"

What could I say or do? I signed, a gnawing fear nagging me, the icy clutch still around my heart. As I drove home, listening to the powerful throbbing engine and imagining envious glances from pedestrians and other motorists, the gnawing fear started to ebb. The icy clutch around my heart melted in the afternoon heat, and all was well in the world.

That car served me well for almost four years, and I have never had another that I loved so much. But when I thought about it, even way back then, I realized that I bought a rectangular sideview mirror for $500 — with a dark blue Buick attached.

You may recall purchases you've made in the past. Many, I bet, were made in more or less the same way — your last-minute gasp to avoid buying: a demand for a certain color, a different-shaped mirror, a corner lot, or some other really inconsequential tidbit. Whatever, it is still a sharp salesperson who will recognize the dodge, and close the escape route.

Direct selling is a challenge and a promise. If you accept the challenge, you can look forward to ever-sharpening skills and increasing rewards. Direct selling promises you nothing — you promise yourself. It is an independent lifestyle, and not for everyone. But if you have talent, courage, and a penchant for hard work, it just might be ideal for you.

INDEX

A

Accident-reporting kit, for insurance companies, 229–230
Account books
  organization of, 44–46
  page from, 52
Accounts
  grading, 41–42
  winning over, 26–28
Add-on sale, 227–228
Advertisements, 7–8, 21
Advertising allowances, 31, 32, 123
Advertising money, 121
Age, power words and, 112–113
Agreements, from buyer, 162, 163
Anniversaries, remembering, 17
Appearance, 102, 256–257
Appreciation, letter of, 152–154
Asking why, 160
Assumptive close, 91
Attaché case, 268
Attention getting, 114
Attitude
  adjustments, for cold calling, 200–203
  cold calling and, 199–200
  positive, development of, 203–204
Audiovisual aids, 224
Authority/responsibility, qualifying for, 79

B

Benefits, 73, 83, 111
Billing, extended, 157
Birthdays, remembering, 17
Body language, 8
Brand names, vs. no-names, 178–180
Briefcase, 47, 268
Brush offs, during cold calling, 209–211
Business
  cost of doing, 168–171
  hours, 206–207
  letters. See Letters
"Buy America" program, 13
Buyer. See also Customers
  allowing to say no, 60
  answering of questions by, 155–156

arrogance of, 2–3
artful dodgers, 19–20
attitude toward competitor, 76
commission, 32
confidence in, 232, 236
decisions of, 2
defensive, 69
dialogue with, 11, 61–62, 155
disagreeing with, 17–18
ecological concerns of, 5
ego, emotional appeal to, 58
extras for, 161
friendship with, 167
getting involvement of, 13
going over his head, 30
hail-fellow-well-met buyers, 16–17
"I-can-get-it-cheaper," 15
impressing, 45–46
initiating dialogue with, 155
intellectual, 17–19
job of, 1, 5–6, 21
know-it-all, 85
knowledgeable, 98
in large retail chains, 3
latitude of, 22
litigation and, 5
new, dealing with, 213–215
payoffs to, 12–14
problem, handling of, 72–74
professional, 12–14
quality of, 4–5
real meaning of what is said, 158–159
refusal from, 162
relationship with, 55–56
relationship with salesperson, 3, 24–25, 172. See also Friendship
respect for, as motivational reminder, 232, 235
responsibility for merchandise, 240
as screener, 207–208
shifting responsibility to, 162
small, 28–29
staying on course with, 159–160
strong, silent types of, 8–12
thanking, 50–51

277

uncooperative, 55
unknown vendors and, 4
very tough, 23–28
Buying by committee. See Committee-buying methods

C

Calling lists, 251
Cancellation, preventing, 92–94
Canvassing, 250–251
Cards, 51
Catalog houses, 192–193
Chains, retail, 22, 164, 175
Clerks, 79
Close/closing
   after close, 92–94
   assumptive, 91
   in creating a need sale, 64–65, 71
   definition of, 86–87
   for direct sales appointment, 270
   emotional appeal to ego, 58
   example of, 62–63
   fear of, 43, 86–87
   as moment of truth, 87
   oblique, 274–276
   opportunity for, 82, 88–91
   "puppy dog," 215–216
   push for, 91–92
   questions for, 57
   readiness for, 87–88
   in selling by creating a need, 64–65
   silent, 160–163
   soft assumptive, 91–92
Close-out merchandise, 15
Cold calling
   attitude and, 199–200
   brush-offs during, 209–211
   developing positive attitude for, 203–204
   embarrassment/shame from, 199
   fear of, dealing with, 200–203
   networking and, 208–209
   overcoming resistance in, 204–208
Commissions, 32, 182, 265
Committee-buying methods, 3–4, 19, 195–196
Committee selling, 224–225
Common sense approach
   for group presentation, 219–223
   with tag-on sales, 227–228
Communism, 37–38
Company image, 14
Competition
   being a little better than, 196–197
   buyer's friend as, overcoming, 173–174
   comparisons with, 59–60
   filling a need and, 73
   ignoring, 71
   separating yourself from, 61
   stature of, 58–59
   value of, 37–39
Complaints, turning into sales, 239–242
Computers, 177
Concept selling, 58–60
Confidence, organization and, 49
Consignment, 163
Consumers
   fears of, 270
   gender of, 111–112
   growth of mass merchandisers and, 22–23
   rights of, 261
   taste, changes in, 60
Contemporary changes, 175
Contests, promotional, 123–125, 129
Contract cancellations, 261
Control, maintaining, 156
Convenience store chains, 191
Courage, 104
Courtesy, 204
Cover letters, 136
Creating a need, 192, 243
   advantages of, 64–66
   closing and, 64–65, 71
   concept selling and, 58–60
   example of, 61–64, 69–72
   failure in, 67
   importance of, 193–196
   meaning of, 39–40
   as motivational reminder, 232, 234–235
   during presentation phase, 85–86
   purpose of, 68
   re-establishment of, 162
   steps in, 73
Creditworthiness, qualifying for, 79

Criticism, insensitivity to, 29–31, 100
Customers
   giant, meeting demands of, 179
   motivating, 242–243
   target, qualifying, 79–80
   tough buyers as, 24

D

Decisions
   objections. See Objections
   previous, questioning/challenging of, 59–60
   simplifying, 16
Decorations, store, 122
Demeanor, appearance and, 256–257
Department manager, 242
Dialogue, with buyer, 11, 61–62, 155
Direct mail, 185–187, 251
Direct sales
   definition of, 247, 266
   discovering leads for. See Leads; Prospecting
   guarantees and, 273–274
   setting up, 260–261
   tips for, 265–276
   vs. street sales, 74
Discontinued models, 15
Discounts, 123
"Discovery," as power word, 109–110
Distressed goods, 118
Distributors, 191–192
Downsizing, 177–178
Drugstore outlets, 191
Dump-bin displays, 191

E

"Easy," as power word, 110
Efficiency, in prospecting, 255
Ego, 58
Emotional appeal
   to buyer ego, 58
   creating a need and, 65–66
   in creating a need selling, 69–71
   generation by words, 107–109
   use of, 63
Employment letter, 145–151
End-of-run merchandise (tens), 15
Endurance, 104–105

Entertainment
   of buyers, 17
   expenses, stretching to limit, 168–171
   of intellectual buyer, 19
   of professional buyers, 14
   as sales contact, 167, 171
Enthusiasm
   for backup source, 65, 95, 96, 105
   of salesperson, 95, 96, 105
   for sales promotion, 132
Excitement, from sales promotion, 132
Expansion of sales, 190
Extortion, 31, 32
Extra billing, 15
Extroverts, 6–8, 16–17

F

Fear
   of cold calling, dealing with, 200–203
   of consumer, 270
   taking away from buyer, 117
Features, 73, 83
Fishbowls, 252–253
Flattery, as icebreaker, 78
Follow-up methods, finding, 50–51
Formal notices, for finding leads, 253–254
"Free," as power word, 115
Friends
   collecting money from, 168
   as leads, 258–260
Friendship
   with buyer, 16
   entertainment expenses and, 168–171
   overcoming the buddy system, 173–174
   taking advantage of, 167–168
Front-loading, 60

G

Garden shops, 191
Gasoline service stations, 191
Gifts, 50
Glitches, handling, 84–86
Goals, keeping track of, 236–237
Goods, "presold," 21
Grading, of accounts, 41–42
Greeting cards, 17

INDEX

Group
  committee selling, 224–225
  presentation, common sense approach for, 219–223
  selling to, 218–219
Growth, business, 175
Guarantees, 81, 273–274

H

Habits, bad, 75–76
Hail-fellow-well-met buyers, 16–17
Hardware stores, 190, 191
Hard work, 97
"Healthy," as power word, 112
Help, asking for, 18–19
Herd mentality, 225
High-pressure sales methods, 56–57
Holidays, remembering, 17
Honesty
  attitude and, 201
  expectations of, 9, 24
  importance of, 97, 103, 105
  need for sale and, 90
  overcoming resistance and, 204–205
  vs. truthfulness, 103
Hope, false, 161

I

"I-can-get-it-cheaper" buyers, 15
Icebreakers, 78–79
Image, of retail organizations, 192
Immediate after close, 93
Industrial sales, 180
Insider deals, 171–172
Insurance
  companies, accident-reporting kit for, 229–230
  issues, for sales promotions, 120
Intellectual buyers, 17–19
Internet, 251–252
Introverts, 6–12
Inventions, competition and, 39
Inventory, after promotion, 122
Involvement, in presentation, 220–223, 224
Itinerary, creating, 42–44

J

Janitorial services, 181
Joke telling, as icebreaker, 78
Junk mail, 185

L

Language, appropriate, for sale presentation, 19
Laws
  on cancellations, 94
  for consumer protection, 261
Leads, 265
  friends as, 258–260
  looking for. See Prospecting
  neighbors as, 258–260
  prospecting for, 247–248
  qualifying, 255, 266–269
  from referrals, 249–250
  rewards for, 250
  targets of opportunity, locating, 269–273
Legal issues
  cancellations, 94
  consumer protection, 261
  for sales promotions, 120, 129
Letters
  of appreciation, 152–154
  of credit, 13
  for direct sales, 140–143
  employment, 145–151
  impact of, 134–135
  to job applicant, 151
  requesting personal meetings, 136–140
  selling. See Selling letters
  shock, 142–143
Life Insurance Marketing Research Association (LIMRA), 249
Listening, for closing opportunity, 88–91
Litigation, buyers and, 5
Lottery laws, 129
"Love," as power word, 113

M

Mail, solicitation by, 135–142
Male ego, 113

Managers
   department, 242
   marketing, 191
   merchandise, 21, 22, 117–118, 121, 213
   production, 89
   sales, 55, 57
   store, 122, 242
Markdowns, 117–118
Marketing manager, 191
Marketing support, 14
Market research study, 191
Markup, retail, 15
Mass merchandisers, 22–23, 175–178
Mechanics of selling, 75–94
Membership lists, as lead source, 253
Merchandise managers, 21, 22, 117–118, 121, 213
Merchandiser, 121, 122
Merchandising trends, 193
Money
   advertising, 121
   as motivator, 101, 243–244
   as reason for not buying, 57–58
Morale, employee, 132
Motivation
   of customers, 242–243
   by helping others, 231–233
   importance of, 101, 105
   negative reinforcement and, 244–246
   pep talk for, 237–238
   reminders for, 232–236
   of sales force, 243–244
Multilevel marketing, 181–185
Mystery Shopper, 125–127

N

Namedropping, 14
Need, 73–74
   assuming the buyer recognizes need, 227
   creating. See Creating a need
   defining for customer, 243
   existing, identification of, 192
   failure to establish, 67
   identifying, 73
   for profit without large cash outlay, 191–192

   trying to fill where no need exists, 189
   vs. features and benefits, 73
Negative reinforcement, 244–246
Neighbors, as leads, 258–260
Networking, 208–209
"New," as power word, 114–115
New calling. See Cold calling
New markets, exploring, 189–190
New products, creating need for, 39–40
Notes, 51

O

Objections
   buying decision, 89
   dealing with, 65
   from first time cold call buyers, 210–211
   price, 98
Objectives, remembering, 238–239
Oblique closes, 274–276
Off-brands, 179
One time sales, 266
Openings, for presentation, 78–79, 269
Opportunity
   for closing, listening for, 82, 88–91
   targets of, 269–273
Organization
   of account book, 44–46
   benefits of, 47–49
   confidence and, 49
   importance of, 102, 105, 263
   of sales territory, 41–42
Outlets, new, 191–193
Ownership, feeling of, 215–216

P

Packaging/marketing idea, 228
Parking-lot sale, 119–120
Payment, for shelf space, 31–32
Pep talk, motivational, 237–238
Perceived value, 228
"Permit," as reverse power word, 112
Persistence, 24–25, 100, 105
Personal interview, letter request for, 136–140
Personalized sale, 114
Phrases, old-fashioned, 115

INDEX

Planning
  for prospecting, 255–256
  prospecting payoffs and, 254–255
  for sales calls, 196–197, 263
Point-of-sale materials, 261
Post-call notes, 45–46, 49, 53, 201
Power words
  age and, 112–113
  gender and, 111–112
  list of, 115, 116
  modern, 116
  old-fashioned, 115
  timeliness of, 115
  use of, 109–116
Praise, 15, 18
Predecessor, knowledge of, 42
Premium market, 197
Preparation
  as motivational reminder, 232, 233–234
  for sales call, 196–197
  for selling to strong, silent type, 10–11
Presentation. See Sales presentation
Price
  discussion of, 57
  higher, appeal of, 71–72
  lowest, consumer insistence on, 22–23
  "meet or beat" proclamations for, 22
  objections, 98
  slush, 123
Privacy, selling to friends and, 259
Production-line jobs, 177, 178
Production manager, 89
Product knowledge, 84, 98–99, 105
Product selling, 61, 64, 68–69
Promotional aide, 120
Promotions, 117–132
  accomplishments from, 241–242
  business letter for. See Letters
  creating, motivation from, 238
  for employees, 131–132
  ideas for, selling, 123–132
  insurance issues, 120
  legal issues, 120
  limits for, 122
  monetary allowance for, 123
  Mystery Shopper, 125–127
  problem-solving, steps in, 121–122
  Punch Card, 131–132
  for retail salespeople, 130
  tie-in, 129–130
  unexpected target, 128–129
Proof of performance, 32
Proof of publication, 32
Prospecting, 247–248
  appearance as demeanor in, 256–257
  by direct mailings, 251
  by directories/lists, 253
  efficiency in, 255
  fishbowl method of, 252–253
  formal notices for, 253–254
  on Internet, 251–252
  making efforts payoff, 254–255
  planning and, 255–256
  questions for, 257–258
  tear-off tag method of, 253
  by telemarketing, 250–251
Prospects. See Leads
"Proven," as power word, 110
Punch Card Promo, 131–132
"Puppy dog" close, 215–216
Purchasing agreements, 21
Pushing for close, 91–92

Q

Qualification
  closing opportunity in, 89–90
  of leads, 266–269
  in presentation, 79–82
Question-and-answer period, 220
Questions
  asking, to draw people out, 11
  closing, 160–161
  define need for asking, 269–270
  "if," 88
  pointless, handling of, 84–85
  for prospecting, 257–258
  qualifying, 79, 267–268
  for securing sale, 93
  what if, 229–230

R

RAN (return authorization number), 117
Reading, writing ability and, 133

Recognition
    forms of, 231
    as motivator, 244
Recordkeeping, 41, 45–46, 50, 201
Referrals, 249–250, 259
Refusals. See Rejections
Reinforcement, negative, 244–246
Rejections, 60
    from buyer, 162
    emotional reaction to, 72–73
    fear of, 87
    handling, 29–31
    insensitivity to, 29–31, 100
    not taking personally, 201
    product selling and, 64
Reluctance to buy, causes of, 156
Repackaging charges, 33
Resistance
    dealing with, 57–58
    overcoming, 204–208
Retailers, 21
    chain, 22, 164, 175
    image of, 192
    massive. See Mass merchandisers
    presale research for, 193
Retailing, mass market, 22–23, 175–178
Return authorization number
    (RAN), 117
Returned goods, 15, 117
Reverse power word, 112
"Reward," as power word, 112
Rewards, for prospects, 250
Rudeness, overcoming, 201

S

Sales force, motivating, 243–244
Sales manager, 55, 57
Salesperson
    advantages of, 1
    as adversary, 57
    as buyers, 28–29
    characteristics/qualities of, 95, 105
    confidence, as motivational
        reminder, 232, 235
    direct, 82, 266. See also Direct sales
    high-pressure methods of, 56–57
    knowledge of, 47–49
    mistakes of, common, 189
    neatness of, 11
    persistence of, 57
    preparation for calls and, 196–197
    product knowledge of, 98–99
    professionalism of, 11
    relationship with buyer, 3, 24–25,
        55–56, 172
    successful, 58
    unorganized, 44
Sales presentation
    analyzing, 223
    close. See Close/closing
    for concept selling, 58–60
    differences in, analyzing, 64–66
    for group sale, 218–219
    introduction for, 203–204
    involving senses in, 216–218
    opening for, 269
    parts of, 76
    presentation phase of, 83–86
    qualification phase of, 79–82
    rehearsal of, 11
    sales method comparison, 60–66
    sales methods and, 56–58
    support materials for, 194–195,
        232, 236
    warm-up phase of, 76–79
Sales profession, 213
    career in, 1
    historical aspects of, 36–37
    importance of, 35–36, 37
Sales territory. See Territory
"Save," as power word, 111
Schedule, respect for, 11
Screeners
    buyers as, 207–208
    gaining cooperation from, 204–206
Seating, for direct sale, 260
Second calls, 202
Seconds, 15
Secretary, 79, 134
Security, 119
"Security," as power word, 113
Selling. See also specific sales methods
    comparing methods for, 60–66
    to extroverts, 6–8
    to introverts, 6, 7–8
    methods, 56–58
    to professional buyers, 14

during prospecting, 255
spots, in-store, 121, 124
tools, transfer of feeling of ownership as, 215–216
vs. cosigning, 163–165
Selling letters, 135–142
and employment letter, 145–147
with hard-selling tone, 143–145
shock type, 142–143
Seminars, group sales, 95–96, 218–219
Senses, using in selling, 216–218
Service-minded stores, vs. mass merchandisers, 176–177
Service sales, 181
Shelf space, payment for, 31–32
Shills, at gaming tables, 220
Shock letter, 142–143
Shoplifting, 119
Shortcuts, taking, 234
Shotgun approach, 203
Show-and-tell method, 58–59
Show-and-tell selling, 60
Sidetracking, during sales call, 16–17
Silence, advantage of, 155–157, 161
Silent close, 160–163
Sincerity, 201
Slotting fees, 31, 164–165
Slush price, 123
Small buyers, 28–29
Small industrial operations, 180
Small talk, in warm-up, 78–79
Social functions, talking business at, 171
Soft assumptive close, 91–92
Soviet Union, 37–38
Speakers, powerful, 96–97
Spiff, 121
State laws, on cancellations, 94
Store manager, 122, 242
Street sales, 74
Success, sales, 95, 97
Support materials, 194–195, 232, 236

T

Tag-on sales, 227–228
Taxi drivers, rewarding, 128–129
Tear-off tags, 253
Telemarketing, 250–251
Telephone directories, as lead source, 253
Tens (end-of-run merchandise), 15
Territory
building, 56
organizing, 41–42, 47
Thanking buyer for the business, 50–51
Thick skin, development of, 29–31, 100
Tie-in promotions, 121, 129–130, 134
Time wasting, 43, 44
Travel agencies, as outlet for point-and-shoot cameras, 190
Trust, 24
Truthfulness, 102–103, 105

U

Unfairness of buyer, handling, 30–31
United States, salesmanship in, 36–37

V

Vendors
off-shore, 12, 13
unknown, buyers and, 4
Videotapes, 262
Visual aids, 224, 225–227

W

Wardrobe, 102
Warehouse fee allowances, 31, 32
Warm-up
importance of, 77
for presentation, 76–79
purpose of, 76–77
small talk in, 78–79
"What if" questions, 229–230
Window designer, 122
Words
perceptions and, 112–113
powerful, usage of, 109–116
power of, 107–109
Work, importance of, 35–36
Writing ability, reading and, 133

Y

"You," as power word, 111, 113